MAGICK TAROT

MAGICK TAROT

by Magick Altman

Published by Magickal Times Books

Book and Cover Design by Sofia Limon
Deck by Aleister Crowley and Frieda Lady Harris
Thoth Tarot © Ordo Templi Orientis.
All rights reserved. Used by permission.

Finishing Touches: Book Shepherding
A division of FinishingTouchesEditing.com
Back cover author photo by Aaron Wojack

ISBN-13: 978-0-9979416-0-9
ISBN-10: 099794160X

Gratitude

I give my deepest gratitude to my daughter April Faith for planting the seed in my mind to write this book and then urging me on, in her unique Aries fashion, until I began the process. This book would not have happened without her wind at my back.

Thanks to my daughter Celeste for her great feedback and editing suggestions and thanks to my daughter Allegra for her helpful input and encouragement.

Many people have given me editing help, each in their own unique voice. Thank you Lee Bloom, Terry Bronson, Judy Walthers von Alten, and Shellie Citron.

Special thanks go to my copy editor Esther Baruch for her careful reading and editing of the manuscript.

Sending gratitude to Sofia Limon, my designer, who brought fresh enthusiasm and excellent ideas for bringing this book to completion.

My greatest inspirations in the field of Tarot have been Mary Greer, Vicki Noble, and Rachel Pollack. Appreciation goes out to Mary Greer for her astute advice during the developmental stage of this book. A bow to Starhawk, I have learned so much from her work as an activist and author.

Aleister Crowley and Lady Frieda Harris, sending out many thanks to the other side for creating this amazing Tarot deck that embodies so many myths and cultures in an artistic rendering that is, to me, the most inspiring of all the decks available today.

INTRODUCTION

*"The Soul rejoices in hearing
what it already knows."*

Like a Fool, I fell in love with the Tarot the first time we met. As a young hippie, my heart was hungry to try everything that opened the doors of perception. As I roamed the Haight, seeking my next mind-blowing experience, the electric currents of rock-and-roll rushed through my veins and the verses of the vagabond muses kept me wide-eyed with anticipation. It was in the midst of this intoxicating dance that I received my first reading.

When the powerful Queen of Swords appeared, enthroned in the clouds, I knew she was me. There I was, reflected in the woman of the clouds, but the really telling part was the star child radiating behind her head whom she will defend at all costs. Just like Kali herself, I was a fierce truth-teller fighting to end the Vietnam War and at the same time expand my consciousness. The calm, cool, and collected wise woman image invokes the principle that when the truth is spoken with love for all that is innocent and needs protection, then Shiva himself surrenders in service to the mother.

This book reflects these two paths of my life, spiritual growth and frontline activism. It is my hope that through this revelation of my intimate relationship with the Tarot, you too will see how to use this amazing guide in your life journey. The cards are not limited to one meaning but can offer insights specifically for your unique story. In this book, you will have a resource to encourage your personal growth as well as a lens to understand the socio-political world around you. It will give you a mirror to contemplate all aspects of your life including love, relationships, family, education, spiritual questions, work, home, travel, health, and pleasure.

In the midst of this fast-paced and overwhelming world, it is both comforting and clarifying to have a "wise friend" to consult, in order to understand our role and our gifts, our challenges and our potential. I have found that, every step of the way, the cards have the uncanny ability to show me exactly what I need to know right now.

We, as a species, are taking an evolutionary leap off the familiar into a still fragile future.

Across the world stage there is great tumult and upheaval as empires give way to the birth of systems of Earth Justice that will bring humans back into balance with the rest of creation.

This book can serve to assist you in giving what no one else can give at this time of transition: your authentic self. You may not be an activist in the typical understanding of the word, but we must all be activated to awaken to our true nature and manifest our life purpose in service to our Mother Earth.

If you are a writer, write; if you are a dancer, dance; the Tarot can help you know yourself and your challenges and gifts. The best reading will confirm your innermost thoughts and invariably give you some synchronistic signposts to guide you on your path. You have a role to play in the theater of life. The Tarot opens a window into your unique drama, involving all the characters, actions, and emotions that make for great entertainment and profound lessons at the same time. I suggest that if you want an in depth understanding of the Major Arcana and the Court cards you have chosen then read the whole description. If you need a quick guide to understand how to apply the card to your current circumstances, then jump to the section called, "When you get this card in a reading."

The Major Arcana will serve to provide the underlying concepts and potential lessons of your personal drama. The Court Cards provide the characters and the Minor Arcana, the actions and emotions. But you are not just an audience. You are all aspects of the story and every card is clamoring to reveal yourself to you.

The cards give you an opportunity to step outside of a reactive mode and see clearly what is actually going on in your life. Because the Tarot is not a religious system, it frees you from the good/bad dichotomy and allows you to see things exactly as they are. The Tarot does not act as a parent or a preacher; instead it speaks in symbols and stories that will aid you in facing the mystery without any pat answers or unknowable future promises.

The most common response, in my experience as a reader for over 30 years, is that the cards affirm an inner knowing and offer my clients tools that have been employed by humanity for thousands of years to work with their current life lesson.

When we leave the mind trap of judgmental thinking, it also clears the way to get outside of ourselves. We can have a sense of humor and let go of our ego-protections and strategies to laugh and cry at all the pathos of our lives.

Throughout the Tarot's existence, to some extent, it has had to reflect the limitations of our societal dogmas. The Tarot is an ever-evolving tool, and in this book I have suggested ways to free it from past limitations. For example, to let the Tarot live and breathe, I have released our Aries archetype from the toxic attributes of The Emperor, allowing him to become The Visionary Activist, a charismatic leader modeling power from within as opposed to power over. He is full of ideas that will aid his partner, The Empress, who is now called Gaia, in the healing of her body, the Earth. Thus they are reborn as an inspirational love affair for us all.

It is my intention that you, dear reader, will also find a lifelong companion in the Tarot.

Magick for the Earth

INTRODUCTION
TO THE TAROT CARDS

The Tarot is the living body of the collective unconscious. The people who created this amazing tool observed inherent archetypal patterns and distilled this knowledge into a map and story of human life. They constructed a universal filing system for understanding any event, person, environment or problem. In fact everything, from an atom to the Milky Way itself, can be studied and understood through the many layers of symbolic language and mythic stories that are contained in the Tarot cards.

This system is not an imposed theory or a dogma that shows us what is right or wrong, but a way of understanding the essential nature of any given circumstance and human condition. It brings us to a conscious awareness of the wealth of human experience and universal principles that will help us learn the lesson at hand.

Traditional methods of rote memorization and simplistic categorization will fail to create a link to this magical map of life. Rather, you will need to take the journey and experience the cards as they connect in a very personal way.

Although it is very helpful to learn the essential nature of numbers, elements, planets and signs as these will serve as a loom on which to weave the story, the Tarot comes alive when you treat the cards like people: recognizing their essential nature without stereotyping them. Then the variables of questions, situations and the person who is consulting this oracle can reveal each reading as unique and time specific.

It is no mistake that the first card in the Tarot is The Fool. Grab onto the shirttails of this fearless optimist and take a leap of faith into the realm of infinite possibilities! The first thing you need to leave behind is that puzzled look when your intellect cannot make sense of everything. Do not police your intuition by demanding pat answers.

When you pick a card with a raccoon in the picture and ten minutes later you walk out the door and there's that little bandit gleefully stealing your cat's food, then, like Alice, you are ready to jump down the rabbit hole and explore the mystery. You need to weave the significance of the cards into your own being through experience and, thread by thread, the tapestry will grow.

The word education is derived from the Latin *educere* which means to draw out. When we trace the roots of words we uncover their essential nature and mine the rich soil that fed the original intention of that thought. The origin of education was to draw out the natural intelligence, interests, passions and talents of individuals. This suggests that each of us, inherently and intuitively, knows our own path and it is the responsibility of teachers to help us follow our soul's desire by giving us tools and resources, offering experiences and telling us stories as they naturally arise. This cannot be accomplished through predetermined curricula primarily supported by rote memorization.

It is of the utmost importance to approach the Tarot as a spiritual guidebook to life, not a manifesto. Just as you would consult a tour book on a trip to understand the history and key sites of a given place, so the Tarot can divulge the landscape of a relationship or a job and tell us how other humans have worked through similar situations to grow as individuals. But that is only a starting point. You certainly don't want to be a tourist in your own life and yet so many of us are. We go where we are told to and have the experiences we can expect, but we never venture into the mysterious back roads of our own dreams and longings. If you stick with what is expected, The Emperor may reward you with a false sense of security and a high position in his empire, but the delightful Child/Fool, who loves to run wild with his puppy yapping at his heels, will be buried below the ego persona of the practical, normal, mature adult. The Fool is the free agent, always beckoning us toward our next adventure. At any moment you can be reborn into this magical realm of the imagination.

Throughout time people have dreamed the impossible dreams of The Fool and made them real. The Earth was flat until it was round; people couldn't fly until they did. So many accomplishments seemed initially impossible, but through imagination, a passionate will and discipline, they became manifest. So much of what we accept as a fact of our daily lives was an impossible dream of some "lunatic." But it is Luna, our moon sister, who relentlessly whispers in our ear as we sleep, keeping alive the dreams we were born to make real.

The best way to gain access to the magic of the Tarot immediately, without any previous knowledge, is to simply pick a card in the morning, read about it and notice how the different elements of the card play out in the events of your day. If you are a visual learner it may be best to refrain from reading about the cards until you have played with the images themselves. In that case, pick a card in the morning and read about it at night, thereby avoiding the intellectual interpretation that reading tends to create. Remember, first and foremost the Tarot is a pictorial language capable of connecting directly to the soul's archetypal web, thereby circumventing the ego intellect that wants to judge everything as either good or bad. The soul is only concerned with what is.

The Tarot will waste no time in pulling you into its dance so get ready for some fun-filled and profound, synchronistic experiences.

THE CREATORS OF
THE DECK OF THOTH

This book is based on the Deck of Thoth created by the illustrious and flamboyant Aleister Crowley. The unique, stunning, and brilliant art was a five-year labor of love by the artist Lady Frieda Harris. The art in these cards speaks to me more than any other deck I have seen and continues to be one of the most popular decks in the world.

Although Crowley was a challenging and complex character, there is no doubt that his genius in creating this deck deserves respect and appreciation. The Thoth deck has inspired many to write books that offer new and innovative interpretations demonstrating that the Tarot is an ever-evolving map of consciousness that is alive and well in the 21st century.

Journey Through The Archetypes:
THE MAJOR ARCANA

JUNG AND THE TAROT

My favorite way to present the Major Arcana in my classes is as an archetypal journey through life. Sallie Nichols's book, Jung on the Tarot, is an excellent resource and my first encounter with this theory. Jung did a great service by recognizing and articulating the symbolic language of the Tarot as a vehicle for self-reflection, as a tool for psychologists and a door to the collective unconscious.

This lent great legitimacy to an art that had long been regarded as mere fortune telling. Until Jung, most educated people had totally ignored this rich treasure, slyly disguised as a deck of cards that only the Romani and some secret societies kept alive during the last 500 years.

This orphaned child of the great civilizations of the past has been undiluted and kept intact by the very fact that no religion or field of study has claimed the Tarot as theirs. Magically it appears and disappears before anyone can force it to be shaped and used for any other purpose than its own.

Its very history is clouded in mystery. Some believe that representatives of many different cultures met to create a pictorial and symbolic language that would transcend cultural and linguistic barriers. If the library at Alexandria had not been burned, we might be able to trace it back to its roots, for the Tarot may actually be one of the few intact resources of those times.

Although Jung's discovery and public acknowledgment that the revelations he was receiving about the nature of the human psyche had a long history in the cards, it still amuses me how little most people really understand about them.

On one occasion I was hired along with six other readers to work at a dinner for the National Association of Psychiatrists' meeting in San Francisco. We were prepped by the woman who hired us with a little talk about our purpose at this function. We were here to entertain the crowd with a kind of '60s sideshow for the out-of-towners; nothing serious, just something colorful to remind them they were where all the hippies lived.

I surprised her by responding that we actually predate the field of psychology by hundreds of years. As it turned out, the psychiatrists respected us as counselors like themselves and it was a wonderful evening.

The primary function of the Majors is to bring the archetypal message of the moment to consciousness. The Major Arcana correspond to the 22 letters of the Hebrew alphabet. For example, Aleph is The Fool and Beth is The Magician. The combination of these specific letters is, in fact, the origin of the word alphabet.

THE THREE LEVELS
OF THE ARCHETYPES

The following diagram shows the three levels of the 22 Tarot cards as defined in Nichols's Jung on the Tarot: the Realm of the Gods and Goddesses (Family), the Realm of Earthly Reality and the Realm of Self-Realization. The Fool stands outside categorization and is a free agent, showing up when and where he pleases. That allows the twenty-one other Majors to divide neatly into three rows of seven cards each. The primary function of the Majors is to bring the archetypal message of the moment to consciousness.

This journey naturally evolves from birth through maturity and, hopefully, to the wisdom of the self-actualized being. It is important to acknowledge, of course, that life is not linear and we often jump all over the map. To begin, we will follow the stages of the journey as they unfold sequentially in the deck.

Note: Each Major is governed by either an element, planet, or astrological sign. For example, The Fool's element is Air, The Empress's planet is Venus, The Hierophant's astrological sign is Taurus.

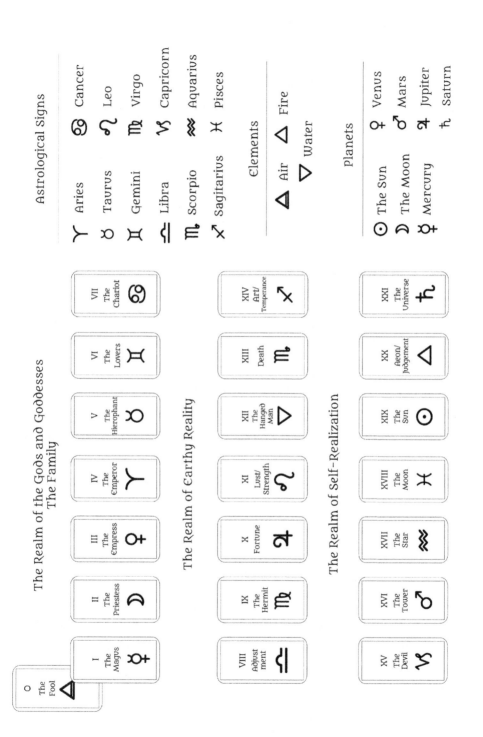

Astrological Signs

♈ Aries   ♋ Cancer
♉ Taurus   ♌ Leo
♊ Gemini   ♍ Virgo
♎ Libra   ♑ Capricorn
♏ Scorpio   ♒ Aquarius
♐ Sagittarius   ♓ Pisces

Elements

△ Air   △ Fire
▽ Water

Planets

☉ The Sun   ♀ Venus
☽ The Moon   ♂ Mars
☿ Mercury   ♃ Jupiter
   ♄ Saturn

The Realm of the Gods and Goddesses
The Family

I The Magus ☿	II The Priestess ☽	III The Empress ♀	IV The Emperor ♈	V The Hierophant ♉	VI The Lovers ♊	VII The Chariot ♋

0 The Fool △

The Realm of Earthy Reality

| VIII Adjustment ♎ | IX The Hermit ♍ | X Fortune ♃ | XI Lust/Strength ♌ | XII The Hanged Man ▽ | XIII Death ♏ | XIV Art/Temperance ♐ |

The Realm of Self-Realization

| XV The Devil ♑ | XVI The Tower ♂ | XVII The Star ♒ | XVIII The Moon ♓ | XIX The Sun ☉ | XX Aeon/Judgement △ | XXI The Universe ♄ |

The Fool 0
Element: Air

Before we enter the first row, let's get in touch with The Fool and his/her essential nature. Crowley called The Fool "the Babe in the Egg of Blue, neither man nor woman, but both in one." Now there's a non-sexist way to start things off! In this interpretation, The Fool is still in the Cosmic Egg, pointing to the awareness of the potentiality of life. He reminds us that everything is possible right now; there are no limitations, only dreams and imagination. He is bursting with enthusiasm for the adventure itself; as he steps forth fresh into the world, he is excited to see and experience everything. Plans are too pragmatic for this vagabond; he is simply glad to be alive!

In the Rider/Waite Tarot deck, this adventurer is dressed in a many-colored loose garb, his bag of tricks hanging on the end of his hobo stick. He is followed by his trusty companion, a little dog nipping at his heels, reminding him of his instincts for self-preservation. Carefree, he looks off into the distance, one foot hovering over a cliff, oblivious to the danger he faces. Somehow we get the impression he's going to be all right, but we don't know how. The rational mind doesn't hold the answers for this young dreamer, so what will save him? Will his dog get his attention in time? Will there be a tree he can grab hold of (so often depicted in cartoons), some opportunity he was unaware of that will offer another chance? Or is the pool of his unconscious waiting for him to take a dive and discover a hidden treasure, perhaps from another time or life? Will he leap across the abyss and make it to the other side where a beautiful city glitters in the Sun?

When you get this card in a reading

The Fool is like the Sun bursting through the clouds, painting a double rainbow on the horizon and, like the perfect playmate, calling us to come out of our caves of worry and introspection and drink in the moment!

He reminds us that life always offers us the opportunity to start over and some of his favorite ways to entice are travel and love. The Fool is a strong confirmation that a change of environment will awaken the soul that has been mired in a narrow perspective inside

0

TRUMPS **The Fool**

the four walls of a boring job or a stagnant home life. So if you want to know if this is a good time to chuck it all and go to Bali, well, why not! But if the question is about an important business trip, be aware that The Fool may take you where your subconscious has been hungry to explore. Suddenly that work on the trip could become unimportant as The Fool pulls you down a dark alley to a smoky nightclub where music and dancing will keep you up all night.

When we ask about certain plans and The Fool seems to be suggesting something quite different, it's important to explore those messages even though the logical linear mind might be a bit resistant, reinforcing our fear of the unknown by suggesting negative scenarios.

Perhaps you could make some allowance for The Fool's desires and extend your trip to include free time to let go and see what happens. Instead of going the typical tourist route, look for where the locals hang out and let another culture get under your skin.

When I first traveled out of the U.S. to Mexico I was surprised by how limited my perspective was in relation to family, customs, time and even the way the air felt and smelled. I realized for the first time that I was a child of the world, not only the U.S. and I became immersed in the gentle pace that slowed me down and let me feel my body and my heart in ways that my speedy mind could not comprehend. My body seemed to have a consciousness of its own and after staying three weeks in a village with no cars or electricity I learned the hardened earth pathways to my palapa (shelter). Even in the dark of night, my feet would take me home. By the time I left Mexico, natives were asking me directions at bus stations. When I crossed the border to come home, the U.S. customs man asked me if I was an United States citizen and I automatically answered, "Si, Señor!"

These experiences offer us a chance to let the world act on us instead of us trying to manipulate the world for our purposes. In these "out of time" experiences we find hidden aspects of ourselves that can awaken our more creative and playful side.

Now let's talk about love. The Fool's appearance indicates that we have probably done a good job of clearing the slate of old expectations about relationships. If this is not the case then it's high time we did so! When the heart leaps it doesn't want to hit a wall from the past that keeps it under wraps.

Let's say you have met a few people and you're trying to make some choice and you're hoping the cards will give you the answer. Well, The Fool loves to open doors but he always forgets to close them—keeping all options open is most pleasing to his nature. He believes things will happen that will reveal the right choice and he doesn't need to give it too much thought.

Until now we've been giving The Fool full reign to cajole us into freeing ourselves from all limitations, but sometimes The Fool is just plain foolish in an irresponsible way and you will need to balance his message with the other voices in the reading to get a complete picture. The card Justice or Adjustment is the natural partner of The Fool for balance (see Adjustment VIII page 74).

When The Fool pops into your life he gives you the gift of experiencing your inner child who is always there, innocent and expectant, and filled with enthusiasm. Don't be too hard on him; he really just wants to play!

THE FIRST LEVEL:
THE REALM OF THE GODS AND GODDESSES / THE FAMILY TREE

The first row represents our heavenly and earthly family and all of the wisdom, traditions and limitations that are part of the social developments of a human being. We encounter our spiritual guides in the forms of The Magician and The Priestess, whose roles are to guide us to the womb of The Empress to be fathered by The Emperor. (This does not need to be literal; there are many ways children enter a family these days.) The Hierophant will be our teacher of the secular and religious traditions. The Lovers card offers us the social and family customs that our culture wishes to instill in us, and, hopefully, our first experience of falling in love. The Chariot is the assembled vehicle of all these elements that will carry us into the world with what we need to survive, and under optimum conditions, thrive!

The Magus I / The Magician
Planet: Mercury

The Magician is our true will written in our hearts by the messenger of the divine himself, Mercury; as opposed to The Fool who has forgotten all that and just lets life unfold moment by moment. The Magician will find ways to keep alerting us to who we are by any means at his disposal. Synchronicity is his favorite method of getting our attention, but he does get a bit discouraged when we keep using logic against the obvious magic of his ways. Not that he isn't a master of reason; he just doesn't believe it should be used to defeat his stellar intuitive skills.

In the corner of the card we see the ape god Thoth, who represents logic, reason and mathematics. Thoth is shaking his fist at the illogical ways of The Magician but he refuses to be dissuaded from his path and turns away from Thoth's protestations.

In the Rider-Waite Tarot deck he wears the lemniscate on top of his hat. This symbolizes infinity as a continuous loop or figure eight turned on its side. The lemniscate is a perfect representation of the two sides of the brain moving as a current through the central intersecting point. When we allow the right and left brain to complement each other the flow is continuous and electric. If we see them as separate, the leminscate would be split into two circles representing a disconnect between left-brain logic and right-brain intuition.

The Magician doesn't see reason and intuition as opposing forces. Intuition is meant to make the choices and reason is meant to make them real. Intuition resides in the heart and must be served by the mind. They are not meant to be wrestling endlessly, but rather embracing each other as perfect complements.

The Magician has one purpose in mind—to keep returning us to our true will by offering us opportunities that develop our skills and our voice in the world.

Each day I start my grounding ritual with an ancient Sanskrit chant, Om Hrdaya Namah, that articulates this principle. The first two lines translate as "First I bow down to my heart, that awakens my mind." (For complete chant and accompanying gestures, see Appendix 389.)

The Magician's message is a powerful one for these times. We seem to be mired in a dualistic approach to everything. An either/or instead of both/and aesthetic leaves us bereft of a holistic world view. In readings, clients constantly ask, "Is that good or bad, should I or shouldn't I?" The duty of the reader is to help reframe the question to go deeper into the present situation and move away from the ego's desire for a concrete answer. It is not good or bad; it just is what it is. It is our work to penetrate into the significance of exactly where we are. Remember all those maps that say, "You are here," with an arrow pointing to a spot? The cards in a reading all have their unique take on what "here" is. Witnesses to an event tell many different accounts and the reader, like Sherlock Holmes, must thread them together into a cohesive whole. The purpose is to gain different perspectives that complement one another, instead of finding where to put the blame and hand down the punishment. Judgment colors the lenses and the obvious becomes evasive.

The Magician's edict is, "As above, so below." In other words, if we can apply the universal principles represented in the Major Arcana (above) and recognize how they are unfolding through the circumstances in our lives via the Minor Arcana (below), a light will shine on the path ahead. One of the great epiphanies of my spiritual development came when I was meditating on the hexagrams of the I Ching as they appear in a circle on the back of Crowley's poetic translation of this text. I had decided to use this circle for the label of a small record company I was a part of in the '80s and when I saw the hexagrams spinning on the turntable I thought this must be the same as DNA!

A few weeks later I was visiting a bookstore called EastWest Books and there was a text called The I Ching and the DNA Code. Although someone else had already discovered the connection, I was thrilled to have confirmation and a detailed explanation of my realization. How kind of The Magician to lead me to this book as I wandered the streets of North Beach and for no particular "reason" found this treasure.

The Magician in the Thoth deck is shown tied to the caduceus, the magic wand of the adept. This wand is his will and all that he juggles before him are the tools or, depending on his mood, the tricks of his trade. The caduceus is entwined with two serpents echoing the same principle of yin/yang with the added symbolism of the serpent as the awakened life force called kundalini.

Mercury is the fastest moving of the planets, completing its orbit around the Sun every 88 days. I am sure many of you have heard of the term Mercury retrograde, which means that the planet appears to be moving backwards in the sky. Many people believe this is a bad sign and during these times we are prone to accidents and mechanical breakdowns. When we remove ourselves from the good/ bad paradigm, however, we can discover the advantage of such times, slow down and tuck speedy Mercury in for a much-needed rest. Astrologer Caroline Casey, author of Making the Gods Work for You, suggests that during retrograde we apply all the "re" words to our lives such as reflect, remember, reexamine, retreat and refresh. Although these periods of inner working are against the dominant paradigm of our culture, this is the very opportunity we need to receive the deeper magic of our soul's journey. And, yes, if we heed this advice we will probably experience fewer accidental occurrences and more synchronicity.

The caduceus is also a symbol of the medical community and that tells us that The Magician has the knowledge of the healing arts at his disposal also.

To combine The Magician's aspects of will, synchronicity and healing, here is a story of a friend of mine whose infant child was very ill. The doctors were unable to determine the cause of the sickness and the child was listless and not eating. The mother was very distraught but had not given up and one day when she was at the hospital visiting her child she noticed there was a lecture on botulism being offered. Her intuition told her to go in and listen. When she entered, the doctor was explaining how an infant under one year of age did not have the ability to fight off botulism. He said that honey often has traces of botulism and this was a very recent discovery. It was common practice for this mother to feed her child honey water and to dip the baby's pacifier in honey as well. Her answer was found because she combined the will of a mother to save her child with the trust in her intuition and the help of the knowledge of the medical community.

This child, who was at death's door, is now a healthy adult thanks to the magic of Mercury.

When you get this card in a reading

The Magician signifies a time to trust in the synchronicity of events and act on impulses that connect you to helpful people or go to places that are calling you. Our instincts tell us to trust in messages that may not seem logical but feel right. It is time to gather all the tools we need to manifest our destiny on another level.

The Magician is a great communicator, so seek out opportunities to speak and write about what you are inspired by. You will attract people who can be great allies.

If you are not clear, do some free writing, speak into a recorder or just talk out loud to yourself to bring what is hidden out into the light of day.

Then, when the clouds of confusion have cleared, follow the clues on your treasure hunt for chances to do your work.

When magic is happening
it's important to seize the day!

But if we are unconscious, misuse of these powers will ensue. Herein lie all the stories of the evil magicians who desired power over this world and completely lost touch with the innocent child who has come to give a unique gift to the world. The true magician needs no empire or control over others because he has not separated himself from everything else.

This shadow aspect attempts to appease the ego's desires for control over the mystery. But in the end the mystery cannot be dominated or even completely understood. The creed of every authentic magician is "to do what thou wilt and harm no one." The best way to make sure your magic wand has not been stolen from the seat of the soul by the ego is to ask yourself if what you are planning to do is for the highest good of all.

When we experience a conflict between our self and someone else it would be wise to ask if it is our will to continue on this path or if there's a way to be flexible and non-confrontational in our choices. Does it appear that the other person is within their proper orbit and are we within ours? Do we need to be more patient, try another approach or must we find a way to change the dynamic with the other person because we are truly being blocked?

To challenge with the confidence of inner truth is to be willing to find a peaceful solution. Sometimes, though, retreat is truly "the better part of valor." Conscious communication is the Magician's forte and one of his many magical tools.

Each of us is gifted with the ability to "do" magic because we have the power to imagine. These two words have the same root, magh, meaning to be able. We are all capable of creating if we are willing to imagine something first.

My favorite song concerning a worldview is the John Lennon song, "Imagine." He addresses very profound issues including the idea that we must dream one world before it is possible. If we cannot see it and feel what it would be like, we cannot create it. Many times in this world we have seen revolutions against what is wrong; but if there is no vision of what will work, the same structure remains with new puppets held by the same old strings.

The methods we use to create something will be the methods that hold that structure in place. Poet Audre Lorde stated this principle very clearly, "You cannot dismantle the master's house with the master's tools." It is important to slow down and make sure your motive is not just a desire for power. Mercury often gets too speedy and we forget to make sure we are staying within our integrity.

Now we need the wisdom of The Priestess to be the receiver of this potential will, to deliver us through the portals of duality, across the desert of the abyss, so we may manifest our destiny.

The Priestess II
Planet: The Moon

The Hebrew letter for the Priestess is Gimel. Gimel corresponds to camel and you will notice that the image of the camel is seen in the Thoth card of The Priestess.

The camel has the ability to cross the desert carrying the waters of life on her back as she makes her way through a lifeless landscape, trusting her nose to bring her in time to the next oasis. This is an excellent metaphor for times when we must go where we have never gone, follow our instincts and trust that we will receive the knowledge we need to go through life's initiations.

I often use this idea to suggest to young people that the wisdom their parents and teachers have given them is like the humps on the back of the camel, available to get them across the desert of their personal initiation. Then there are those who must take the journey with little assistance from family and community. These people have to go to a deeper place of trust, to tap in on their own intuitive nature and learn by experience to recognize their authentic voice.

The Priestess is ruled by the Moon, the ever-changing reflection of the constant, life-generating, Sun. Our lunar goddess has manifested the counterpoint to the yearly cycles of the Sun with the 13 months in the traditional lunar calendar perfectly aligning to the year of the Solar King. We see in her cycles and rhythms the essence of all life by witnessing the waxing, full and waning phases of her light. These correspond to birth, fruition and death, or in mythological terms Maiden, Mother and Crone. All cultures honor these cycles in the form of the Triple Goddess. For example, Persephone, Demeter and Hecate in Greek mythology; in Tarot terms, The Priestess, The Empress and The Crone (Hermit). In the women-centered interpretation of Persephone's journey into the underworld, it is told as a coming-of-age initiation.

She journeys to the underworld, to the land of the dead, leaving her mother, Demeter, to mourn her disappearance. Demeter doesn't know what fate has befallen her beloved daughter. She is the harvest goddess of bounty and agriculture, but bereft of the will to go on, she turns the earth into a barren wasteland.

II

The Priestess

It is Hecate, the crone aspect, who finds out where Persephone is and informs Demeter. She gets her attention by telling bawdy stories and lifting her skirts and showing her vulva, making Demeter laugh and bringing the life force bubbling back up through her body.

Finally Persephone, the fruit of her own womb, returns, and spring bursts forth again. But Persephone, who has seen suffering and death and learned compassion in the process, will have to return for the winter months, symbolizing awareness that comes from growing up and separating from our mother's protection.

These three phases are exemplified in all aspects of human life and The Priestess is our guide, calling us to come to her ritual and participate in the celebration of our births, our accomplishments and our return to source.

I am a child of the '60s and I have participated in my generation's redefining of these phases of life. It is very important in these transformative times to honor and give authentic meaning to these phases of our beloved Moon that have made life possible on planet Earth. Without her sister the Moon, the Earth would still be barren of life and the waters and tides that we take for granted would not have materialized. The pull of her heartstrings is the life force of fertility and the mystery of birth.

When I turned 16 it was 1966 and the San Francisco Bay Area was sizzling with new visions of the Age of Aquarius. Like a young Persephone, I ran off to The City every chance I had to be part of this dance of the dawning of a new era. Along with so many of our sisters, we left our poor Demeters mourning for the loss of their innocent children. As carefree as The Fool, we were dazzled by The Magician and all the muses of that unforgettable time.

Forces beyond our control called to us to fulfill a destiny of freedom and a desire for individuality and community that had been simmering underground since the end of the Second World War.

Our mothers had become models of normalcy. Life in the suburbs was the height of success, defined by gadgets and two-car garages, bridge parties and church on Sunday. The boredom of this false security was smothering our adolescent hearts. Every generation has to leave their Demeters behind and take their chances, but I think we all can agree that the '60s were a very extreme example of this phenomena.

At each stage of our initiations we can call on The Priestess to give us comfort by opening to her compassionate and eternal knowledge of these profound lessons of the soul's journey through the dark of night. What doesn't kill us makes us stronger. After all, the night is her domain and she knows beyond all human doubt that the Sun will be born again and she will move through her many phases and hold our hand at every stage.

To hear her gentle voice is to be able to open to silent wonder, to receive and accept what is happening without always knowing the answer. She is the unfathomable mystery and no matter how many of her veils you try to tear from her face with the probing of the scientific mind, you will never penetrate her essence.

She is not The Magician, full of ideas and schemes, but the holder of a space where knowing comes to awareness in its own way and in its own time. If we hold rituals to honor her cycles of waxing and waning we will have access to solutions regarding our individual conundrums.

I use the word ritual not to imply that you must join some pagan group and dance naked before the full moon, although I can say from experience that can be a truly ecstatic and enlightening experience. I do suggest you become aware of her ways and moods and find time in your life to honor the changes you go through that correspond to her cycles. Although women have the unique experience of following her cycles by the rhythms of menses, all humans and indeed all life are affected by her powers.

The world would be a safer place for all our teenagers entering into adulthood if we had some initiation rituals to honor and welcome their coming-of-age. Many high school graduates get drunk and test their immortality driving at high speeds, or join the military, or have an unsafe sexual experience. Every year I pray for the safety of our young ones and wish we would have more ways to help them take this step into the world.

One of the innovations that the counterculture rediscovered was the concept of a vision quest that has been used by cultures all over the world to help the young find their own relationship with the mystery of life. It sure beats fraternity beer binges that often end in humiliation and sometimes death.

These extreme daredevil adventures are rooted in a youthful sense of immortality. In seeking extreme experiences we are pushing the moon to tell us her secrets about love, sex, and death. The instant you demand her favors, she will cover her face and leave you begging for mercy. But if you can come to a place of surrender she will probably hear your prayer.

Mercy is one of her attributes and that is why the other goddesses associated with the Moon are Kwan Yin, Tara and Mother Mary. The Beatles wrote the song "Let It Be" to exemplify this principle.

"In my hour of darkness…Mother Mary comes to me, speaking words of wisdom, let it be. …There will be an answer, let it be."

The '60s counterculture proceeded to define new ways to live in all aspects of life. We changed the way we ate, exercised and grew food, listening to nature as our guide every step of the way. The Moon has always been a great guide to farming and raising animals for humans all over the Earth and she was smiling down on us as we rediscovered the different Moons for planting and harvesting. Native tribes have a different name for every full Moon to help them remember the seasonal changes. There's no getting away from the moon if you are going to live a life that moves in a natural way. Most of the "new" ideas of our generation were actually a process of unearthing the ways of all indigenous people of the Earth.

One of the most significant ways the patricians tried to hide the ways of our lunar guide was to change the calendar from 13 months to 12. The word "month" is from the same root as the word menstruation, i.e., menses: to measure. The first measurements of time were clearly connected to women coming to consciousness about their own innate connection to Luna. The awareness that their body's menstrual cycles coincided with the phases of this heavenly body must have been an awesome epiphany!

To hide and discount this fact of life was a tool used to discredit the power of our original priestess process. The number 13 became unlucky and cities renamed 13th avenues, like Funston St. where I lived in San Francisco when I gave birth to my second child who was born in my Priestess year (see page 370 for the formula to figure out your Priestess year).

Apollo fails to trick Luna

Here is a fascinating tale of modern mythology as revealed by our space program, NASA. The only time the government used the number 13 in any of its projects was for the ill-fated Apollo 13 mission to, where else, the Moon! Many people are unaware that there were 8.7 pounds of plutonium on that missile, to be used to eventually create a nuclear-powered space station on our beloved sister. So they pulled out all stops to use the persuasive powers of the love god, Apollo, to deliver this unwanted poison to Luna.

But Luna was not to be fooled by these trickster black magicians and she sent the death god Pluto's potion (plutonium) right back to Earth. There are many such tales of modern mythology you can discover if you look at things through the lens of the Tarot and other mythic resources. Try picking a news story or event that lends itself to a mythic interpretation and see where it takes you.

When you get this card in a reading

It's time to let go of your determination to get from A to B and come fully into the present moment. The camel cannot decide whether he will go to the next oasis by charting a course; he needs to follow his nose.

The Priestess is a signal that you are going through an initiation into another stage of your life and, therefore, familiar logic and reasoning are now in the unknown and cannot take the lead.

Time to receive the guidance from within.

If you are in a relationship and you keep trying to determine whether or not to stay, it is time to let go of decision-making and see what happens when you respond authentically to the other person.

Remember all those times you didn't say what you really felt? Do it now and do it consistently. The truth will be out in the open—not through some decision but through being present with this person you have shared your life with. Then you may learn what your partner feels, may agree to seek help, or may see clearly that the end is already here.

In terms of life purpose and work, you are being called to go deeper in your journey because you have learned the lessons of your current situation and now you want to grow. This could be testing your skills in new ways in the same work or returning to education to learn new skills.

The Priestess could also be calling you to another line of exploration on your life path. Be still and listen, consult the cards, and listen to wise counselors. Then be true to yourself. "There will be an answer, let it be."

Since The Priestess is a lunar card, it is helpful to pay attention to your dreams to see what insights naturally arise. Keep a dream journal or have a dream friend whom you share your dreams with.

The Empress/Gaia III
Planet: Venus

We have already touched on some of the aspects of The Empress in the previous card but now let's explore her in her own right. She is different from The Priestess in that she is not the spiritual guide that brings us across the abyss on the way to our mother's womb. Rather, she is the actual fertile mother, Venus, in all her aspects of loving, creativity, sensuality, nurturance, abundance, and beauty.

Traditionally The Empress has been relegated to the role of wife and mother, completely defined by her relationships to the other. But in the '60s she also spawned a wave of feminist fire that tore down the four walls of suburban boredom. Here we see the remaking of an archetype. Yes, the key word associated with the Mother/Empress is birth, but birth is also the creative process; every idea is conceived, gestates and is born.

The mother is the archetype of the gestating womb of creation, endlessly birthing new babies, and new and exciting ideas. Venus is the patron of the arts, sending out her message of beauty and pleasure as an integral part of the celebration of life. Life is not just a biological imperative but also an arena where the goddess of love creates art and beauty. She dances ecstatic rhythms in the many festivals of the world. For a long time the divine feminine has been reigned in by The Emperor and kept in her place as a vessel of his lordship. It is time to let go of this aspect of The Empress label and just call her Gaia, Earth Mother herself.

In the older Tarot books you will mainly find references to fertility, pregnancy, mothering and courtship. But now The Empress is emerging in all her glory to reclaim the crown of creation in all realms of life.

Let's examine how women reclaimed the act of birth itself. The entire process of birth in Western culture, especially in America, had been co-opted by the male medical establishment. In fact, women of my mother's generation were often scheduled for delivery to accommodate the golf game of their physician. Labor was induced and the mother rendered unconscious and completely disempowered during this miraculous and life-altering experience.

III

ז The Empress ♀

The baby was also affected by the drugs and, listless, taken away from the mother to be slapped, hosed down, and isolated from the very source of its existence. Bottle feeding and rigid schedules were imposed by the all-knowing male doctors, who were considered expert in all things female.

Natural home birth and alternative birth clinics were the result of the flower-children-turned-earth-mamas who declared to the world that birth was a natural, beautiful and deeply bonding experience. Women began to rediscover the old ways of the wise women and their herbal remedies that eased the labors. Birth was not scheduled but unfolded in its own time and in its own way, with every experience unique and profound. Partners were no longer pacing the waiting room. Having practiced breathing techniques and learned about birth, they became active participants, often cutting the cord and catching the baby and gently placing the newborn on the joyous mother to breastfeed immediately. The struggle to have this natural process fully reinstated and under the authority of the mother is ongoing, but the changes instigated in the '60s began this process.

When I gave birth to my first daughter I went to the hospital because I knew my baby was going to be born that day. I had no symptoms of labor and the hospital staff thought I didn't know what I was talking about. I arrived at 10:30 on a rainy Friday morning and they said if I didn't start labor by noon they would send me home. Immediately my instinct as a priestess of the door between the worlds was doubted. But around 11:30 the contractions began and I was taken to a room and told to lie down on the bed.

While I was lying there a strong contraction shook my body and I instinctively got up on my hands and knees. I had never been told anything about what to do in labor but I was happy to feel that I was in sync with my body. I felt I was inside an altered time and I would just keep going with the flow. I was only 21 years old and I was so excited to be giving birth my heart was wide open and very innocent. At that exact moment a doctor I had never met before abruptly entered the room and boomed in a loud voice with a thick German accent, "Vat do you think you are doing?!!" I crumbled in embarrassment and felt so small and ignorant that from that moment on I could not recover my own intuitive connection with this age-old process. Up until that point I felt guided and confident, but after that I helplessly surrendered to their concept of a medical procedure that shunted me aside.

What had originally felt like hard work became agonizing pain. They proceeded to give me medication, including a saddle block that hurt like hell and was too late to help anyway, and then they used forceps to pull my baby from me. I watched the people move around me and felt they had stolen my experience. I am happy to say my child was fine but I can still hear that cruel, cold voice in my head as if it were yesterday.

It's ironic that the hospital was called St. Mary's. If I had been allowed to continue to commune with the archetypal mother, represented by the divine Mary, I think I would've done just fine.

The next time I gave birth I decided to take matters into my own hands and did not go to the hospital until I had labored for over twelve hours and felt the birth was imminent. The birth was hard work, in other words, labor, but it was not what I would call painful at all. I stayed right with the whole rhythmic flow and was ecstatic and fully aware when my second child was born. By the time I gave birth to my third child I had a home birth with a midwife.

As soon as our children reached school age the same parents who had reclaimed the birth process began to examine the educational system and, remembering the intense boredom of our own school years, set out to reinvent the learning process to save our children from the same experience we had suffered through. Most of us can remember teachers and activities that really inspired us, but we felt that the system as a whole was very dysfunctional. The propaganda of history lessons alone that started with the glory of Columbus was not what we wanted for our children.

Many parents in my community decided to start homeschooling our children to respond to the natural curiosity and interests of our children. When I discovered that the word educere meant to draw out and not to stuff in, such as much of my experience had been, I used that concept as my guiding principle. If we could bring up one generation of children uncovered by our propaganda and our prejudices we could change the world, proclaimed my Indian guru.

To give birth in a loving way, women need to be honored, listened to, and served.

To create education in a loving way, schools need to feed the natural curiosity of the child and to reveal the resources that will help the child be an integrated part of life, a place where creative expression is of paramount importance. The Empress of today wants to see her children playing in the garden, experiencing the miracle of planting and growing first hand, and enjoying the harvest of their own efforts combined with her miraculous bounty. This, more than any other factor, will create healthy children with lifelong wholesome dietary habits.

The Empress is calling you to remember your love of life, nature and your own inherent instincts as an artist. We are all artists. In other words, we are all creators in our own right, and each time we awaken to this reality, life opens doors for us to demonstrate and offer our creative gifts to the world. The Hebrew letter for The Empress is Daleth, meaning door. She is the doorway through which we pass to enter this life and through which we return when we die. She is also the doorway through which we birth our creativity. Her ground is fertile, rich and capable of growing anything we have the inspiration to plant.

To learn the lesson of The Empress/Gaia is to discover that all life is interconnected and the garden is communal and cyclical. We will often experience an idea re-surfacing, just like a weed in our garden. As Henry David Thoreau stated, "Weeds are plants whose virtue is yet to be discovered." Sometimes our own ideas are uprooted like weeds before they can come to maturity because of ignorance or prejudice that doesn't allow us to nourish our virtues and our wildness. All my life I was told dandelions were weeds to be destroyed and now I know that they are a wonderful, spicy, and nutritious addition to any salad. I always loved to make wishes and blow her seed pods into the air and now I make a wish that dandelions will be liberated from the ghetto of weeds and be valued for all they're worth.

The Empress calls us to mirror her expression of unconditional love to those around us. This is something to aspire to and is much easier said than done, but when we employ her principles it becomes easier with practice. Just like Mother Nature, she never rejects any form of life, considers all beings her children and never takes personally our unconscious behavior. When The Empress card shows up, it's a good time to reflect on the idea that the cruel and heartless things people do to us has to do with their own struggles and life lessons. To stop loving them will only perpetuate and validate their actions. Unconditional love does not mean we are meant to martyr ourselves but that we can hold a place of compassionate detachment. We do not want to let our ability to empathize be limited by the limitations of those around us.

I personally never thought I would be able to be friends with my ex-husband and I am sure he felt the same way about me. But The Empress knew we both held unconditional love of our children and eventually that opened the door of shared parental love once again. Now we have family gatherings together and our children are no longer caught in the middle.

The Empress is also here to remind us of her wonderfully sensual aspects. She tells us to love ourselves and indulge in the many scents of her flowers, warmth of her waters, and love of her sexuality. She is always reminding us, with every rose we smell and every soft breeze that caresses us, that she wants us to celebrate the joy and pleasures of our human forms.

Vicki Noble and Karen Vogel chose to emphasize the luxuriating lady in their interpretation of The Empress card of the Mother- peace deck. We see her with a mirror, the same tool I use on my altar to remind me I am She. I have used this at home and have attended rituals where the attendees are each asked to look into a mirror and recognize the face of the divine in them. Whether they are male or female is irrelevant. We are all born out of the divine feminine and when we are able to see and honor ourselves we are much more capable of sharing our love with others.

On a physical level The Empress is definitely signaling us to not only wake up to our fertile minds but, of course, our fertile bodies. On a social level she sends a green light to those wanting to marry and have children, but it is important to take into consideration all the other factors in a reading to make this blessing truly fulfilling.

When The Empress is present we are ready to experience abun- dance and plenty in our lives, and be as generous as our Mother Earth in sharing what we have with others. The Empress tells us that the more we love and the more we give, the more we shall receive.

The Empress's shadow can be over-indulgence, as seen in the Seven of Cups, called Debauchery. Here Venus loses her dignity and that manifests in our lives as addictive behaviors. Desires that are not sourced in love can lead us into some dark Scorpionic caves if we are not careful. As Yogi Berra said, "There is never enough of something that does not satisfy."

In our culture the feminine is too often limited to the relationship realm. Her only value is in what she does to serve and nurture oth- ers. While this is a wonderful aspect of women throughout time, women also need to value their creativity, leadership and power as a voice in the world and on our own terms.

When you get this card in a reading

It is time to drink in the abundance of nature and all her delicious pleasures. Feast, dance, sing, swim, and make love to each other and the world.

If you are considering letting yourself open to a new relationship, Venus says, "Come on in, the water's fine!" If you are contemplat- ing having children, this is the ultimate fertility card.

Considering a new creative venture? The patron of the arts extends her blessing. Everything about this card exudes pleasure, celebration and abundance.

But if you find that you only feel important if others think so, or if you are taking care of everyone else, it is time to take a step back and find out who you are and what unique expression you offer to this world.

You are the fertile ground for art, writing, poetry, dance, music and imbuing every project with beauty and your unique expression of truth.

On the shadow side you may be confronting challenges that deal with your own biological mom, your relationship with the big Mama Earth herself, or your own children. Ask yourself how you can be both loving to others and true to yourself.

Take the time to reflect on how you nurture yourself and others around you. Make sure you do something to bring beauty into your environment, whether it be picking a bouquet of flowers or purchasing a work of art from a local artist you have long admired. We can all be patrons of the arts in our own way.

The abundance of Venus is not measured in dollars but in the simple joys of a baby's smile, the scent of a rose, the sound of laughter. Don't get caught up in the manufactured world of buying things to feel you are adequate. As Bob Dylan said, "Money doesn't talk in swears."

Now that we have met our divine mother in all her beauty, let's get acquainted with her partner, The Emperor.

The Emperor/Visionary Activist IV
Astrological Sign: Aries

———————————— ◖●◗ ————————————

The Emperor is a challenging card because many of us do not believe in the idea or necessity of emperors. It does not mesh with the principles of democracy. But it is necessary to transform this archetype, not merely condemn or reject it. So let's examine his inherent nature and how he was actually perverted into this dominator role. Hopefully we can retrieve him from his cruel heights and, at the same time, find the leadership powers from within each of us.

A good place to start in our discovery is through the astrological implications of the card. In the Major Arcana, all the visible planets, constellations and elements are designated to a particular card. We have already encountered the element of air in The Fool; the luminaries of Mercury, the Moon and Venus in The Magician, The Priestess and The Empress, respectively. Now we encounter the first zodiacal sign of Aries as the lens through which we can get to know The Emperor.

Aries is the sign of spring, the birth of the Green Man in European folklore and the time of rebirth and renewal. Ideas that have been gestating during the winter months are ready to be activated and made real. The profusion of nature abounds, exciting our desires for passionate lovemaking and promising projects that will fulfill the dreams of our winter mind.

To parallel nature's green and golden parade of beauty we find our hearts and minds excited about planting seeds of family and community that will give us opportunities to build and create new ways of learning, working and celebrating together. The ram is ready to charge forth with his determined horns to lead the way to get things moving.

Not all the seeds of our spring planting will come to fruition but a time of enthusiastic brainstorming within our communities can send a scatter of possibilities out into the world. Letting our minds be innocent and free is a great relief after the dark introspective winter months and we are ready to reconnect with The Fool in his dance of delight. Time to participate in the endless potentiality of life and accept his invitation to take a leap of faith. Every dawn and every spring, hope rises in the human spirit and we are engaged in the process of creation once again.

So where do the principles of The Emperor come in? Aries folks are natural leaders, with the charisma and enthusiasm to inspire others. When we let go of the toxic version of "power over" and move into leading by example, then The Emperor becomes The Visionary Activist. This is the name of astrologer Caroline Casey's radio show and a perfect evolutionary take on the authentic nature of Aries. Starhawk, a Visionary Activist in her own right, has proposed that we work with the concept of power from within; that we evolve out of the Dominator model of "power over" as defined by author Riane Eisler in her book, The Partnership Way: New Tools for Living and Learning.

The Visionary Activist does not seek personal power and profit. He loves to be an innovative and active force for change.

He is an inspired speaker who can voice the vision of his people in a way that serves to focus the energy out of chaos into order. He is practical and realistic in his determination to get things done. These are the qualities that all of us need to access if we are going to actually manifest our dreams and not just talk about them. He offers a plan within the parameters of possibility and suggests realistic ways to take the brainstorms of The Fool and lead us towards forging what is actually possible at this time.

The key word is order. Here we encounter the nature of the number four. The Emperor is often pictured sitting with one leg crossed over, looking very much like a four himself.

When we consider the nature of numbers in their geometric progression we discover that four is the cube, foursquare, the idea of structure and limitation. The indigenous peoples showed this reality in the idea of the four directions that contain the sacred hoop or circle. We need to follow certain laws of nature, represented by our mathematical systems, in order to construct or build our projects.

How do we create the structures and follow the laws of nature to build these new projects? Limitation is a necessary part of the building process and The Emperor is here to remind us of how to impose the limitations needed to proceed. We need to be guided by the laws of geometry as well as the laws of our society that are already in place. Sometimes when new ideas surface, old laws or customs must evolve and change to accommodate the times.

But how did this Visionary Activist become The Emperor and rule over us in ways that are dominating, cruel, and even violent? We humans are often too willing to give our power away to someone who is charismatic, strong, and willing to take charge. In the

IV

ℵ **The Emperor** ν

beginning we are glad to have our leaders help us to focus and direct our energy toward the improvements and projects we want to implement. But if we give up our rights to stay within the decision-making process then, little by little, corruption seeps in to undermine the original intention that was for the benefit of all.

The Emperor can start out as someone who is willing to do most of the work and our laziness lets him gradually be in control of everything. The visionary who spoke words that sparked our imagination is now demanding that we do it his way, and is excited and deluded by his new power. He finds satisfaction in his position rather than his purpose. The monster that is created is latent within each of us. To want to either control or be controlled is often an unconscious power dynamic that this card brings to light.

Returning to the myth of the Green Man we can apply some of the wisdom of the ancients. The Green Man is birthed each spring and is sacrificed at harvest time to be recycled and composted during the winter months. He does not hold a permanent position. He is born, plants his seeds, tends them, brings them to fruition, and dies to go back into the womb of the Great Mother and be gestated and filled with the new seeds for the coming year. The Emperor in his evolved form as The Visionary Activist sheds his role when the harvest is reaped, the initial task accomplished. It is the male cycle that moves with the seasons just as the female cycle moves with the Moon. The Green Man becomes the sacrificed god or The Hanged Man. The King is Dead! Long Live the King!

The divine will of the masculine is immortal because it is born and reborn, not because it is rigid and immovable.

It is this rigidity that incites the many violent overthrows of repressive regimes. But such conflict can be avoided if we learn as children that leadership is not a person but a transitory position occupied by individuals aspiring to facilitate the will of the people. Leadership is evolving to be a more flexible rotating position according to the needs of the community and not according to the needs of the leaders. The position is available to all of us when our skills and the necessity of the time coalesce. Within our spiritual mythologies and actual religions and governments we have the opportunity to participate in new ways that could bring out the leader in us all.

The Major Arcana represent aspects of each of us. Whether or not we are introverted or extroverted, we can still exercise leadership in the realm of our personal power. The chef is the leader for the feast, the architect for the building of structures, and the monk for the example of quiet meditation. Each of us is here to activate our vision, whether it is in the quiet of the artist's studio or the arena of politics and government. When the feast is done and the building built then that particular role of leadership is over. This is referred to as task-oriented leadership.

We are maturing as humans when we don't expect our leaders to have all the answers and make our decisions for us. Instead, we can temporarily surrender some of our power in cooperation to get things done. But the modern world is rife with leaders who started out as visionaries and became despots.

In the mythology of Egypt the hieroglyph for Isis is a throne. This is a profound symbol of the principle that the position is held in the realm of the divine and occupied by those who are in service to the divine. The throne is not to be possessed by humans but served by them. This signifies that a ruler was meant to serve what was considered sacred by the people of Egypt and not act as The Emperor who only answers to himself.

When you get this card in a reading

We are being asked to examine our relationship to power, both internally and externally. Do we like the structures within which we live our daily lives? Do they serve us or are they oppressive? Power structures that have been in place a long time often become dysfunctional bureaucracies that are bent on their own self-preservation rather than an open channel to coordinate activities for the good of all.

The Emperor asks us to examine our own ability to exercise power in our work and our relationships. Many times this character will bring to the fore our relationship to our own biological father and how we have internalized him and are unconsciously playing out that relationship in our adult lives as well. This can be especially true if your life card is The Emperor or you are in an Emperor year.

The Emperor often makes an appearance when an individual is in a hierarchical structure, specifically a corporate job. Many people work in these jobs because of the perceived security they offer and sometimes this is limiting their ability to create a structure that would be more cooperative and serve their needs. Sometimes we as young adults overstay our time in our parents' home for these same reasons. Do we still want daddy to pay the bills and keep the system in working order or are we ready to do it for ourselves?

Fear and indolence coupled with an indulgent father can keep us from our true potential as an independent person. I did a reading for a kind woman in her mid-thirties whose life was really defined by her relationship to her father. She was living rent-free in one of the buildings he owned and her bedroom still looked like a teenager's with cutouts from magazines, hearts, bunnies and stuffed animals everywhere. These are signs of arrested development and demonstrate that when we give away our power to make life "easier" we are often just avoiding growing up.

Many of our institutions and religions promote the idea of a father figure that will answer all our questions and our prayers and all we must do is surrender ourselves via faith and funds. It is not until we enter the second row of the Majors that we really encounter the archetypes that will reconnect us with our inner link to the divine. The Hermit and Strength/Lust are examples of self-empowerment. The Hermit does the work of finding confirmation from within, turning away from gurus and organized religion. In The Strength/Lust card we see the self, free and uninhibited, in the outer world.

The transformation of archetypes of The Emperor and The Empress into the Visionary Activist and Gaia allow us to still honor the father and mother without being dependent and infantilized by them. We need the gifts of unconditional love, abundance, and creativity from the mother aspect; we need order, protection, and leadership from the father aspect. These gifts can be received from parents of either sex or other caring adults. There is a big difference between receiving these gifts and incorporating them into our lives versus looking for surrogate moms and dads in our jobs, religions, and relationships. Deeper analysis of this stage in our evolution is explored in the excellent book by Joel Kramer and Diana Alstad called The Passionate Mind Revisited (see my review in Appendix 385).

To truly understand our parents is to grow beyond both dependency and rebellion and understand them as human beings just like us. In their positive role they are guides but they can be unprepared and wounded themselves. As we become adults we can then understand and forgive our parents and not unconsciously take on their psychological limitations.

The Hierophant V
Astrological Sign: Taurus

The Hierophant is the guardian of the socio-religious heritage of our many different cultures. He has been called The High Priest, The Pope, The Teacher. Sometimes he is simply called Traditions.

The Hierophant embodies the function of our educational and religious institutions to pass on the knowledge, wisdom, and mores of our society. We encounter him as the teacher or coach in our schools and the priest, minister, rabbi, guru, or other guide of our family's spiritual practice.

In The Emperor we confronted our relationship with power and now we are looking at our relationship with truth. Our teachers and priests pass on to us the "truths" that are intended to reveal the underpinnings of the history of our community, tribe, and world at large. History is presented as facts but they are usually told from the perspective of the ruling class and, therefore, are inextricably bound to the moral messages of the cultural norm. To give a simple example of this we need only look at the history of colonization and the Crusades to see how the stories support the propaganda of the ruling institutions. When the state, as represented by a despotic Emperor, is reinforced by the precepts of The Hierophant, we are in danger of losing sight of the higher functions of our cultural traditions. This is why it is so essential to democracy to have a separation of church and state.

So, then, what is the higher purpose of our religious and educational structures? The answer to that question lies in the word itself. Hierophant literally means sacred fantasy, i.e., hieros = sacred, phantos = fantasy. If the true function of our educational and religious institutions were to help us uncover our sacred dream and give us the tools, resources, and past experiences of our ancestors, what kind of world would we be living in today?

Here, as with The Emperor, we have created dogma where we need inspiration; moral imperatives where we need encouragement to make rational judgments and choices. If our teachers inspire us to discover life for ourselves, to become scientists without pre-conceived theories, exploring life with our own perspective still valid and intact, we would create more Madam Curies and Einsteins.

It is, of course, a part of the tradition of all cultures to want to instill in the next generation the values, morals, and lessons of the society. But it could be possible to pass on the lessons of the past without indoctrinating our youth through propaganda and fear of eternal damnation. A child could easily understand that to do unto others as he would have them do unto him is a win/win situation. To develop morality from within by encouraging respect for others, to help allay fears of that which is alien or different, and to reveal the interconnectedness of all life, is an evolutionary leap that is taking place in many alternative educational and spiritual organizations.

Incorporating the above principles can lead us to look at The High Priest/Hierophant as a channel to the divine, a link to source, and a guide that confirms and encourages our inner voice, rather than an unquestioned authority. When examining this card it is important to recognize both aspects.

The Hierophant in the Motherpeace deck shows women supplicating before a priest with breasts and a skirt. He has usurped the power of the feminine and declares the authority of the church over all life. The Pope and the priests claim a direct link to "god" and therefore cannot be questioned.

The study of mythology reveals that religions have often retold the stories of the goddess to denigrate and disempower her role. Artemis, the goddess of wisdom, becomes the goddess of war and Eve becomes the temptress and creator of original sin as opposed to the one who initiates us into the knowledge of good and evil as a necessary step in conscious evolution. Isis becomes Mary, a passive receptacle as opposed to a wise, magical, and powerful female archetype. This poem, called "Hail Mary," exemplifies this attempt by patriarchal, warring tribes to disempower the goddess as they spread throughout Europe.

V

The Hierophant

HAIL MARY

I was walking by a church one day
    it was nearly the twilight hour,
A gust of wind blew open the door,
And the light of the votive candles
    drew my eyes to the sterile room.

An old woman was kneeling
    and whispering prayers
    before the Virgin Mary.

I pulled my coat against the cold,
    and tried to hurry on,
But the statue's sad and lonely stare,
    called my soul to enter there.

As I walked in,
    to my amazement,
The statue came alive!

Tears were falling from her face,
She looked into my heart,
    and Mary's voice both trembling,
    and infinitely kind
Spoke as if inside my mind.
"I want to leave this place!" she said,
"I cannot breathe, I have no life,
No one understands me here,
The people come because they fear
The wrath of a jealous god.

I miss my sisters, where is Artemis,
Athena, Isis, Kali?

The stories they tell about the brilliant Eve,
That the knowledge of life,
    she used to deceive,
Denies the initiation we all must receive,
To live a life of truth.

And then there's Ruth
and the Magdalene,
Treated like a whore obscene,
When I know she is a Priestess.

I want all those priests
To now confess,
Take off their skirts
    and their crucifixes
And clean up this ugly mess!"

Well, the smile spreading across my face,
 I wanted to see on the whole human race,
So I rushed to take her hand,
"Come with me, Sweet Mary,
I'll take you home," I held her in my arms.

She whispered, "I am a Virgin,
But not the way they think,
It once meant we were autonomous,
    not sexless and anonymous,
I want to dance in the world!"

We ran for the door,
    her mantle unfurled
    and fell upon the floor,
And the weight of all
    those Darkened Ages
Was lifted from her shoulders.

She sparkled in anticipation,
        of her sweet Emancipation,
No more lies about temptation,
        the snake slithered from under her foot.

The Kundalini current entwined us
Both in ecstasy,
And as we stepped into the street,
        we turned back to hear the sound of feet,
And spied the old woman
        skipping quick and fleet,
To catch us in our dance.

She said, "Mary! You forgot the Apple!"
We laughed and took a bite!

The Moon looked down on this epiphany,
        and bathed us in her light....
"Tonight, Tonight, is a Holy night,
Let it never be forgotten,"

When all the Pagans
        danced for Joy!
And even Jesus, as a little boy,
Came home to Mary,
        when he beheld,
The Moon beneath her Feet,

So, Every day, Every church you pass,
Hail Mary! As she leaves the Mass!
Hail Mary! As she leaves the Mass!

By Magick

When we are liberated from the internalized voices of our parents, teachers and religious guides we become more capable of dialing direct to source. This is embodied in the card The Hermit/Crone, which we will experience in the second row of the archetypes.

Another way to understand The Hierophant is to look at him as Taurus the Bull. Just as The Emperor/Ram represents Aries, here we find the second sign in the zodiac portrayed in The Hierophant.

Taurus is the sign of passion, feasting, agriculture, animals, and the abundance of The Empress, Venus, who rules Taurus.

May Day, or Beltane, a cross-quarter day that lies exactly between spring equinox and summer solstice, is a celebration of the fertility and sexual magic of all life's creatures. Hieros Gamos, the sacred marriage, was enacted by many European pagan tribes. During this celebration, large bonfires would shine brightly from the hilltops calling all the people to the feast of consummation.

It was believed that nature's crops were enhanced by human ritual enactment of sexual union. On this day The Priestess, dressed in her finest apparel, was led to a tent to await the Green Man disguised as a deer. There the sacred union was enacted while outside the tent many people coupled without concern about normal relationships. For one night, sexuality for the continuance of the tribe and the crops was celebrated by all.

What happened in Beltane, stayed in Beltane.

The union of the masculine and feminine (not necessarily male and female) as an offering and prayer to the spirit realm was a powerful message of our connection to nature. The institutionalization of religion banned this kind of ritual and deemed it satanic. That is why naked people dancing on hilltops around a fire became associated with black magic when it was actually a life-affirming celebration.

The phrase associated with Taurus is "I have" but what it is that the bull possesses is up for debate. Is it the Papal Bull or the Golden Calf? The power of the church to declare edicts from above or the desire for material pleasure that was condemned in the story of the Golden Calf?

"I have" can also be just the obsession with possessions as an end in itself. This card represents the paradox between Taurean earthly pleasure and the religious condemnation of an embodied life.

When you get this card in a reading

The Hierophant asks you to consider your lifework. Are you doing what you "should" according to your parents and teachers or are you listening to your soul's yearnings and manifesting your unique work in the world?

My daughter, Celeste Hirschman, has an M.A. in human sexuality and works as a sex and intimacy coach, helping people free themselves from the judging, condemning "should" of religion and dogma to reclaim the Taurus sensual embodiment that is our birthright. As it happens, her life card is The Heirophant and she likes to say: "Stop shoulding all over yourself!" Humor is one of our most effective tools in breaking the ego/mind's stranglehold of judgment, guilt, and inhibition. (www.celesteanddanielle.com.)

Before Celeste became a "sexpert" she had in mind that she "should" become Dr. Hirschman. She enrolled in a five-year Ph.D. program and after a semester that cost her $12,000 she could not stand the cold, sterile heights of academia; she wanted to be in the nitty-gritty of real sexuality. It was well worth it for her to have this experience and forever put to rest the "should" voice that had diverted her from her heart's desire and lifework. Now she is a teacher, coach, trainer, and author in the realm of sexuality and intimacy.

Here are some questions to ponder to explore the deeper meanings of this card.

- Do you need more education or training to become who you truly are?
- Are you intimidated by educational institutions because of negative experiences of the past and therefore need to face and overcome this fear to further your development? (See the Seven of Disks.) This would be a great time to take a class in something you are passionate about without the need to prove anything to any one else, including the teacher.
- Is there an imbalance of power between the masculine and feminine within yourself or your relationships?
- Is there an aspect of obsession and desire to possess that is unhealthy and never satisfied? Greed and overindulgence is the shadow of just enjoying the pleasures of the sensual world.

Another aspect of the bull is to volunteer to shoulder the weight of whatever needs to be done. You can count on a Taurus to do the heavy lifting. But as we mature, our greater gifts are not to take on all the physical and repetitive tasks, but instead to share our experience and wisdom. It might be a good time to take on an apprentice or find other ways to share your lifework so your legacy serves future generations.

Many times this card indicates a strong connection to the animal world, agriculture, and the preparation of food. These may be fields you need to work in or at least enjoy and experience on a regular basis.

If you have been thinking about starting a restaurant, garden project, or work with animals, this card is a green light to all of the above.

The Lovers IV
Astrological sign: Gemini

Here we see the first card in our journey that is not about just one character. The Lovers are introduced under the appropriate sign of Gemini, The Twins. In The Lovers, our young Fool encounters the beloved, his/her divine mirror and partner in the dance. In other words, he/she falls in love.

In the image we see a marriage taking place within a cultural milieu that encompasses myth, religion, and class. This ceremony often symbolizes a fulfillment of our socialized role as passed down by previous generations to maintain the current order and structure.

Or will it be the first step in individuation represented by the separation from the parents as the all-knowing authorities? It is like finding a twin spirit, or at least a projected belief in a soulmate, who is now holding center stage in our lives.

When I fell in love as a teenager, my relationship to my parents, The Emperor and The Empress, and my teachers, The Hierophant, changed drastically. I rebelled against anyone telling me what to do or what to think. I found an ally in my boyfriend and we explored new ways of thinking and acting that challenged the people who had influenced the development of my young mind.

No one understood me better than my lover and the time we shared was the focus of my life. I questioned authority in school, church, home, and in the world.

Our love was energized by the times we lived in. I was a freshman in high school and it was 1964. The hippie movement was just breaking through the two-dimensional world of postwar materialism and we were ecstatic to be a part of the awakening.

We felt like a young Bob Dylan and Joan Baez and, as such, we rejected our parents and teachers and embraced The Priestess, The Magician, and The Fool. They beckoned us to be initiated into a new way of perceiving our lives. One path was the use of mind-altering substances. Although now it is clear that any long-lasting shifts in consciousness need practice and dedication, these substances catalyzed a shift by literally changing the way we thought.

VI

ʼ **The Lovers** II

The psychoactive substances catapulted us into an awareness that everything was alive, dancing, rhythmic, and interconnected. As Allen Ginsberg explained, you could meditate for 15 years or drop LSD!

I am not advocating anything here by telling an experiential truth that mind-altering drugs catalyzed an explosive energetic awakening. Like the song "White Rabbit" by the Jefferson Airplane that called us to feed our heads, we jumped down the rabbit hole and there was no going back.

We were hungry for something more than the two-dimensional lifestyle of suburban boredom. We threw off the yoke of our parents' emphasis on acquiring things. We wanted to be alive, dancing, and creating a new world.

Young lovers everywhere were rejecting the limitations of the parental version of the institution of marriage as represented in The Lovers card. The mythology, represented by Cupid, religion represented by Cain, Abel, Eve, and Lilith, and the dualistic nature of the whole picture was being ripped apart at the seams!

Cupid seemed like a romanticized joke to sell Valentine's Day cards; Eve was becoming the goddess of initiation into the knowledge of good and evil; Lilith represented the autonomous and sometimes lesbian woman; and Cain and Abel were the divided brothers of the war in Vietnam. One brother following the blind patriotism of the hero's path; the other radicalized in opposition to serving the state, rejecting war as a crime against humanity.

Our spiritual parents, represented by The Priestess—dreams and intuitions, and The Magician—our will and imagination, had taken the reins from The Emperor and Empress. There was no turning back for the young lovers of my generation.

The Lovers card has historically been a backdrop to tell the stories of lovers such as Romeo and Juliet whose tragic demise was a result of their failure to be released from the last generation's limiting prejudices and controlling expectations.

In some older decks, this card was called Decisions or Choices and asked us to not only evaluate our feelings about romance and family, but also our connection to the community at large.

Hippies rejected the dead zone of suburbia and flocked to the cities to express the rebellious urges to create a new sense of communal living. The soundtrack of those times was a motivational element for the politicalization of our generation as well. Songs like "The Chimes of Freedom" by Bob Dylan, "For What It's Worth" by Buffalo Springfield and "Imagine" by John Lennon were anthems of change that called us to take to the streets.

We were creating a new mythology of fools, feminists, tricksters, shapeshifters, earth mamas, and sexually liberated men and women. At the same time we leapt over the monotheistic, patriarchal, and militaristic systems and reached back into the primal cultures of the goddess and indigenous tribes worldwide.

We discovered cultures that did not accept or believe in the enslavement of the Earth or other species. The Gaia theory became a widespread concept that saw the Earth as a living, unified being that we are all a part of.

So we see being "lovers" has the power to awaken us to all kinds of evolutionary changes that can be joyous as well as filled with profound challenges in a world mired in hatred, prejudice, and war.

To truly let love awaken us is to be reminded of the interconnectedness of the universe, the one song, the vibration of life itself.

When you get this card in a reading

It is time to assess your relationships and bring a fresh awareness to all facets of your life. If you are to make wise choices instead of unconsciously reacting, then shedding a light on your story so far is paramount.

Four relationship questions to ask yourself are:

- What have you learned from your family and community growing up that you still value and respect?
- What have you chosen to release from your upbringing that does not serve you now?
- What do you want to invite into your life now that you have learned from your own experiences?
- What models of relationships are useful to ponder in literature, myth, and society that resonate with you currently?

It is helpful to look at ourselves as an evolution, not a rejection, of where we came from. Even when there is abuse in our past, as is so often the case, it is most healing to find ways to take care of ourselves that we lacked within our family and community. The kindest way to proceed is to find a way to become whole in ourselves and find synthesis in the duality of male and female. We can care for our wounds by being our own parents, often with the help of some form of therapy such as Hakomi or Somatics.

Studying and practicing meditation to gain the ability to witness our mind instead of being plagued by old reactions is really essential. There is a common misconception that meditation's goal is to stop the mind. It is really a practice in patience and self-love to gradually loosen the grip of our brain that is always judging and assessing from the standpoint of survival. It is the witness that can grant us the spaciousness that empties out the old patterns.

Creating intentional circles of friends where we share our personal stories has also been very useful to millions of people. These are all ways to get out of the cycle of reactivity and blame.

Often we are told to forgive and this can be very challenging. Forgiveness does not have to mean we accept the cruelty of our past, or have contact with abusers. Forgiveness really is recognition of the human condition. We are all broken and as Leonard Cohen said, "There's a crack in everything, that's how the light gets in."

We also do not want to be reductionist about karma and assume we deserve what has happened to us. Karma is best seen as the roster of lessons we need to learn. Once they're learned, we are released from further circumstances that repeat the same story.

The Lovers card shows up when an integration of our duality needs to deepen. The Gemini twins need new ways to communicate. Since Gemini is ruled by Mercury, the messenger and healer, we might delve into his magical tool box for some assistance.

His magical wand (fire) would suggest action and play.
His cup (water) calls us to do a cleansing, taking time for reflection.
His sword (air) invokes a deeper expression of our truth.
His disk (earth) reminds us to ground in individual life purpose so we don't get lost in the other/beloved.

Examine how these elements in the Minor Arcana show up in the reading to chart a course of renewal and healing.

Often the Major Arcana, The Emperor, The Empress, and The Hierophant, show up in conjunction with this card to bring into our field the challenges of our upbringing.

It is self-limiting to hold the people of our childhood in a fixed idea of who they are. When we say someone will never change we are holding on to an unchanging idea in an ever-changing universe. We do not need to know how they will change, only that it is always possible. If not, we are magnetized to that fixed idea and we will continue to attract that story to us in myriad ways.

Although we might think this would be simply a romantic card, it is much more complicated and concerns all our relationships and a need to continually re-evaluate and grow as we go.

This card also asks us to bring clarity to our connection with our community so it is a reciprocal relationship that feeds us.

The Chariot VII
Astrological Sign: Cancer

The Chariot is the first card in our journey that is named after an object. Even though we see the charioteer seated or standing in the chariot, we are called to focus on the vehicle. What vehicle will take us into the world? Is it a job in our father's business, joining the army or the Peace Corps, going to college, taking a trip abroad, or possibly getting married?

If there was no real rebellion or individuation in The Lovers stage then we may still be unconsciously or begrudgingly following the plans of our family. The job at the father's business or a prearranged marriage would fit this category. Going to medical school to be a doctor because we were always told we were supposed to is within the constructs of our familial influence.

The chariot could be the old jalopy we buy to elope with the lover our parents didn't like. Or the drugs we take to try to understand our expanding consciousness, to kill the pain, or escape reality.

There is a middle road that is not rebellion or acquiescence, but rather conscious choice to honor the useful gifts that our family and community have given us during our developing years. If our mentors have taught us and allowed us to reason and think for ourselves, and to acknowledge the murmurs of our heart, then we do not need to be in constant reaction to our parents and elders.

The Chariot is a very complicated card in that it exemplifies both our physical and spiritual choices. On the spiritual level it represents our will, our personal grail, the core of our being.

In the Thoth deck, the charioteer is seated in a meditative pose holding a blue disk with a red center. This is meant to represent the Cup of Life (the Ace of Cups), the Holy Grail. It is turned on its side and facing outward, a whirling disk of energy. The red symbolizes the blood of the womb, the mystery of the dream-creating Moon within. To find out what's in our blood, our DNA, our destiny, we need to be still and listen.

The spiritual vehicles that can help us to hear our inner voice are meditation, prayer, or simply writing in a journal or taking a walk by the sea. Many of us find clues while dreaming, relaxing in a bath, or just being in nature and fully present.

There is a voice within each of us that is our true will and with practice and in time we grow to recognize this voice. To ignore it, rationalize against it or to mistake our ego's longings for our will is to lose direction. We come in touch with ourselves and lose touch in a continuing search for the truth. If one vehicle doesn't work we must find another way to amplify the message of The Magician, our true will, and bring it into the realm of our conscious mind.

When we act on the intuition of the still small voice, we reinforce it and give it validation and weight. The more we do this, the more capable we become of recognizing it and distinguishing it from the false urges of our desires and fears. This is not to imply that desires are wrong; life is meant to be satisfying, but not at the expense of our conscious purpose. There is a time for pleasure and a time for practice, and to honor both creates a healthy, balanced outlook that makes the journey in our newfound vehicle more authentic.

Another aspect of The Chariot can be understood through its astrological sign of Cancer. Cancer is ruled by the Moon and is, therefore, related to the feminine aspect of nurturance. The original home of all life is the sea itself so it is called the sign of the home. The easy way to remember this is to take a look at the crab, the totem for Cancer, who always carries his home with him. He lives inside his shell and is protected so he can have a cozy scene with everything he needs right there. Some Cancer people can take this to an extreme and become pack rats, feeling they are safe and in control the more stuff they have. We can be led astray by this Cancerian urge and if it becomes an obsession it may be a cover for the deeper, emotional need to love and be loved.

Cancer is the sign of feelings and these crabs also carry their shell as a symbol of protection when they are hurt or misunderstood. The need for appreciation is strong in these creatures and a few words of thanks can turn their claws into castanets!

The Chariot presents a paradox, leaving home and creating home at the same time.

The more we follow our true will the more we will, like the crab, carry our home with us and be present in the moment wherever we are. When we look at the image in the Thoth deck, we see that it projects a feeling of movement created by the wheels and the circles of blue coming from behind, yet all the elements are in stasis. Look at the charioteer and the animals, all seated and still. When we are truly manifesting our will and are fully in the present moment, we are moving in and with time and the concept of linear time dissolves in the eternal moment of now.

VII

ה   **The Chariot**   ♋

This is not a state we can stay in so we spiral out and back in over and over in the course of our lives. Each time home becomes more like home than the last time. Maybe someday we will never leave, and in an enlightened state become a compassionate witness and benevolent soul who feels his heart beat with the heart of the world. We will feel as at home as the crab in the currents of his mother, the sea.

In the traditional Tarot decks we see the conquering hero careening through life, fighting for the state and following the orders of The Emperor, defending all he was taught to believe is right. This is very much connected with the concept of the quest that runs through many of the world mythologies. When we set off into the world we are full of ambition and determined to be victorious. It is a wonderful feeling to set a goal and accomplish it. But it takes a lot of focus and honest self-reflection to be clear about our true will. Victory is hollow if it is only a demonstration of bravado. After all, we can be a conqueror in the world and still not know ourselves at all.

When you get this card in a reading

The Chariot calls you to examine your real focus and purpose. Are you trying to win or conquer to prove something to yourself or others, or are you on a journey of self-development? Are you sacrificing the feelings of others to elevate yourself?

The interpretation given to this card by the seated meditator as opposed to the conquering hero is an evolutionary remake of the hero's quest. Now he/she holds the grail within the feminine sea of dreams that exists in all people, male and female. Even though women bleed in synchrony with the Moon, men are also capable of tuning in to the receptive Moon aspect.

The following inquiries explore the different themes within this archetype:

- What vehicle will take you to the next level of understanding?
- What does a true home feel like or look like to you? If this is your life card you need to ask yourself what feels like home to you.
- Have you ever actually created a home as an adult that you are proud of?
- What do you need to do to own your space?
- Does your home reflect your tastes and interests? Does it give you a cozy feeling? Or is it a crash pad, a temporary way station, or a party scene?
- Do you want your home to be a sanctuary? A good place to entertain, to work, or to raise a family?
- What are your wounds that you cover over with bravado instead

of bravely acknowledging the pain and compassionately mothering yourself?
• What do you need from others in order to let go of control and
feel safe, appreciated, and loved?

Whatever vehicle we have chosen will now take us into the Realm
of Earthly Reality where things are often very different than anyone ever told us in church, school, or at home. Our direct relationship to the reality of self-determination is about to take us for a ride.
Will we choose the freeway of love or the combat zone, the arena
of physical accomplishment or spiritual development?

The biggest danger can often be on the path that seems the safest
and most familiar (note that family is the root of familiar). This can
manifest as an unconscious urge to just go along with the status
quo. It is imperative to take responsibility for our own lives. No
matter how much privilege or poverty we have experienced, we still
have a choice. To go off in the world only to fulfill the dream of
the previous generation is to deny the evolutionary nature of this
life. Each generation is meant to generate the next stage of growth;
there is no safety in hiding within the limitations and prejudices of
the past. Take the precious gifts like The Fool with his knapsack and
The Magician with his tools but remember you are unique in the
entire universe and, someday, with a little luck and a whole lot of
determination, you will have a chance to give your gift to the world.
The Mayans said that human means one who owes a gift.

At the end of this first stage of the Majors you have the gifts you
will need to go forth. Remember that, like the camel crossing the
desert, you have within those humps the stored waters of life, the
transmission of the wisdom of your community and your ancestors. Ask for help whenever you need it. The benevolence of The
Universe is always there, even in our darkest hour.

THE SECOND LEVEL:
THE REALM OF EARTHLY REALITY

Justice/Adjustment opens the second row of the Majors as we try to get our footing in the world. In the Realm of Earthly Reality we are now facing choices, responsibilities, and possibilities of the vast world without the constant guidance and direction of our family. It is a time in which anything can happen. This is often a time of uncertainty and doubt, as we weigh our choices on the scales of justice.

Possibly the young Fool has stepped out as a traveler, off to let the world reveal her charms as she sees fit; or maybe the serious student has decided he should get a Ph.D. in astrophysics.

As we take our Chariot out into the world there are many road signs that are not familiar; they may throw us off course; but each experience is an opportunity for learning.

Life is the larger school we now attend, and the more we are aware of this truth the less painful and repetitive the lessons become. Life can be a joyous revelation one day and a school of hard knocks the next, so finding our center of gravity, the place of balance and integrity, is the first major challenge to the young explorer.

Justice/Adjustment VIII
Astrological Sign: Libra

One of the first things we learn about the world: it isn't always fair. When we are thrust into confrontation with obstructions to our progress it is necessary to make adjustments. If not, The Chariot could career out of control, crashing and burning down the highway of life, as we refuse to recognize the need to slow down and take heed.

The first experience of this balancing act is often literal, such as the frustration of bounced checks as we learn to balance our checkbook. Questions arise. How do I balance work and play? How do I eat a balanced diet now that mom isn't here to help me out? How do I apply my own limits to stay centered now that freedom of choice has expanded immensely?

Drugs and alcohol are a huge temptation and the need to understand how to use them responsibly is an adult lesson that is often learned the hard way when our young immortal faces a police officer and he can't walk that line.

Facing justice in a court of law can be a daunting lesson, but this lesson could save our young protagonist from a life-threatening accident later on.

It is in fact the highest form of justice that teaches the proper lesson and sets things right. Too often we find that our modern day justice is obsessed with punishment that often fails to teach anything at all. Those who would want to impose a sense of justice on our youth, using a whip instead of wisdom, are surely not teaching by example.

Rupert Ross, who spent 14 years working as a member of the Canadian mainstream legal system in northwestern Ontario, found within the tribal communities of the Ojibway and Cree an excellent example of restorative justice. He argues that social order does not result from creating fear of punishment but from working to heal the whole community and the transgressor at the same time. Read his book, Returning to the Teachings, and your idea of true justice will be altered forever.

Now let's examine the deeper symbolic level of Justice. We see pictured in this card a woman, balanced perfectly on her toes (en

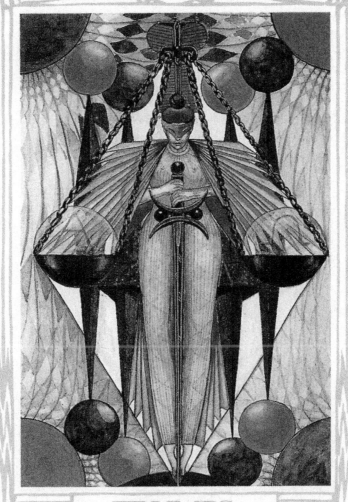

VIII

Adjustment

pointe) holding the scales of justice and girt with a sword. This is actually the personification of Venus, implying that since there are no absolute truths, the sword of truth is only authentic when a loving heart wields it. Justice is only justice when the full picture is considered, the Alpha and the Omega (written on each side of the scales). Venus rules the sign of Libra whose symbol is the scales. But Venus is not limited to the realm of humans. In reality it is the larger picture that she holds in exquisite balance by the infinite interfaces in the dance of duality. Night and day balance each other, as do fall and spring, summer and winter, the Sun and the Moon. She does not perceive these polarities as good or bad, any more than she sees life as something to be exceeded, or death as something to be avoided. This is the dance of light and dark that plays itself out across the ever-expanding universe. She delights in the endless possibilities; from the tiniest ladybug to a supernova, her beauty is expressed.

She is also the Patron of the Arts, revealing her beauty as a constant inspiration to the artistic spirit in each of us. She does not sit in judgment of our attempts at creation, but rather encourages us to see beauty in everything. For to truly love is to accept wholly the beloved. We cannot have the blackberry without the thorn or day without night. Our innate desire to explore the mystery of this palette of possibilities is her gift to us all. She surrounds us with the profusion of her creative impulses, thereby compelling us to be creators ourselves.

All expression can be elevated to the realm of art by the intention we infuse it with. Or to look at it another way, all life is art. This is exemplified by the Balinese who do not have a word for art—for life is art, and to separate it is to diminish its spiritual essence.

If we always stay in our critical mind we won't be able to explore the intrinsic beauty of all life. She invites us to know and experience John Keats' poetic revelation, "Beauty is truth, truth beauty—that is all ye know on Earth, and all ye need to know."

Her natural partner is The Fool, leaping into life believing that all things are possible. And he is right! "If it can be imagined it can be done" is a seldom believed, but infinitely demonstrated, truism of this plane of existence.

The most palpable example of this is that people said we could never fly and then we did. All things are impossible until they happen. A baby can't walk until it does; we cannot walk our talk until we grow in wisdom gleaned from our ancestors and learned through our own life experience. This is the wisdom she expresses to temper The Fool's imagination when he throws out a wild dream that we desire to make real. Venus does not laugh but helps him understand the different laws or structures of the universe that must be respected and applied to bring a dream into reality.

So she dances with The Fool and presents our young adventurer with the Magician's tools that will help him recognize the laws of cause and effect and other universal principles. Justice softly whispers in his ear, "Ah, but if you do that, I must do this." And on they waltz, separating and uniting in the spiraling dance of The Universe. They are secretly wed in the card called—what else—Art! (Temperance in other decks.) This card of synthesis shows the transformation of opposites into complementary elements of the whole in the cauldron of alchemy. We will hear more about that later in the section on Trump XIV, called Art (see page 108).

Another aspect of balance is in our connection with the natural world. To actively honor the Earth, we need to literally ground ourselves and shed some of the layers of our constructed world.

When you get this card in a reading

It's a great time to take more walks in nature or find some outdoor activity to experience the simple miracles of life that will realign the body with the living body of Gaia. Recently, a study revealed that "tree-hugging" actually boosts our immune system. When we hug a tree there is a measurable exchange of energy that helps us de-stress and make adjustments to find inner balance. Mother nature always loves to take us in, and it only takes a little time to come to a timeless place.

When we experience all our allies, the raccoon and butterfly, the flower and the brook, we also remember that to stay in balance with the Earth we must tread lightly and treat her kindly. By using her resources with care we are offering true respect for this living being. Offering our work in honor of source is a powerful act that keeps the channel of inspiration open and increases the life force running through our veins. If you are interested in protecting and healing the Earth, Cormac Cullinan's book, Wild Law: A Manifesto for Earth Justice, proposes recognizing natural communities and ecosystems as legal persons with legal rights.

When we find ourselves connected with Gaia, releasing our belief that we own her, our whole being vibrates in a harmonious, balanced way.

Balance is not a rigid or permanent state and the naming of this card Adjustment brings with it the implication that justice needs to be a fluid action of assessing the situation and our present responses and reactions.

To evaluate is to become aware and centered. Only then is it possible to respond from integrity.

There are many ways to find balance, such as yoga, tai chi, meditation, or even walking a tightrope. One simple way to feel alignment is to try balancing rocks on one another. This is not a logical, mental activity. All the mind needs to know is that everything has its center of gravity; then let the hands feel the back and forth motion until that exquisite moment when we feel viscerally that balance has happened and we let go.

I had just seen a rock balancer on the bay in San Francisco before I went to the river with my teenage daughter Allegra and her older sister April. Next to us was a campsite of teenagers who were partying loudly throughout the first night.

The next morning I went down to the shore and balanced rocks. That night there was laughter from the next camp but the vibe was different, more light-hearted and fun. The next morning my daughters and I looked out at the shore and there was a mini Stonehenge of balanced rocks created by our teen neighbors.

This story links many levels of this card:

- How do teenagers find balance in the world away from the guidance of family?
- How do they deal with intoxicants?
- How can they get high on life!
- How does being in nature, and creating within nature's class room, help us find inner balance?

On a practical level this card can literally mean dealing with the justice system, being arrested, going to court or making contracts for work or living situations. If this is the year you are in it is important to make conscious agreements that make you feel valued and respected.

It is not a good time for "handshake" agreements; instead it is an excellent time to learn about legality and contracts and how to negotiate and adjust them to your needs.

On the emotional level, stay in the dance, but be honest and forthright; speak up when you feel disrespected, invisible, or misunderstood.

It may be a time to fight for the justice you believe is necessary to protect the rights of people and the Earth. You might find yourself called to stop racism, sexism, and other isms that denigrate life on Earth.

Remember: this can lead to legal repercussions so it is best to decide whether or not you want to push the envelope. Sometimes anger, which is rooted in our personal story, calls us to deal with discrimination in the broader world. Try transforming your anger into actions and be the change you want. Reactivity needs to be converted into response that is present, flexible, and coming from a sense of inner balance.

This card is often an indication of divorce if a marriage is in jeopardy, but you might try the approach of the next card, The Hermit, and take some time alone to hear the still small voice of truth before you make any rash decisions.

The Hermit/Crone IX
Astrological Sign: Virgo

Now that we have experienced the need to find our center of gravity, we are starting to develop our own perspective about the world and life in general. We are seeking to understand who we are in direct relationship to life, nature, the divine; in fact, to everything.

Much of what we learned from our parents and our teachers brings more questions than answers to our minds.

We hear so many conflicting points of view that it can be overwhelming. Beliefs that we took for granted are now showing cracks that let in new shafts of light. We wonder what it all means.

When we meet the Hermit, it is the first point on our path that we will consciously choose to seek our answers within. Traditionally this card shows a hooded man with a lantern held high, searching for the honest individual. This image is derived from the story of the Stoic known as Diogenes, who believed that men and women lived a life dictated by rules and taboos and, therefore, no one was really truthful or honest. He searched the streets, carrying his lit lantern night and day, on his quest for an honest man.

This story suggests that we need to question the taboos and rules of our society when they run up against our own conscience. For example, what if our young Fool, who is now in the Realm of Earthly Reality, gets to know a young man and they become best friends. Then The Fool, who was brought up to believe that homosexuality is wrong, both religiously and morally, learns that the young man is gay. He finds himself in a dilemma because his heart feels love for his friend while the voice of judgment from his parents and religious teachers blares in his head.

It is at these moments that the individual needs to search his soul and know what is right for himself. This is not a challenge he sought, but there it is, and he must deal with it. Has this possibly made him question his own sexuality as well?

Will he disown his friend, confront his parents, or withdraw from the whole situation? These are the lessons that we must learn on our own. The hounds of hell at his heels can be the voices of his cultural imprinting. He may be activated to try to change the way

IX

The Hermit

people think, he may reject his parents for their prejudice, or he may perpetuate this prejudice.

But self-righteousness can be a lonely stance. How do we determine what is truth? He was taught that homosexuality is wrong. If that is true, how is it possible that his friend, whom he respects and cares about, is in a loving relationship with a person of his own gender?

So he asks himself, what is truth? Is there an ultimate truth we can all agree on? Is the word of "God" as given to him by his religious mentors "The Truth" when his heart tells him something quite the opposite?

These are questions we will ponder throughout this realm as different contradictory stories call us to make choices. If there is no ultimate truth, then is it possible that loving intention is the foundation for truthfulness? This is what Venus intimates in the Justice card.

The feminine form of The Hermit is called The Crone in the Motherpeace deck. The image is of the goddess, Hecate, the guardian of the crossroads.

Hecate calls us to slow down to the pace of guidance and tune in to our "old soul" aspect. She is not a parental voice but an archetype that represents our own internal sense of integrity and wisdom. The Hermit/Crone wants us to focus through silence and listen to the mystery until a sense of knowing arises.

To complete our journey from maiden to mother to crone, it is now time for the baby boomers to deal with old age and death. There are people all over reclaiming this final passage as sacred, beautiful, and very personal. People are planning their own ceremonies and shunning the death industry and its vampire ways of preying on the grieving family; it uses the leverage of guilt to extort ridiculous amounts of money for a box that is seen for one day and buried in the earth forever.

A local woman in my area named Jerrigrace Lyons is doing workshops and helping people plan rituals that truly honor the life that has been lived and the mystery that is yet to come. Hecate stands at the crossroads lighting the way. She is the embodied wisdom of the postmenopausal woman. It is she who now contains the blood mystery and the wisdom of life's younger phases as maiden and mother.

Hecate is very pleased and appeased to see the conscious ceremony that is beginning to develop around death. Society tries to shoo away the old women in our culture as having no function or purpose. Hecate knows that in honoring death as a profound and very individual transition we may well start honoring the elders as well. Old age and death, in a youth- and beauty-obsessed culture, are hidden from view and from the common experience as much as possible.

Hecate asks us to pause on this journey to contemplate life and all we have experienced. She calls to our culture to wake up to this incredible resource of our senior community. As my generation enters this finale, you can be sure that we are going to find a way to reassert the power, authority, and wisdom of the elders. So slow down and listen up!

When you get this card in a reading

It is time to turn away from external pressures and internalized voices that are not your own and listen to your soul. Discovering this voice and trusting it is the work of a lifetime, but even in our first experiments with inner listening, we may find a sense of integrity and courage to make choices that we can live with.

These times of soul searching can be heart-wrenching; but in the end they are times of great inner growth that will weave in us a stronger moral fabric of our own making, and not a mantle placed on us by society.

Some of the simple tools to help us clear away the obstacles to accessing our own truth are also connected to the Virgo traits that are represented by this card.

Virgo comes from virgin, which originally meant autonomous and also carries the connotation of purity. To be alone, to fast and purify the body, is a way of cleaning the temple before sitting in contemplation of the divine to receive our answers.

Virgo is the sign of the healer and physician so we need to take a healthy approach to our soul searching. If we do not, we often make ourselves delusional, sick or diseased (not at ease) by becoming isolated within the limitations of the ego/mind.

Many cultures send their young on vision quests to enter the Realm of Earthly Reality. These rites of passage are important vehicles for creating courageous and self-reliant individuals who can think for themselves.

Another tool that is suggested comes from the ruler of Virgo, the planet Mercury. Mercury is the messenger but he can also be the trickster; so purifying our body and stilling our mind gives us a better shot at knowing which message is authentic.

Mercury is also the god of writing so journaling will help us to clarify and understand our own feelings. Often it is best to just let stream of consciousness happen, unedited by the Virgo critical mind.

When we let the critic take a nap and we open up to receive, what comes through can be surprising and enlightening, often an epiphany. The art of writing at its best is a process of self-discovery where new insights can arise.

If this writing takes us deeper into our lifework and we decide to make writing a profession, the critic can be employed to polish up the work. Inspiration is killed by judgment and criticism so it is important to use these tools in their proper order.

When our lives are filled with too much busyness, a hot bath scented with lavender can help us find ourselves. Light some candles to represent the lantern of the Hermit in his search for truth. Knowing is very different from deciding.

When we spend an afternoon in the woods and let go of our reasoning mind, it's remarkable what small miracles can unfold.

If you are trying to solve a problem and feel stuck, it is valuable to distract the logical mind and just take a walk, listen to music, and stop searching. Many great discoveries and breakthroughs have come from this very process. Inherent in every moment is the problem and the solution, but when we are desperately searching, we cannot see the obvious.

In "The Charge of the Goddess," (See Appendix 390) we find this gem: "If that which you seek you find not within yourself, you will never find it without."

In the Hermit card, we find ourselves face-to-face with the mystery. We can run back inside the safety of answers and institutions from our parents, teachers, and religious leaders; or we can rest in awe and wonder and see what comes.

HECATE

There she was impassable
I could not see her face…

Everything was grey
And blue, and black
              Large, Looming
She was blocking my way,
There was nowhere to go.
      No way to lie and say
      I had the energy to get past her,
She was going to slow me down.
Actually, no, what she did was
Stop me dead in my tracks.
Finally I knew there was no way
Around or through this one.

I had to stop and take notice.
Slow down and listen up.

Hecate was sternly
      Holding me in her gaze,
Arms akimbo,
Feet spread `wide and firmly planted.

At first I thought, this woman really
Knows how to take up space,

Then I knew She was Space…

And She was showing me my place
In Her matrix, Her web, Her cave,

She had a fix on me…

And suddenly I did not feel so brave.

She said, " I am not your shadow,
Your inner wise woman, your grand
mother,
Other than you,

I am you, look at me,
You've earned it," She said.
Then she let me breathe in…
….this lived in, loved in, laughed in
place,
that stood at the end of the race.

This time She spoke
      Inside me, to the rhythm
          Of my pulse,

She said (brittle as breaking bones),
"Don't speed by me
When your body's aching,

Don't pay no heed
When your heart is breaking,

Woman take care of yourself
      Right Now!

Honor Yourself.
Even as the consumed world
Places all its purchases
      On the altar of youth,

Nurture the gifts of experience,
      Feel the deep weave
          Of your integrity,

And know your voice will rise
When you look into my eyes
      And see Yourself."

And then She vanished, Dark
into Dark.

You know, I never saw Her face,
But I faced Her just the same.

By Magick

Fortune/The Wheel Of Fortune X
Planet: Jupiter

The goddess Fortuna never stops spinning out new variations on the themes of life. Then she dazzles us with enthusiastic presentations of these exciting opportunities, offering us the golden ring on the merry-go-round of life. Fortuna is an offspring of the goddess Vortumna, she who revolves the year. This suggests that our fortune is directly linked to the rhythms of the seasons; thus, there will be times of great flowering, Aphrodite's season, as well as periods of introspection and thoughtful consideration that will need more prudence and austerity, as when Hecate rules. Fortuna's father is Jupiter, the great teacher, father, and the element of luck and change, incalculable yet ever-present.

Speaking in these terms, personifying an aspect of the universe, we humans are able to relate more easily. When we tell stories in mythic terms we give richness to the learning of life's lessons. Cultures use stories to pass on values while including the fallibility of the human dimension. These ways of transmitting values carry compassionate empathy; whereas edicts or laws that command us to obey feel harsh and demanding.

Something in us will always initially reject orders that come with the threat of punishment.

She may offer a job or a home, a trip or a lover, because she loves to see our faces light up when we grab the golden ring and take the ride. We may find ourselves flung into the far reaches of the world or sent back home to our place of origin.

If we know what we want, we will wait; we will listen to the inner guidance we have gained in the cave of The Hermit, until the opportunity presents itself that aligns with our inner will.

We need not be rigid in our definition of how that will look, just that it resonates on the soul level. Fortuna cannot be limited to our ego's expectations of what the perfect opportunity would be for us; she is not a slave to our imagination; she has one of her own. When we hear a story about how our young fool sets out to become a writer in the world after his hermetic experience and ends up falling in love and traveling to Egypt, we can relate to the Wheel of Fortune, as Fortuna dancing before us.

X

ℷ **Fortune** ♃

It is also helpful to examine the image in the card showing a giant wheel with three beasts that symbolize phases, or Gunas, as defined in Hindu mythology.

The Gunas are directly related to the scientific terms inertia, action, and stillness. All life forms participate in these phases. We can move through them in an hour, a day, a year, or a decade. When we are able to recognize which mode we are in, our consciousness can stay in the center of the wheel as the axis of motion instead of being tossed about by "the slings and arrows of outrageous fortune."

This axis is also known as the Eye of Shiva or, in Egypt, the Eye of Horus. This third eye sees beyond dualism and holds the whole picture in clear perspective so we may use the highest aspect of each phase to fulfill our soul's purpose.

The action phase, called Rajas, is symbolized by the monkey. He represents the natural curiosity, excitement and busyness at the onset of a project, the start of a new job, a relationship, or a journey. In Rajas we are passionately involved in manifesting all our expectations and our life is filled with activity. Our modern culture is totally enamored with this phase of relentless action and basically does not acknowledge the need for anything else. It's always more, more, more. To acknowledge the other phases takes personal strength.

When the action phase begins to wane, we can respond in two different ways. We can refuse to read the signs that signal a slow-down and try to force things to stay at the same pace. If we do this, we can be caught in the throes of desire and become too greedy and too speedy.

When things stop going our way, we can become discouraged and angry, cursing Fortuna for seemingly taking away what was so recently offered. But, as the I Ching states, the universe moves in a zigzag pattern and it is the steady vision of our third eye that holds us to our course. If we can stay grounded in knowing we have chosen well, then we can move into one of the two other phases without regret.

The other two Gunas are Tamas, inertia, and Sattvic, stillness or essence. We visit one or the other depending on how we acted in the state of Rajas. In other words, we will go where we need to go next depending on our own stage of growth.

Tamas, the Guna of inertia, is represented by the crocodile that lives in the deep waters of our unconscious. If we arrive here out of exhaustion, anger, or disappointment, we will end up living out our worst aspects. An example of unconscious Tamasic behavior would be sitting in front of the TV eating junk food and bemoaning our fate. Or we can take this opportunity to develop inner discipline, practice our craft, and learn new tools in preparation for the next outward thrust. This Guna invites us to go deeper into ourselves and be willing to acknowledge our need for inner growth. Otherwise we can fall into depression, illness, or self-indulgence. It is an excellent time to sit with our shadow patterns of flight or fight, addiction, anger, and frustration.

The deep waters can renew us or we can drown in self-pity; there is always a choice.

The third Guna, called Sattvic, is represented by the Sphinx, the all-knowing soul that holds the answer to our next riddle and helps us sit in contemplation and witness the situation. In times of meditation we can return to the seat of the soul and dwell in peace. Then, when the next action phase calls, we will be grounded, renewed, and ready.

And so it goes, around and around, action, inertia, stillness. If we fulfill the function of each phase as it comes, we will spiral. Otherwise we may rise and fall, propelled only by external forces.

When you get this card in a reading

Fortune's number is ten so it is definitely the end of a cycle in your life, especially in the arena of career. Note your accomplishments as well as the limitations you were dealing with in the last phase.

Then ground yourself in a clear assessment of what kinds of possibilities would offer you ways to grow, expand your realm of influence, and bring more abundance into your life.

Too often, when this card shows up, we get lost in looking outside ourselves before we set a clear intention of what we are seeking. Fortune dazzles us with the chance for fame, fortune, travel, and romance. These can all be wonderful, but not if it is only your ego that will be gratified.

The Hermit/Crone calls you to contemplate the opportunities and focus on those that mirror your true vision and allow you to act with authenticity.

Sitting in the seat of inner calm provides you with a non-reactive awareness of the people and circumstances surrounding you so you can see the light that will guide you forward.

In the relationship realm, you may find when you slow to the pace of guidance that your lover was calling you to awaken to a deeper love and not rejecting you at all, or you could learn that you have ignored how you have affected others in your desire to fulfill your dreams and there may be some bridges that need mending. There could be challenges if your partner is focused on living in one place to pursue career opportunities and you have a chance to get work you want somewhere else.

Opportunity is knocking. Open the door, but take a moment before you leap like The Fool and check in with yourself and your loved ones to see if this chance matches your inner purpose.

Infinite possibilities rise and fall on the horizon of our vision. Choosing wisely is the key to understanding the Wheel of Fortune, lest you spin out of control.

Fortuna can lead us to our fate but we alone can fulfill our destiny. By integrating opportunities with true will we become our true selves actualized.

Lust/Strength XI
Astrological Sign: Leo

We have now arrived at the very middle of the path of life and, full of passion and at the height of our power, we relish the joy of just being alive. This card is the archetypal Leo, the lion king of the jungle, leader of the tribe and the activated courageous heart. It is also connected to the seasons as the height of summer when all the fruits and vegetables are bursting with life, juicy and delicious.

It is time to be fully who we are, uninhibited by what others think of us. We should be willing to push the envelope, to test our strength in the world.

In the Thoth deck image we see a voluptuous woman riding a lion with many faces. She holds the reins, symbolizing her direct connection to her animal instincts, while still retaining her capacity to control and choose.

The many faces of the lion are an acknowledgement that humans are not just one personality throughout life but have many faces that show themselves in different circumstances.

She is the transformation of the classic image of the secretary, with her hair done up primly, wearing glasses. When this same woman goes out dancing, off come the glasses and her hair tumbles sensually around her shoulders.

We all need to find this release for our many desires and personae. This is not to say we must succumb to every desire. Remember, she holds the reins. We can enjoy this luscious physical existence without becoming addicted to or obsessed with it.

Balancing passion and reason is a constant challenge that many solve by subjecting themselves to a fundamentalist mindset in which the rules are preordained. This subjugation is usually coupled with the threat of punishment and damnation if the disciple strays from the fold.

In the Lust card we are called to deal with our choice on our own and not to judge or reject the lust for life as evil and wrong.

Many people would rather be told what to do than take on the responsibility of living fully while not hurting ourselves and other living things.

Only through embodying love of this world can we feel our full strength, and like a roaring lion know what it is to be truly alive.

Otherwise we might as well return to the first row of the Archetypes and find a priest, parent figure, or boss who will tell us what to do.

Many religious practices that are not fundamentalist welcome thinking individuals who use the teachings of the religion to guide them in their choices. These practices will keep us in the Realm of Earthly Reality, as mature humans willing to experience and learn from our own mistakes.

Lust is a loaded word to many people. Crowley lived in a very Victorian society so he intentionally chose to shock and offend many times in his life. He himself wrestled with addiction and his inability to control his desires.

But in his willingness to explore this realm, he discovered a profound truth: "Lust, without lust of Result, is in every way perfect." To love being alive is not dependent upon a constant gratification of sensory desire. But to enjoy desire itself, there lies true strength, freedom, and an authentic human experience. So many people hide from the realm of desire and so many more drown in its tempting waters.

Here are some examples of Lust without lust of Result that will clarify this point.

Let's say you are very attracted to a woman and you find her to be everything you desire. To be in your strength and not lust for a result would be to just tell her that you love being in her presence, that just to know she is alive is a gift. But the usual pattern is to say everything you can to get her to feel the same towards you, and to ask her to be with you alone.

This desiring is a result of not enjoying your feelings for this woman. When we express our enjoyment without needing to possess the object of our desire we are in our power; we are Strength personified.

A great example of this archetype is revealed in the movie The Philadelphia Story. Cary Grant hangs around Katherine Hepburn on the eve of her marriage to someone else. He just keeps loving her and understanding her without expressing any jealousy or trying to change her mind. In the end she re-marries him.

In taking this idea to the level of finding our true passion in life, we can take to heart the words of the great mythologist, Joseph Campbell, who said, "If you follow your bliss you will find out who you are." Clients often ask me to help them figure out what their lifework should be. Although it is helpful to suggest from the cards certain talents or assets they possess, it is always best to encourage people to discover their path through confirmations, experience, and synchronicities that are signposts on the map of life.

I often ask the client to tell me what they love to do, not in terms

XI

ל TRUMPS **Lust** ♌

of work but just what their passions are. It is surprising how difficult this question is to answer. If this draws a blank then it might be useful to remember what you loved as a child or what you have always wanted to try, just for the fun of it.

If we do what we love to do without a need to make money or be successful, we send a message to our soul that we are listening. It may not be that the actions one takes in manifesting these desires will end up being connected to your lifework but it will set you on the path of joyous action that can lead you to meaningful work because you are taking your cues from within.

I personally never planned on being a Tarot reader. I just worked with the cards and did readings for friends and myself because I loved the Tarot from the first time I was given a reading. I knew instantly it was an amazing tool of self-discovery.

One day I was offered a job as a hostess at a psychic fair and the woman who had hired me, Mala Kabbala, suggested I do a reading since there were more clients than readers at the event.

My first reading was an epiphany, and the rest is history.

When my daughter, Celeste, chose to test her courage by skydiving, it opened her to levels of herself that were hidden behind her fears. So when you get the Lust card in a reading, it's time to do what you love to find out who you are. Whether you love to dance, travel, sing, sew, garden, or collect stamps, it doesn't really matter. Just do it and a light will shine through to take you on your path to self-discovery.

Since this card is a manifestation of the sign of Leo, it is also a time to show leadership and express your ideas with passion and determination. Leo is the sign of drama and the many faces on the beast also reflect the many roles we play in life (or in the theatre for those who choose to make this their life work).

Many people who are Leos or have this as their personality card can be unconscious of its deeper significance and they will tend to be drama queens, playing out their desire for excitement by creating unnecessary melodramas as a way to release their flair for the dramatic.

When one witnesses this in young children, it is often helpful to direct them toward performance opportunities where they can explore all their different faces in a growth-oriented, guided environment.

We love to try out different forms of expression that break us out of the everyday, mundane aspects of life. That is why costume parties and Halloween resonate with children and many adults as well. Halloween is especially powerful as a vehicle to bring out the shadow in our society and play with it. Shadow aspects that we fear are often quite amusing and harmless when they are allowed to be visible.

In the children's story, There's a Monster Under My Bed, the monster turns out to be afraid of the dark and the little boy lets it crawl in bed with the light on to comfort it.

That is really what all our shadow selves need—understanding, comfort, and a place to be.

The shadow self is hidden from our consciousness often because we were told to be something other than what we are and, therefore, made to be ashamed of our natural self.

I am sure you have witnessed children who are wild, playful tricksters and who are told often to be quiet or be nice. By the time they are teenagers they are more than ripe for some seriously rebellious and often self-destructive behavior.

Other children are told to repeat certain "cute" behaviors for every relative who drops by. They are sent the message that certain behavior that is socially acceptable and creative will be rewarded, while spontaneity will often be frowned upon. This lesson tragically imprints on the child the idea that being herself is not acceptable but repetitive performing of the expected is highly commended.

Allowing children and the child in each of us to experience daring adventures and spontaneous acts of random joy helps us love ourselves as we are and even discover unknown creativity that is always ready to spill out into the spotlight of a free environment.

The Sun, the center of our solar system, is the celestial body that rules Leo. It calls us to shine uniquely for all to see and allow our many facets to be like planets circling our own energy-generating soul. Therefore, a well-adjusted Leo will have a sunny personality and a passionate approach to work and life in general.

When you get this card in a reading

It's time to pull out the stops and take a walk on the wild side. You will feel, now more than ever, that you don't want to be what everyone else wants you to be. You want to unleash your passions for the sheer joy of being alive. You want to see yourself and be seen in all your glory.

As Jim Morrison said, "Break on through to the other side" and open to the free spirit trapped within. When you do some outrageous acts that have been simmering on the back burner for a long time, you get rid of the backlog of possibilities. Then your soul, realizing your mind/ego is finally listening, will send up some more great ideas, until one day, voila! you will know your true will better than you ever have before.

If you tend to be introverted, then play out your fantasies through writing, reading, or having a secret lover whom you exchange love letters with or meet in exotic places. Or dance naked in your own home with your favorite sexy songs turned up a notch! It will feel wild even though no one will see. If you always wear muted tones, just buying a sexy red dress or wearing an outrageous tie can make you feel more alive. People will definitely notice.

When you run up against obstacles, duck around the corner and keep going. When those obstacles are within and presenting themselves in the form of inhibitions and self-judgment, it's time to take yourself to a place that gives you the space to spread your wings. Check a few items off your bucket list. You won't regret it. Listen to Dylan:

"Yes, to dance beneath the diamond sky
with one hand waving free–
Silhouetted by the sea, circled by the circus sands
With all memory and fate driven deep beneath the waves
Let me forget about today until tomorrow."

The Hanged Man XII
Element: Water

In the Thoth deck, the image is of a man hanging upside down, suspended from an Ankh with a snake entwined, his feet and hands nailed to a cross-like grid suspended over a sleeping serpent.

This definitely brings to mind the Christian crucifixion as well as the pagan story of the sacrificed god. But the two stories are diametrically opposed and say much about our relationship to the concepts of sin, inhibition, sacrifice, and our relationship to nature's revolving seasons.

Let's start with the pagan story since it predates the Christian tale.

The sacrificed god is a seasonal story connected to the Green Man who is born each spring and grows to maturity along with all of nature's profusion. But as the seasons change and harvest time arrives, we cut the plant life down to the ground once again, so the Green Man is sacrificed to return to the earth, decompose and be reborn again in the spring.

This is not something to be mourned but to be celebrated. The analogy to the cycles of human life is that there are periods of passionate growth and opportunity as we saw in the last two cards, Fortune and Lust. Now there is no more we can do in the outer world. We need to surrender to what is and drop into the underworld with the sleeping serpent of our own life force and rest and resurrect anew.

This cannot be forced; it must be accepted and experienced, even though it can be uncomfortable and painful.

Remember the monkey speeding around the Wheel of Fortune? He needs to know when his run is over, but surrender is extremely challenging to our human nature. There is an old fable called How to Catch a Monkey. Take a coconut and cut a hole just big enough for the monkey's hand to fit through. Fill the coconut with rice. When the monkey reaches in to grab the rice he is caught and unable to pull the rice out because now his hand is full. All he has to do to gain his freedom is let go of the rice, but he fails to get the message.

If he can surrender to what is, the monkey will have lost his next meal but when he lets go of the rice, he will have his freedom.

What ties you to work or a relationship that you can't let go of even though you have lost your freedom?

Are you willing to surrender to the truth of your current situation and drop deeper and breathe life back into your kundalini life force? It is time to be resurrected into a new world, free from the shackles of your own creation.

It is interesting to note that the number four, symbolizing law, order, and structure can be seen in the shape of the Emperor's body and again in the reversed position of The Hanged Man. So we see that leadership is meant to be an activity, not a permanent position. The Emperor, who is born in the spring and plants the seeds, dies away as The Hanged Man when we harvest in the fall. Transitioning into the Christian myth it is helpful to remember the song, "Turn, Turn, Turn."

"To everything (turn, turn, turn)
There is a season (turn, turn, turn)
And a time for every purpose, under heaven
A time to be born, a time to die
A time to plant, a time to reap."

This song was adapted from the book of the Bible called Ecclesiastes, and put to music by Pete Seeger. It shows how the Bible also acknowledges the need to recognize the nature of the seasons as a metaphor for cycles in our own lives.

In a Tarot reading, the particular cards we receive are meant to awaken us to the truths that are most important for us to focus on now. All the cards embody essential truths but each cycle needs specific tools that will help us on our way.

In examining the Christian myth of the sacrificed god we encounter the idea that each of us reaches a point in our lives when we must surrender to the higher and deeper power of the life force and let it act on us without resistance. In the mythic story of Jesus he was a vehicle for transformation, but being human, he, too, asked if the cup could pass from his hands. But this was not to be. In life there is self-determination and destiny, and a wise man knows the difference. His answer came to him and he chose to surrender to the circumstances of the world he lived in and have faith in the divine. He let go of attachment to his human body and trusted in the promise of resurrection. This does not have to be taken literally.

When we surrender and drop into the waters of the collective unconscious, we arise with renewed energy and passion to truly be dead to the past, like a serpent shedding the skin it has outgrown.

XII

↩ **The Hanged Man** ▽

Another version of the Christian myth says that Jesus died for our sins, placing a dogma of judgment and a burden of guilt on all who believe.

This limited perception is the continuation of the Adam and Eve myth of original sin, allowing churches to be the arbiters of morality and deciding for the layperson what is good or bad and what will send you to heaven or hell.

When we take on guilt and sin as our mantle we are nailed to a cross of inhibitions and suffering that keeps us from allowing the life force to move freely through our bodies.

Thus, this card is also about the inhibitions that bind us to our parents and religious pundits who use fear and guilt to impose rules and moral codes that make us feel revulsion towards our natural human instincts.

When you get this card in a reading

It is important to explore the reasons you feel like The Hanged Man in the different arenas of your life.

Career

Is it because you have chosen work that you do not really like but feel you have to do? Do you believe work is meant to be a burden and a form of subservience to others because you were taught this as a child?

Are you unable to hear the voice of your own true will sleeping in your unconscious because you only hear the voices of what you "should" do echoing through your mind?

Are you unable to access your creative will because you were taught that artistic endeavors aren't really legitimate work?

Relationships

Are you staying in an unhealthy relationship because it would be a "sin" to divorce?

Do you feel guilty because you want to have an open relationship and your partner doesn't?

Are you ashamed of your desires around sexuality? Have you been taught to believe that talking about sex is taboo?

Are you staying married because of the children?

Personal growth

Taking the more pagan approach you can see that it is time to surrender and go deeper inside yourself for answers. When I teach Tarot classes I often have my students create a picture of a Tarot card to symbolize their understanding of its meaning.

My daughter, April Faith, decided to draw The Hanged Man as a young woman hanging by her knees from the branch of a tree, suspended above a beautiful pool of water in a lush forest.

She felt The Hanged One (not gender specific) meant it was time to let go and just drop into the healing waters and find renewal there. In fact, she often practices this quite literally by going to her sacred pond, diving in, and replenishing her soul. Nature has the power to heal in mysterious ways that we often forget in the bustle of life.

Learning to surrender to what is gives our ego a rest and lets us witness the universe at work. Often this card shows up when we are in a state of limbo between the past and the future and there seems to be nothing we can do about our outer circumstances. When this is the case and you can't find an answer in the logic of your mind,

"There will be an answer, let it be!"

Death XIII
Astrological Sign: Scorpio

Ah! The most dreaded card in the deck. The one that evokes questions like, "What if the Death card comes up, am I going to die?" Or, "I'm afraid the Death card might come up, I don't even want to know my future!"

This response represents the pathology that our culture has about death. We don't want to talk about it, and many of us live in a state of denial about the whole mystery.

But there is a way to understand death that helps us to see it as a gift.

When I hear these fears arise in people I answer that death offers us an opportunity to get out of stifling and stagnant situations in our lives.

For example, "Aren't you glad that you can completely end a bad job or a negative relationship in your life? What if we could not let these negative times truly be over, how would we then have a chance to start anew and be reborn?"

Any legitimate Tarot reader will tell you that the Death card is not meant to predict literal death and it is morally reprehensible for a reader to "play God" and make that prediction. But for the Tarot to be a complete story about life it must include death. There are times when death is looming in our lives and when it shows up in the reading it offers an opportunity to talk about it. The realization that life ends is what enriches and gives more value to this brief, beautiful gift we are given.

There is a time to be born and a time to die and these cycles of life are unavoidable. When someone we love dies unexpectedly, we learn that there is no way to make sense of it. We could ask "Why? Why? Why?" until our dying day. But even without understanding why, there are ways to give meaning to someone's death.

I recently read a story about a young mother of two who lost her husband when a drunk driver hit him while he was riding home on his bike.

At first the woman abhorred the man who killed her beloved, but after a while her 10-year-old daughter said she was curious about him and wanted to know who this man was.

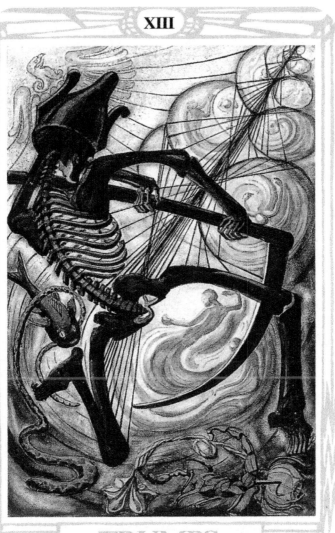

XIII

♃ TRUMPS **Death** ♏

Eventually the mother went to visit him in jail and brought a letter from her daughter forgiving him.

She felt empowered to be able to look him in the eye, share her suffering, and witness him having to feel the awful pain he had caused her family. He was completely humbled by the grace of her forgiveness.

This is an example of a way to give some sense of closure and is an excellent tool to end painful relationships.

Forgiveness of someone who has hurt us helps us immensely in the process of moving on. Hatred, disappointment, and judgment keep us tied to that person and we find our thoughts endlessly circling back to the past.

If we can pinpoint the lesson we learned from the experience then we won't have to do it again. But continually blaming the other person is just inviting the experience to repeat itself. In fact, the next level is to be grateful for the lesson and then move on. We all make many mistakes in life; it's just one of the ways humans learn and we all need forgiveness.

To truly experience death in life we need to let go. Many people physically die, embittered and lonely, because they were incapable of going through the small deaths along the way.

To physically die in peace is to die many times to old ways of thinking, living and acting. In fact, if we were to really see our lives for what they are, we are living and dying everyday.

Like the Sun rising full of promise and the night dropping a curtain on all that was possible in that brief time we call a day, so our lives are filled with beginnings and endings. When we give full participation to our deaths and births as rites of passage, we can evolve consciously, instead of feeling that everything is just happening to us.

The image in the Thoth deck is of a dancing skeleton stirring the stagnant waters with his scythe to bring new possibilities bubbling to the surface.

We see the snake that was latent in The Hanged Man slithering along, released from his old skin and ready to start anew. The dancing skeleton is derived from the story of Shiva the Hindu god of creative destruction. He hangs out in graveyards covered with ashes and offers himself willingly in service to Kali, the fierce mother goddess.

He is often pictured with her dancing on his corpse or holding his severed head in her hand, showing that the male aspect can sacrifice itself on Kali's altar of change when old forms need to die. Spirit does not die, only its manifestation. These images can seem rather gruesome and not very "religious" to the western mind but maybe we need to be more willing to see images of death as a metaphor for change.

In our culture, if you want to see death and gore just play a video game or watch a violent movie. But what do we learn from this experience?

Shiva and Kali are also lovers and represent the divine union of all opposites in the synthetic cauldron of sexual union.

It is in the sexual realm that to truly experience ecstasy we must surrender and let go. We are called to become free of fear and shame and be present in the dance of union.

This card represents Scorpio, considered the most sexual of the signs because it is the intersection of life and death, the place of the great mystery, where the first signs of life appeared from the stagnant waters where land and water meet.

The French call sex la petit morté, "the little death," recognizing the profound surrender and release inherent in this act of transformation. Scorpio rules the season of death and transformation in the fall when all plants have exhausted their ability to give fruit and the energy moves underground until spring.

It is actually a profound relief to let go and actualize our passions, whether in the sexual realm or other aspects of our life.

What a relief to quit an oppressive, stagnant job and decide to do something that inspires and empowers you. There is often a need to take a leap of faith and remember that The Fool is the free agent, always ready to burst through all our masks and disguises and live for the adventure itself.

So it is that death always posits life in this ever-evolving dance.

Shamans say that death is their friend and they always hold him next to them, shoulder to shoulder, to never forget that life is precious, temporary, and constantly changing and renewing itself.

You can be the compost or make the compost, it's up to you!

So when Death dances into your life, embrace it and open to life's mysterious, infinite potential to grow and change. It's either going to happen to you or happen by your own will; there is always a choice.

When you get this card in a reading

Resistance is futile, transformation is at hand, the old story is slipping through your fingers, and it's time to just let go. In fact, The Death card in some decks is actually called transformation or letting go. Other cards in the reading will clarify in what arena that death is occurring. For example, if the Eight of Cups, a dark image of stagnant waters, appears, it's time for Death's scythe to stir things up. In this situation it may be that the relationship can be resurrected but there can be no crawling back inside the old story. New ways to communicate need to be employed to face the challenges that have been ignored or denied. Love calls us to be courageous and be with tensions and painful truths until a new understanding and tools for change are discovered. This can be facilitated through therapy, temporary separation, or sharing responsibilities in new ways.

If the emphasis is in the suit of Disks then it can signal the end of a job or a career direction. Coupled with the Two of Disks, there is promise of new possibilities on the horizon. Notice the snake that shed its skin in death is now revived as the infinity figure eight, charged with renewed energy. The call is out for you to find your creative spirit and Jupiter will gift you opportunities to do just that.

Then again, if Death is partnered with cards that show energy trapped in the suit of Fire represented by the Ten of Wands, you are probably exhausting yourself trying to make something happen when resistance is all around you. It's a wake-up call that your body will soon send you a message that enough is enough unless you take heed. Our bodies can be pushed only so far until they show us that something is seriously wrong.

Where Death appears in a reading is also very telling.

In the past? This can actually be a blessing, acknowledging that you have completed the process of letting go and it's time to embrace the process of being reborn. Ask yourself if there is anything else you need to do to fully be present. A simple ritual of acknowledging the death that has taken place can be very helpful. Maybe a dream you held onto never truly manifested. Write it on a piece of paper and burn it, offering it up to the past and/or trusting it can come back in a new way you never imagined.

In the present? You are in the midst of change and there's no going back. You may need to grieve the loss of a relationship or a home you have loved as you pare down. Like a snake that hasn't fully grown its new skin, you are very sensitive right now so take special care of yourself and ask for support from trusted friends and family. We often try to just get over it, and stuff our feelings. But unresolved emotions will always find a way to the surface again. Best to honor the process instead of rushing past it.

In the future? This is a wake-up call to prepare yourself for major changes by doing some soul-searching. Where in your life do you know that change is inevitable? You are probably going to feel fear when this card appears in this position because of course death is literally in the future for all of us. But if we are willing to find ways to end old stories and dream a new narrative, it can be a very exciting time especially if The Fool appears to beckon you to take a leap of faith onto a new plateau.

Death appears a lot when middle-aged folks are facing the reality of their parents' passing. If this is the case, ask yourself if there are unresolved issues or old grudges that need to be worked out. Often death brings grace to challenging relationships between the generations. Acceptance without old judgments can happen when we recognize each other's humanity as people and let go of the parent/child dynamic. If resolution is not possible because of diseases such as Alzheimer's, it can be useful to do your own work through writing, therapy, or dream work.

Death can appear when we have had a life-threatening experience and we discover gratitude for the precious gift of life. In the end, life is a mystery, but in experiencing the deaths in our own lives as we would that of a loved one, we can experience anger, grief, loss, and hope. These emotions have their own rhythms; embrace them as you would a sad or angry child. Through acknowledging instead of trying to fix things, healing is possible.

Art/Temperance XIV
Astrological Sign: Sagittarius

In the Art card we are at the last stage of the Realm of Earthly Reality. It is time to integrate all we have learned in order to step into the final path of Self-Realization.

To do this we need to own our duality and recognize that the apparent opposition is in reality an interaction of complementary forces that create the illusion of separation. In the image of the Thoth deck we see this clearly depicted by a figure that is half man and half woman, pouring out the opposites of fire and water from two cups and mixing them in the cauldron of transformation.

Fire and water do not mix literally as the image shows, but rather in the chemistry of their interactions. For example, fire boils water and water extinguishes fire. This card is a deepening of the dance of opposites put forth in The Lovers card where all the twin energies were still depicted as separate. We met male and female as separate and here they are one. We met the lion and the eagle and here their colors are reversed, to demonstrate their synthesis of air (eagle) and earth (lion).

This is the true meaning of alchemy, the discovery of what used to be known as the Philosopher's Stone. There is a phrase in Latin written around the head of the figure that basically translates as: Visiting the interior of the Earth, we discover the Philosopher's Stone.

Alchemy's superficial and mundane meaning has become crudely defined as the ability to make gross metals into gold. In truth, it is the synthesis of any and all opposites that combine to make something new and unique.

When we can hold in our hearts and minds that opposing forces are really an illusion, we experience life as dynamic. It is an awakening that can be likened to falling in love. When we fall in love we lose the feeling of isolation and the whole world shines brighter because of it.

This card asks us to take that process into our individual selves and heal the internal battles of yin and yang, light and dark, active and passive, and to become whole. Through this healing, falling in love takes on a meta-manifestation of wholeness uniting with

wholeness. We can feel the falling away of yearning and longing for the external beloved to fulfill us.

When we do this work for a while, the next time feelings of fear and hate arise we can practice integration by first owning and allowing these feelings to exist. Then we can explore how they affect us in our heart, mind, and body. This will diminish the power of these emotions to rule over us. Once we have identified and investigated their effects, we can stop identifying with them as who we are.

We are often caught in the rut of always blaming the other. These negative webs of thinking about our parents, relatives, and teachers generate thoughts like, "I will never be like them." When we do this, it is a way of holding them imprisoned in an unchanging and painful place in our hearts and minds. Sadly, this static stance of judgment actually magnetizes us to this aspect of our own heritage. The ironic result is that this sets us on a path of repeating their mistakes instead of learning from them. We find ourselves endlessly returning to this black hole of unconscious rejection of that which is a part of us.

When working with clients, I suggest a different approach. First of all, own that your parents are your gateway into this world and you are a synthesis of them as well as a unique expression beyond the generation of their story. You are not a clone; you are more than the sum of your parts.

Then try to imagine yourself in their place and see around you the limitations they experienced and the ways they tried to free themselves, or how they were unable to. Send them compassion. There is no need to forget or deny their mistakes. Mistakes are only mistakes until the lesson is learned and then they are just a lesson and we can move on. Perhaps they were not capable of learning the lessons. It is possible that you can.

Forgiveness and compassion are not meant to justify or rationalize any action. If there has been serious abuse, then forgiveness is not the first step in your process. Instead, it will be valuable to find a therapist to help you find wholeness and probably stay away from or limit contact with the abuser until a level of healing has taken place, to avoid re-wounding yourself.

When you are ready to work on forgiveness, it is useful to start with a more universal form. The idea that we are all flawed, that the human condition itself needs compassion, is a good premise with which to begin the process. I often use Jesus's phrase, "Forgive them for they know not what they do." It is ignorance that is often the source of mistakes as well as the reality that abusers have almost always suffered abuse themselves.

So we begin to see that life is school. Punishment, condemnation, and judgment will never help a soul to learn and heal. Only love and forgiveness can do that. Self-love before forgiveness safeguards against re-wounding and martyrdom.

The final step is to consider yourself an evolution, not a rejection of your ancestors. Then you are healing yourself and them simultaneously.

In their heart of hearts they want you to succeed. Their failures need not be yours, for they have shown you the tragic results of that.

To practice this alchemy, we can notice in our daily lives when we react strongly and contemplate what part of ourselves we are rejecting that is being presented to us externally.

Love is truly all we need; it is the stuff of life. When we love and become whole in ourselves, then life takes on a lightness and joy that is punctuated by creativity, discovery, invention, celebration, and art. All are aspects of the Sagittarian nature.

In truth, the answers are simple, but the application of these principles is challenging, difficult, and endlessly rewarding.

Another aspect of the Art card is discovered through examining more deeply the astrological influence of Sagittarius. Like the planet Mercury that is the messenger and communicator, Sagittarius is the sign of communication within diversity. Their combined energy is revealed in the Eight of Wands, called Swiftness. It is the card of electric dynamic speech that exemplifies the nature of both the sign and the planet.

Sagittarians are great teachers, writers, and motivational speakers. They are usually adept at mediation and negotiation. All of these skills are enhanced when we do the internal work laid out above.

When you get this card in a reading

It is helpful to examine the influence of this card in the different arenas of your life.

Relationship

It is time to go deeper into an integration of all the different voices that have been internalized as our own board of directors. If we can find a neutral voice, a non-judgmental witness to listen and mediate, we may separate the dross from the gold in this alchemical process.

In The Lovers card we heard the voices externally as parents, ministers, teachers, and mythic figures, influencing, and even dictating what we should do. Now we have experienced them for ourselves in the real world and can recognize and mediate them in our own consciousness.

When we can witness the mother who neglected us and move away from reactivity we can become our own mother. When the father judges us we can transform him into a voice of discernment and kindness in making choices.

This prepares us for deeper love connections on a soul level that exceeds the immature projections that often define our first infatuations. This card is also referred to as the soulmate card. In other words, when we have become conscious of our own inner workings, we are more prepared to meet on a soul level where appreciation of the beloved is not just defined by what we need.

Love that expresses appreciation for the beloved without expectations of what we will get, allows us to actually see them for who they really are.

Career

Mastery of negotiations and communication skills is highlighted in the workplace.

If things don't go well the first time around, it may be that the timing is wrong, or this is an opportunity to explore different modalities and approaches.

Group games or exercises can loosen up a rigid situation and help people know each other better. A letter or email may work as it gives the other person time to think and not just react. Active listening or storytelling are other options.

Consider this a chance to grow in your verbal and written skills; you may be rewarded with deeper connections and win-win outcomes to difficult situations.

Personal growth

In the Thoth deck it is called Art. I often suggest that clients take this quite literally and we talk about what creative ventures they have attempted in their lives. There is a sad paradigm in our culture that tells us some people are artists and some are not. But is it not true that all of us are creating all the time? Cooking is an art; gardening is an art. We become artists when what we do is intentionally imbued with our unique expression.

A cook becomes a chef when she infuses the food with a conscious intention to use and trust her own understanding of the ingredients and techniques that will render a unique meal of her own invention. First came the education, then the owning of the information as one's own and then the application that creates a special synthesis that carries your signature style.

To truly complete the path of Earthly Reality is to discover we are an extension of the creative life force, integrating our many faces and manifesting our gift in the world.

This card is the crucible of all opposites and therefore contains endless lessons and insights into the human condition.

My eldest daughter, Celeste, who has a Master's in human sexuality, named this card the bisexual card.

This can be understood on many levels. One interpretation is that when we understand the wholeness within ourselves, we are able to be more open to our authentic urges of attraction that will allow us to validate feelings that we may have denied or held in an unconscious place for a long time.

I have seen this card appear in the subconscious position in a reading and on occasion my intuition has told me to suggest that there may be a need to consider attractions that have been judged or misunderstood in the past.

This card invites us to talk about and explore feelings that may have never been explored before. This opening to diversity without judgment can be a portal to healing and honoring our sexual desires.

Bisexuality on a spiritual level acknowledges that we are all really souls manifested in a rainbow of genders. The spectrum of possible relationships of love and desire is infinite. The possibility that re-incarnation exists is worth exploring also. If it is true, we have probably all been both men and women and everything in between.

Bisexuality opens up the expression and exploration of the full spectrum of negotiated relationships of consensual adults. This archetype invites us to be present with our sexuality and discover who we are when judgment and self-loathing are stripped away.

It could be argued that we are all bisexual because we each contain both the masculine and feminine within ourselves.

Delving further into the astrology of the card we find that one of the symbols for Sagittarius is the rainbow that embodies the full spectrum of all the color vibrations. This relates to the chakras within our bodies and the multi-colored spectrum of cultural diversity as well. That is why it was chosen to represent the queer community.

Sagittarians love to travel and experience the many ways that humans create culture, art, and language. When this card appears in the reading, and especially when it is in the environment position, it implies that the client needs to experience cultural diversity. This can be fulfilled through travel, learning another language, going to cultural events, or joining a group that has racial, sexual, and economic diversity.

It is a joyous card that gives us a vision of how to combine opposites into a new synthesis just as parents welcome the child who is a union of the two that creates a new one.

THE THIRD LEVEL:
THE REALM OF SELF-REALIZATION

Now we are standing on the final plateau and our first encounter is with The Devil. To take the next evolutionary leap it is imperative that we face this shadow aspect and recognize it as a part of our self, in a way our greatest and most challenging teacher.

All of our addictions to power, sex, drugs, food, money, and possessions are guardians on the threshold of our personal freedom. Many religions of the world judge this aspect of human nature as evil incarnate. Demanding that we restrict, condemn and reject this shadow side as a way to conquer it. Pan offers another approach to these crippling addictions. He sees desire as an inherent aspect of human nature that only becomes a disease when it is judged and suppressed.

As we learned in the card Lust/Strength when we embrace our animal nature and enjoy and celebrate the sensual we can learn to see pleasure and pain as part of the play of life. It is the ability to be present in each moment that frees us to be celebrants in this ritual of seasons and cycles. Fully embodied and exceeding the either/or dimension of the matter/spirit split, we are released from thinking anyone or anything will bring us ultimate satisfaction.

Grasping and clinging is the root of all suffering as they take us out of the moment, either by regretting the past or reaching for the future. When we see the transitory nature of existence we will be ready to burn down our false towers of security and liberate our life force. As the fire and smoke of this destruction clears we can once again see our guiding Star and remember our unique gifts we came here to give as an offering; a healing and inspiring balm for the world.

Then one final dive into the birth canal of The Moon to bring forth our inner child, now reborn thanks to our own self-parenting. This stage liberates us from the limitations of our family and the collective consciousness to shine like The Sun and dance with the rhythms of The Universe as all the barriers fall away and we are free!

The Devil/Pan XV
Astrological Sign: Capricorn

Now we are welcomed into the final path of Self-Realization by the old Devil himself to let us know that we are now going to have to look at our shadow and deal with it.

It may seem that with all the work of synthesizing opposites in the Art card we would be done with this, but now is the time to practice what we have learned.

Hiding behind our shadow are the powerful urges of the potent yang aspect that has the down-to-earth goat-like ability to take on any mountain and not give up until the summit is reached.

This card is also called Pan in many decks because when we un-mask the scary Devil we find underneath the very human and, in fact, animal aspects of our life here on Earth.

Pan winks at us, the old goat that he is, and beckons us to dance under the full moon, stripped of the external lies that deny our po-tent urges to create. He scrambles up the mountain; tenacious and daring, he is determined to reach the top!

The card is governed by the sign of Capricorn and therein lies the connection to the goat god, Pan. When he reaches the top of the mountain he has a panoramic view of the world and feels the wild freedom of the wind and the sky.

In the image of the Thoth deck we see a goat with a third eye and a bemused smile on his face. Behind the goat is a very large phallic symbol and within the testicles are bodies, like sperm, trying to find their way into the world. The unique thing about this image is that it is drawn in such a way that, throughout years of working with this card, only a handful of people have seen the phallus. I didn't see it myself for many years. Yet when you do, you will never look at the card the same way again!

This is a good analogy for uncovering our deep creative urges that seem invisible until they are activated; then it is impossible to forget them.

We are all sexual beings and Pan is proud and potent in his pre-sentation of his drive and determination to fertilize the earth with his imagination. He is often pictured playing a flute and proudly displaying his erect phallus.

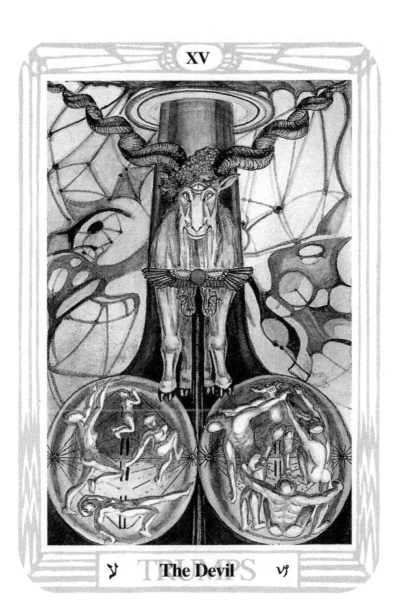

XV

The Devil

This was anathema to the Christians who condemned sexuality, other than for procreation, as a vice; who considered the free expression of sexuality a sin. They called the horned goat the Devil and condemned all those who celebrated this joy and ecstasy.

In our culture it was Pan who was converted into the Devil, making the horned god and lover of the goddess an evil and dangerous force.

When we repress our natural sexual urges and refuse to acknowledge the animal in us all, we get mired in self-judgment and condemnation of others as well.

This sexual energy must go somewhere and so it is usually played out in other aspects of our lives, such as addictive desires for power, possessions, sex, and drugs. This is even evident in the field of sports. Take, for example, the world of football. The word penetration is used to describe entering the opponent's territory.

In the locker room it is clear that to be weak is to be like a woman, sissy being the kindest of the derogatory words used to condemn other players. This is a toxic form of manliness that demeans its own internal feminine that we worked to synthesize in the previous card, Art.

This is how our shadow is fed. When we negate our essential nature, it comes out as a perversion. To own one's shadow is to look at our urges and see that the creative urge is inextricably bound with the procreative and these feelings are meant to be manifested in conscious, healthy, fun, and dynamic ways.

Whether the urge is to unite sexually, to complete a project, or to write a book, without the tenacity of our authentic Pan we are really bereft of our root life force.

So the question arises, what are those ideas and projects that you have held captive underneath all your earthly responsibilities and judgments?

Capricorn is considered the most responsible of the signs and many Caps can be the ones who always get left holding the bag because they have such perseverance and determination.

But what if "responsibility" is transformed into "ability to respond" to their own deepest will to create? Then the goat could gaily leap into the fray with purpose and joy, facing challenges as opportunities to grow and climb to the next level instead of burdens to carry through life.

Another way that these urges get misdirected is especially manifested in women. When a female Capricorn starts to exhibit fierce determination, it is usually judged as not feminine. The female child learns to be manipulative to get what she wants. Learning to lie or use what people call feminine wiles is often how this shows itself. This is often labeled passive/aggressive behavior in both women and men.

Only an honest assessment of our deepest urges can uncover our true will and then this potent force can be exactly what we need to make real our dreams.

The Capricornian Pan is not a flighty dreamer; he wants to take on the very real challenges of the many mountains that we all climb in our lives. He refuses to accept that, like Sisyphus, we are merely here to push boulders up mountains, watch them roll down, and just do it again and again.

He wants to work and play and have a juicy, dance-filled earthy existence, and he's winking at you!

Goats are known to eat almost anything to fuel their fire. Will you feed him the stolen, cruel satisfaction of dehumanized sex, or the healthy food of your dreams?

Will you try to keep him locked in a pen? Or will you let him surge through you to feel the way Michael Franti describes in his song: "Sometimes I feel like I can do anything, sometimes I feel so alive!"

When humans fall into the mistaken belief that our dreams can be separated from the natural urges of our physical bodies, then we are losing the very fire that can bring us to success.

So don't panic when you hear this satyr's flute. He is the Lord of the Dance and he leads us all to our own true will.

This is not to say that every desire is to be followed. In fact, that would be a nightmare for ourselves and devastating to others and the planet itself.

It means that we need to delve into our desires and find a way to the core of our heart's desire so that love holds the central focus, and just being alive is our greatest joy.

To control negative desires, we have to acknowledge them without judgment and then try to understand where they come from and what they are telling us about ourselves. This is the work that we do through therapy, writing, or meditation.

Our true will is not a string of unconscious desires and we must work hard to get to the root of our reason for being here.

The greatest danger we face with The Devil is when we project all of our negative thoughts externally and find a scapegoat to blame everything on. This is what fundamentalist religions preach. They give you all the answers, tell you how to be saved, and put all the evil on the chosen "Other."

This primal lie is the cause of most of the suffering in the world today.

When you get this card in a reading

This is the beginning of your path toward self-realization. First of all, notice when you are projecting your shadow on others. The world can get pretty dark and dangerous without the light of self-awareness, the lantern that The Hermit offered you a while back in your journey.

Raise it high, meet your demons, and look to all the other cards in the reading for tools you have already acquired to understand and find acceptance for all that you are today.

Be careful not to confuse seeking power and control with accomplishments that are manifestations of your true will. Notice that the wand/will of The Magician is firmly placed in front of the goat, reminding you to wield your power from within, not over, to fulfill your destiny. Many people get lost in the megalomania of ego-gratification, convincing themselves that they hold the answers and therefore have the right to rule over others.

Manipulations, lies and cruelty are all tempting tools of the deluded ego that seeks only its own glory and control over the world. If you are rationalizing acts that trouble your mind, ask yourself if you are wielding power over others without their permission. There is no right reason to control and oppress others.

Any means to an end is the road to hell.

This card shows us that we have reached a level of power and awareness that comes with grave responsibility. Remember "Do what thou wilt, but harm none" is a credo of The Magician that can serve you well. When you are tempted by your own ego to control, use or abuse other life forms, ask yourself if love is at the root of your actions.

All those partially formed bodies trapped inside the spheres want a way to manifest in the world. It's time to create for the shear joy of it and at the same time find out what you are made of through challenges that call for creativity and imagination. Ask yourself what project you want to manifest and employ flexibility, determination and the discipline and structure of Saturn to make it real (Saturn rules Capricorn).

When Pan is unashamed, free, playful and creative he is the epitome of yang tenacity and joy. But when our desires become ego instead of animal based we become unnatural. We can enjoy and play in the realm of desire without being chained to these natural urges. The Devil is the cultural shadow of Pan and will show us our addictive, manipulative, and power hungry aspects. When we lie or go into denial about our addictions then they rule our lives.

Most people need help with addictions so don't let shame and denial stop you from seeking the help of professionals, friends, and family.

The Tower XIV
Planet: Mars

After The Devil there is not a moment's respite as we confront The Tower and find that all hell is breaking loose!

In fact, the safety zone that we have constructed to give a false sense of security has become our prison and it's disintegrating before our eyes.

The Tower is blasted apart when we are stuck in a situation that is not fulfilling the creative urges we have just encountered in The Devil.

This card, even more than Death, creates a very strong reaction in almost everyone. In the Death card we do not witness actual destruction, but here there is no denying that fiery Mars has blown apart the safety of our fortress and made us look in dismay at what is happening in our life.

When we examine the image further even more possibilities arise.

Yes, the building is falling and we see figures crashing to the ground, but above The Tower is the third eye of awakening and illumination. Now Pan's third eye (seen in The Devil card) is seeing a new way to create the future and in the destruction we see the dove of peace flying free and the kundalini life force dancing in the sky.

All is not lost! As the lyrics of Jimi Hendrix so aptly state, "Castles made of sand, slip into the sea, eventually." All of life is transitory, but we connect to the eternal life force when we dare to let go. As Crowley states, "Change equals stability." This is truly one of the great paradoxes in life and it is in the Realm of Self-Realization that we learn to hold opposites as complements, paradoxes as both/ands, and recognize that all life is energy and motion.

When our fortress has become our prison, the question arises: Will we awaken to a new vision and let this tower fall and move on? Or will something external have to happen to bring the tower down?

One month before 9/11, I was invited to see a performance piece done by the traveling "Living Tarot" ensemble. This amazing cast of actors did readings spontaneously. Each actor had worked out the basic characteristics of two or three of the Major Arcana, and they proceeded to show you your reading live and in full costume. It was a dynamic experience and before the performance an astrologer with the troupe gave a short analysis of the current state of affairs. She stated that The Tower was the most powerful symbol of this time and we could choose to let our own individual towers fall and, therefore, be prepared for any external destruction, or we could get caught up in the fear and confusion of a larger cultural event about to take place.

When the Twin Towers fell, I remembered her words and was able to better understand this shocking event through her astute analysis.

Note that she did not "predict" a specific event but gave insight to help us become conscious about the nature of what was about to happen.

The story of the Twin Towers is the perfect example of a false sense of security being totally blown away.

But if we could have, as a people, not been overcome with fear, we would have been able to become aware of why this happened to America.

The fueling of our fears by the media and the government allowed us to be swept up in revenge and to lose connection with our grief and our reason. Heightened fear allowed our own civil rights to be undermined by the building of yet another "tower" of false security.

On the path of self-realization it is imperative to take responsibility for the events of one's life. Here is an example of this kind of consciousness on a national level. The Balinese people responded quite differently to an act of terrorism in their own country.

A terrible bomb blast ripped through a tourist area of a major city, killing over 250 people and sending shockwaves through the country and the world.

But the Balinese did not seek revenge and took time to mourn their dead and then set to work to restore balance between the forces of light and darkness by performing specific rituals.

They took responsibility for what happened, by demonstrating the ability to respond from a deep spiritual tradition that infuses the daily lives of the people of this amazing island.

In this largely Hindu country, the people do not project all that is wrong outside themselves. Unlike fundamentalists who are hell-bent on destroying what they call evil, the Balinese believe that there must be a balance between good and evil; that to attempt to destroy evil is to deny the natural order of existence.

What if we, as Americans, had taken this approach, asking why we were attacked. How had we drawn this violence into our midst?

We might have been able to acknowledge the shadow of our collective consciousness and realize that our exploitation of the rest of the world had created great hostility towards us and we were now suffering the response to our cruel destruction by facing destruction ourselves.

XVI

The Tower

Then we would not be ruled by fear that allowed us to enter into a preemptive invasion of Iraq and see our freedoms that we are supposedly fighting for be stripped away one by one.

If it is on a personal level that your Tower is falling, take heed.

The choice is this: make the change or the change will happen to you. Either way, things have been rigid so long that something has to give.

"When an inner situation is not made conscious, it appears outside as fate." —Carl Jung

Patching up the walls or fortifying the army can no longer save the day. It is time to see that to stay in the old dream is to call the winds of change to do our work for us.

There is no going back from here. As Joni Mitchell sang in the "Circle Game,"

"We can't return, we can only look behind from where we came and go round and round and round in the circle game...."

But then she adds in the last verse,

"...There'll be new dreams, maybe better dreams and plenty Before the last revolving year is through And the seasons they go round and round...."

It is the natural course of life. We cannot capture and secure our safety zone from the onslaught of time. When we have stopped growing and evolving in a given situation, the natural law of life says move on or become compost for the future.

This card is governed by the planet Mars and everything we have just discovered about the positive and negative aspects of The Tower are a reflection of the positive and negative aspects of this warrior god.

Mars for too long has been cast as the violent, fierce, and forceful god of war. But his evolved nature is that of a shamanic warrior on the path of enlightenment.

It is time for the people of the Earth to transform their concept of power. The power of love comes from within; the power of ego projects itself outward and wants power over others to prove its greatness. True greatness is manifested in the flexible, resourceful, and imaginative warrior who sees challenges as chances to grow, and so-called enemies as the greatest teachers. (See Mars Story, in the Appendix page 387).

The archetype of Mars is awakened in us when we feel angry at being oppressed, abused, disrespected, or just plain lonely. When a child is not loved the result is all too often an angry young man or woman, who will constantly strike out against the people who have not given love and support or any authority figures in their lives. This is usually done in ways that are self-defeating (see The Princess of Swords, page 156).

As Thich Nhat Hahn so clearly states in his book, Anger, "…all of us carry the seed of anger and when it starts to grow we can water it with our reasons for striking out against a world that doesn't seem to understand, or we can hold our anger like a child, listen to its frustrations, and try to give compassionate help in finding constructive ways to change the current situation."

Marge Piercy says it well in her poem, "A Just Anger," "A good anger swallowed clots the blood to slime." Anger is a tool of liberation, a mechanism in the human emotional toolbox to wake us up to oppression.

Piercy further states, "A good anger acted upon is beautiful as lightening and swift with power."

It takes great discernment to be able to distinguish hostility and righteous anger. A true warrior will not let him or herself be consumed by the fire of anger, but will instead transform it into the fierce actions needed to bring about change.

There are many who feel that anger is wrong under all circumstances, but I would side with the Balinese that it is another aspect of our emotional palette that must be understood and utilized. Suppression only makes us diseased and sick inside.

As an activist most of my life, I have found that anger is a great teacher. I have had to do a lot of work to differentiate between the unconscious acting out of my personal anger and the work of bringing a conscious, loving, and often fierce voice for change.

One tool that has helped me on this path is to not make the person wrong or hate them but speak about how the person could change their behavior. As Martin Luther King, Jr. so aptly stated, "Let no one bring you so low as to hate them." Most immoral actions are rooted in fear. Logic cannot be heard clearly until the heart stops pounding. Fear can only be deflated by love and a sense of belonging. Then education, coupled with an invitation to join in community, can be very effective.

The awakened Mars does not use force or create fear. He is flexible and imaginative, employing the gifts of his brothers, The Magician, The Fool, The Hermit, The Hierophant, and, yes, even The Emperor, in his evolved form as The Visionary Activist.

These are the mentors of our warrior. May we embody this archetype by finding the courage to serve the great goddess Venus in all our challenges while confronting injustice and oppression in the world.

When you get this card in a reading

The Tower is a wake-up call that demands we recognize the false and limiting structures in our lives and embrace change even as our world is falling apart. Pema Chodron's book, When Things Fall Apart, reveals ways to move through these troubling and transformative times and a chance to see more clearly than we have in a long time. The following quotes from her book are clarifications of the meaning of The Tower.

"Only to the extent that we expose ourselves over and over to annihilation can that which is indestructible in us be found."

"To be fully alive, fully human, and completely awake is to be continually thrown out of the nest. To live fully is to be always in no-man's-land, to experience each moment as completely new and fresh. To live is to be willing to die over and over again."

Remember, we are in the Realm of Self-Realization where we must stay in the flow, in the river of change, and relish the joy of just being alive and awake.

On a practical level it can mean the end of a job, the loss of a home, the tumultuous end of a relationship, or an intense internal shock and illumination.

Be careful not to lash out and blame others or shake your fist at the world. Somehow you were trapped and now you are in the process of regaining your freedom and your true power.

Your inner Mars can either do battle externally or transform internally. It is up to you. There is a whole storehouse of energy that will be available to you once you let go of the false gods and false securities that were actually suffocating your soul.

Then, you will no longer be appalled by the fire and brimstone. After the dust settles, look up to see your Star. That will remind you who you are.

The Star XVII
Astrological Sign: Aquarius

WILL NOT TIRE OF LIFE

Other forces are reaching in to protect us
All of us
She, He, It has not left us alone to kill and cry
and beat our breast at the hopelessness of it all
There is only hope and the momentary loss of it
only brings us closer to its source
Depression is only a longing for hope
So rage cry crash and fly again, the wings are there.
Though swords of uncertainty dance in your mind,
The heart opens wings ever wider,
Remember the force that
pulled you drifting from formless to breath
It has not left you
That is only your star,
Which you ever orbit, getting closer and then retreating
so you can feel the active force
of longing again,
Spirit refuses to let you be lazy in your reverent love.
She is holding us delicately with unquestioned strength
He is singing to us in the song of all tongues
Spirit is shining ever stronger now
Though the dramatic tide has crashed
The ever-quiet ocean goes about its ways
tendrils swishing
crabs lurking
The natural world singing natural ways back to life.
If we continue to worship life,
To pray to it, to smile to it,
To make jokes in her honor,
We together will not tire of life.

By April Faith Hirschman

At last The Star, your guiding light, shines forth, bringing you to the next stage of your destiny. Through all your work and play you are truly prepared to take a quantum leap into the next stage of Self-Realization.

When I teach the Tarot, I often use art to explore the meanings of the cards, since, in fact, they are works of art in their own right.

One student of mine, Mua, used a very creative approach to her painting of The Star card. Traditionally, The Star shows a woman pouring water from one cup that is filled from the heavens into another cup that she pours out onto the Earth. In the Motherpeace deck she is shown bathing in a pool of water surrounded by nature with a hawk flying overhead.

In this student's interpretation she was bathing in a "woman-made" pool that was constructed from the recycled bricks of the fallen Tower in the preceding card!

This was a brilliant way to show the continuity of the journey and that we can always find a way, like the phoenix, to rise from the ashes and build anew.

The Star Maiden is pouring out the waters of life to heal herself so she can help the healing of the world by offering her authentic self and her unique gifts at this crucial time of the dawning of a New Age.

Many believe this is the dawning of the Age of Aquarius and this card is the archetypal Aquarian card in the Tarot.

Whether you believe in this idea or not, almost all cultures on Earth recognize this as the beginning of a new era for all life forms.

Following the idea of the Aquarian concept, we are offered a big clue by the astrological term for this card, The Water Bearer. Aquarius is an air sign so it might seem contradictory for it to be The Water Bearer, but since air is the element of thought and water the element of emotion, then The Water Bearer can be seen as the harbinger of Intelligent Love. It is time to reunite the heart and mind, as is traditional in most eastern cultures. The name for heart/mind is usually one word.

If we are to move through these tumultuous times with grace, then love cannot be trivialized. So much of our modern interpretation of love is possessive, blind, aggressive, idealized, falsely romanticized, and sadly, even abusive.

Look at such common phrases as, "You are the only one for me," that gets played out in a stalker mentality like The Police song lyrics: "Every breath you take, every move you make, I'll be watching you."

The idea that love is some state that is achieved and then will remain statically the same is just a setup for disappointment.

Then there is the love that can be bought by investing in products

XVII

ח   **The Star**   ≈

that will get you your man/woman. This immature approach to love is rife in our society and makes love a selling point.

Intelligent love is the willingness to be honest, communicative, and authentic; to recognize that love is a process that takes commitment, patience, and the courage to face our fears of vulnerability. True love goes beyond the ego's desire to feel good about itself because someone is saying all the right things.

In many ways the human species is moving through its adolescence into adulthood and this is most evident in the realm of relationship.

Love in adolescence is very similar to disease; we can't eat, we can't sleep, all we can think about is the object of our desires. We are obsessed.

This is largely a chemically induced phenomenon to keep people procreating, something that is in fact in need of conscious control at this time of limited resources.

But on a deeper level it is that point in our journey that was epitomized by The Lovers in The Family Row of the Major Arcana.

The first time we saw love as something outside the cocoon of our biological family was in The Lovers card.

We experienced a profound pull to the beloved, above all else.

Now that we are in the stage of Self-Realization it is time to be conscious of what we have learned about love on the journey and apply it to our relationships. Since this card represents our individual path, then self-love is the core that allows us to experience love in healthy ways with those around us.

Intelligent love pours out of the cup of the goddess Venus onto the world as a healing balm and the gateway to ecstasy. To feel oneness with other life forms, be they animal, vegetable, or human, is to have the core experience of this earthly existence.

As Alice Walker stated at a Solfest event, "It is time to tune into the frequency of ecstasy, and be like a sunrise to the world."

And as the Sun is a Star so each of us a Star; a unique expression of the divine in human form, capable of expressing the awakened knowledge of this joyful universe.

When we are willing to find the clarity that The Star offers, we are capable of being change agents as we move into a shift in consciousness. It is our work, like Quan Yin pouring her compassionate waters on the Earth, to be healers of the wounds of a brutal time dominated by war, greed, and selfishness.

It is extremely important to know, at this time of the great turning from empire to earth community, that we must hold space and witness the death of the Piscean age. We will encounter and move through this treacherous landscape as we descend one final time into the birth canal of The Moon, the archetypal Piscean card. It is time to leave behind the nightmare of separation and loneliness to bring forth the new dream of interconnectedness with all life.

It is not easy to witness the death of an age, but we cannot leap over this experience. Our only way forward is through the fall of The Tower. If we love this world, and we love the experience of love itself, then we must have faith in its power beyond all else. We may not always see the way through. The canal is dark, but our instincts are strong and our guides from all planes of existence are present and willing to serve. We need to ask and to trust and to know that there is no power greater than the power of love.

Then the intelligence of love will shine through the clouds of uncertainty, and a light will show the way.

As the I Ching says, "It is only when we are willing to see things exactly as they are that the way through will be revealed."

The I Ching also posits a law of nature that when evil has darkened all, then the light must return.

We can all hold the circle, hold each other's hands, and know that the dawn will come. The Sun will rise and we will rise like a million suns, if we are not overcome by fear.

Our Star, our personal destiny, guides each of us. Trust your instincts and your heart to be where you know you need to be. Michael Franti, a San Francisco musician, chose to go to Iraq and bring his healing and uplifting hip-hop/rock music.

In this war-torn country Michael was safe because he was called to be there to help by uplifting the spirits of the people. This knowing is the greatest protection from accidents and so-called "bad luck."

Another important aspect of the Aquarian age is that it is electric and filled with technological advances, such as the computer and the Internet. It is important to remember that all these forms of connection and communication are already inherent in the human matrix and, in time, we will exceed the limitations of the physical tools and reconnect to nature's ever-present web of life.

When you get this card in a reading

You are being offered the opportunity to take a quantum leap into the next phase of your personal destiny. Now that The Tower clouds of confusion have cleared, you can see your guiding light and set your course. It is not a rejection of others, or a focus on them, but a time to regroup and receive the next messages from your own soul.

This is not a time to be concerned with results as much as purpose and authentic action. Since this card is about the Aquarian Age we are transitioning into, ask yourself what is your unique gift. Receive from the heavens and give to the Earth.

No one else can give your gift to the world, so measure your choices by how they show the world who you really are. It is not about perfection but about the willingness to offer yourself, uninhibited by others' perception of you.

We have seen so many "stars" of Hollywood lose their way when they get caught in the web of success and become a pawn in the game. If you are guided internally, whatever happens will be your choice. Your lessons learned and your growth will be paramount.

As Joni Mitchell so aptly writes in
"A Free Man in Paris,"
"I was a free man in Paris
I felt unfettered and alive
There was nobody calling me up for favors
And no one's future to decide
You know I'd go back there tomorrow
But for the work I've taken on
Stoking the star maker machinery
Behind the popular song..."

The word disaster means not of the stars, and you can avoid them if you trust yourself above all outside influences. As synchronicity would have it, as I was writing this section a young woman came up and needed to pick a card about her relationship with her love of the last year and a half. She picked this card and knew she needed to get back on track with her own life. It was not a rejection but a grounded refocusing.

As she said herself, "I need to follow my path now as he does and we'll see where that takes us." Even when there is love we are not meant to lose ourselves in relationships that are bringing us down.

Since this is also an age of healing, take time out to nourish and replenish yourself, as in the image in the Motherpeace deck that was described earlier. Go to a pond, lake, stream, or the ocean and dip your toe in like The Star goddess herself. Feel the revitalizing powers of water.

It is also a good time to revamp your website to reflect who you are now and reveal your aspirations to the world so people can find you and offer you the perfect opportunities.

It is always heartening to see The Star card in conjunction with The Universe card in a reading as it implies that your individual point of light is moving in harmony with the larger spiral of The Universe The microcosm and the macrocosm have synched up and you are on your way!

The Moon XVIII
Astrological Sign: Pisces

Now that we have found our way again by finding the guiding light of our heavenly body, The Star, we are ready to be our own mother and rebirth ourselves into our cosmic skin.

For women and men alike, The Moon represents our deepest visions and our darkest nightmares. In our work through the earlier Trumps (another name for the Major Arcana) we have in a sense triumphed over the limitations of unconscious behavior and are now armed with the tools of a warrior on the path of learning, awakening, and victory. We have shed the physical and ego armors of our former self. The egoic mind is now much more in service to the soul. Like a planet orbiting the Sun, it serves, not rules, our will to create.

Now the monsters and ogres of the moon's dark landscape are friends and messengers in the telling of our own myth. We have found new ways to comfort, listen, and care for all the facets of our human condition without judgment.

The Moon calls us to see her phases as the phases of our own lives. She is the great teacher of cycles. Through witnessing the waxing, full, waning, dark, and return of the new moon, we are able to relate to the beginning, growth, and falling away of the many stages of relationships, jobs, and projects.

Nothing lasts forever in stasis, and the only constant is change.

It is a profound time of wisdom when we recognize this paradox as a fact of life. This allows us to evolve into a place free of judgment, beyond either/or and into the place of both/and.

When I was only nineteen, I dated a young African-American man who took me to a jazz club called the Both/And on Divisadero St. in San Francisco.

It was a soul-warming experience for a young hippie girl up from the suburbs to see Miles Davis, Herbie Hancock, and the rest of the band play amazing improvisational music in this dimly lit, little hole in the wall.

What struck me most, being the only white person there, was that this was different than any musical performance I had ever heard. In fact, the difference was, I wasn't just seeing and listening and applauding at the end, I was a part of a happening!

Everyone was moving and shouting out phrases of encourage-ment: uh huh, go man, that's right! We were all riding the electric current of music being born in the moment. We were not passive observers, not even an audience, we were all one. It was truly a both/and experience I will never forget!

Out of the dark womb all is born. Out of the mystery comes the new child, idea, song, dance. Everything comes forth from the dream world that our beloved Luna calls her realm.

Are we willing to face the dark hour of the soul and venture into the wilderness on our own, letting go of our need to have parents, religions, and teachers lead us? It's not that we are now alone but that we are capable of recognizing our oneness that allows us to feel our way in the dark.

There is no turning back now, no way to crawl back inside the womb. Whatever form our life has taken till now, we must now go where we have never gone before: Into the internal landscape of our personal destiny to bring forth our authentic gift to the world.

The pageant of our victorious return awaits us if we can just keep breathing, breathing, breathing. Every great tradition teaches us to follow the breath and we will find ourselves where we have always belonged, and where we have always been—right here now!

The Moon, astrologically, is represented by the sign of Pisces, the most empathic and compassionate of the signs. To really become compassionate to others is to first be willing to accept ourselves as we are. Only then can we truly find empathy with others.

I know from experience that the biggest mistakes I ever made in my life have allowed me to learn forgiveness for myself so that I can acknowledge the deep need in everyone to be forgiven. "To err is human, to forgive divine."

The shadow of Pisces is when we go overboard in feeling the pain and the needs of others and unconsciously take them on as our own. This results in a sacrifice of our purpose and path to live for the beloved. There is nothing wrong with selfless acts of service, but it is key that we are making this choice in a way that aligns with our nature and allows us to breathe and grow as well.

When we go overboard we can literally drown in the Piscean swamp. You cannot really give another person a hand up when you are sucked into the muck and mire of their personal limitations.

Listening and acknowledging, nurturing and encouraging must not slip into the martyrdom of self to other. In the end, both people

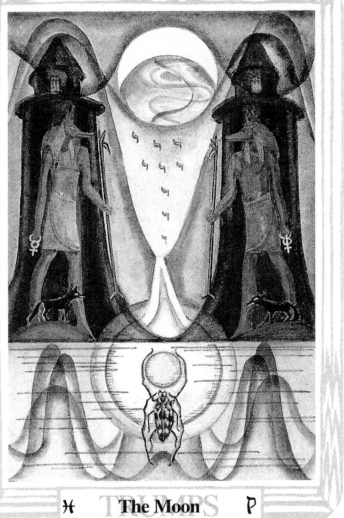

XVIII

ℵ **The Moon** ℘

can become lost and flounder without any ground to stand on.

We are now leaving the Piscean age and moving into the Aquarian age, and to create a bridge over the troubled waters of our times into this next wave, we need to recognize the difference between compassion and self-destructive sacrifices. Martyrdom takes us off our own path and actually robs the ones we are trying to help of their own life lessons by taking them as our own.

These are subtle differences and it might be helpful to look across the zodiac to the complementary sign of Virgo to find the tools of The Hermit.

The Hermit knows when to retreat and go inward, possibly praying or holding a positive image of the ones we wish to help. We need to use critical thinking to see where our healthy boundaries lie.

In fact, it is useful for all signs to take a journey across the zodiac to their complementary sign and ask, "How would my polar opposite deal with this?"

Opposites become complements when we consciously witness their divine interplay.

For example, a Virgo sometimes needs to lose its analytical bent and swim into Neptune's Piscean dream world for a while.

When you get this card in a reading

It is time to go through a profound initiation, a birth that must be fully experienced. The Moon offers no guarantees so you must want to go deeper and face even the dark hour of the soul, otherwise there is no reason to venture into this landscape.

Find your inner courage and give up any desires for specific results. You are on uncharted ground and the logical mind will serve you only to the extent it serves your intuition.

Sometimes you will feel you have no choice and find yourself lost and unable to see any guiding light. Life is pulling you deeper into facing your shadow and your limitations. Acknowledge them and keep breathing. Make mistakes, learn, and keep moving.

Hesitation can leave you wandering in the desert of illusion and fear. Trust yourself and that still small voice within. Even as the jackals of your demons howl at The Moon, know that she is showing you a mirror of yourself so you may bring from within your own dreams for the future.

The Moon may bring depression, fear, regret, and doubt. It is a test of your ability to see that these are illusions of your own making and therefore only you have the ability to dispel them.

It may be helpful to keep a dream journal and track the themes and characters that present themselves during the night. Mugwort is known to enhance dreams and help you remember them. It is only necessary to smell this herb although some choose to smoke it or take it as a tincture or a tea.

This is an excellent time to ask your dream self for answers to questions before you enter the dreamtime.

All manifestations begin with some form of dream or imagination, so take time when you first awaken to gather what you can from your night journey.

Remember, the ever-returning Sun is just a breath away.

The Sun XIX
Planet: The Sun

In The Moon card we saw the sacred beetle pushing The Sun through the birth channel. Now that we have gone through the initiation of the Moon and connected with the unfulfilled dreams that were hidden in the inner world, we are ready to rise like The Sun, and bring those dreams out into the physical world.

In the past this card was referred to as the Crowned and Conquering Child. Although these terms may be archaic, the underlying message is that to become self-realized is to become wise enough to release your innocent, playful child. Healed and released from the limitations of the Family Realm and the Realm of Earthly Reality, it is time to radiate self-awareness and the joy of embodied presence.

Now the wise, experienced part of ourselves has released blame and shame and found that the whole life journey was exactly what was needed to bring us to this moment in time. Bringing us fully present, shining in joy and happiness like The Sun itself. Inwardly we always knew, even in the darkest hours of the lunar night, that the love and truth we needed would eventually "dawn" on us.

The Sun does not actually die each night, but it can seem like the night of unconscious behavior will never end and that we are dying in the darkness. It is only another layer of our old skin that we leave in the Moon's night cave as Venus, the morning star, calls us with her loving song to re-emerge.

The Thoth deck card shows two children with wings dancing with each other. They have earned their wings by remembering that all opposites are complements and the separation from the beloved is an illusion that can no longer keep us apart.

We are liberated children of The Universe, having passed through all the difficult trials of a dualistic mindset. We now see the divisions as the joy of diversity. Within this many-faceted creation we can experience union and creativity. We can explore the many dimensions of this unfolding, ever-changing world.

In The Star card we were reconnected to our individual destiny in this life. The Sun is also a star, and now we have found that after the healing, forgiveness, and the journey through the dark hour of the

XIX

ℷ TRUMPS **The Sun** ☉

soul (Moon), we are fully activating its magnetizing and life-generating qualities. There will be other liberated souls calling to us as we
leave the cave because we have left our solo Star journey and are fully
prepared to collaborate, be it team work or team play.

We are ready to feed others with our dynamic fiery life force and
to be fed by theirs. Imagine interlacing circles of solar systems, like
molecules, giving light and receiving energy.

We are now fully activated generators radiating and creating in
community with others who are ready to fully embrace the New Age
of freedom and creativity. Recognizing each other's unique creative
abilities, we focus on supporting, inspiriting, and appreciating each
other. One day the architect is the central inspiring force; the next
day, the musician. We are all leaders in a healthy way when we express power from within instead of the old paradigm of power over.

In a way, The Sun is the simplest of the Major Arcana as it is the
spirit of child-like innocence. It reveals that in reality life is a divine
play of discovery, creativity, and love.

When you get this card in a reading

You have reached a stage of development that is elevated beyond
competition into the place of mutual cooperation. It suggests that
self-employment or partnerships and cooperatives are the structures
that serve truly self-realized individuals. We no longer need or want
to be ruled by the "should" of parental or dominator institutions,
whether they be in work, spirituality, or our personal relationships.

We are wise fools, liberated from our own limitations and ready to
create. Freedom is really the willingness to take full responsibility for
all that we do and all that we are.

In Hebrew the letter for this card is Resh, which means head. Finally
we have a good head on our shoulders, a head that, like Juno, sees the
past, present, and future, and can be fully in the present, radiating bril-
liance to all who enter our orbit.

The Sun literally calls us outside to play and dance on the verdant
green hills of Gaia. We are no longer eclipsed by society's imposed
judgments and inhibitions. It is not a time to be dependent on others,
but interdependent and mutually supportive.

When looking at your work world and how it connects to this tran-
sitional time, look at the solar power industry as a prime example of
positive use of the very source of life on Earth. It is a template for other
businesses that will help us leave the age of oil and the rape of the
Earth and transition into a time of sustainable stewardship and respect
for Earth as source, not resource.

Ask yourself if the work you are doing or the business you would like
to start fits these criteria.

The Aeon/Judgment XX
Element: Fire

In almost all decks this card is still called Judgment and the images usually reference the biblical story of the Apocalypse in which the angel Gabriel appears and blows his trumpet to announce the end of the world. The card shows corpses rising from their graves praying for redemption.

According to the Bible and the Koran, all sentient beings are held accountable for their deeds and judged by god. This predicted event is central to the Judaic, Christian, and Muslim religions.

The Angel or Messenger of god was instrumental in the beginning of these religions and is the central figure at the end of the earthly part of the journey of humanity.

Crowley, however, received revelations of a different nature that inspired him to radically change the meaning and significance of this card.

He strongly believed, as I do, that instead of the end of the world we are entering a New Age where a judging, punishing god is recognized as an unnecessary and ineffective method of creating a peaceful and loving humanity. Instead of fear of eternal damnation as a motivation for "good," we will evolve into an age where love is recognized as the creative force in the universe and forgiveness and compassion will be the way to help us discard judgment. It signals an end to the externalization of the shadow side of the human condition. We are awakening into a conscious awareness that all of us are at different stages of our personal path and no one is superior or right, while others are inferior or wrong. We are growing up as a species and reinventing our spirituality, guided by the doctrine of love and its instrument of truth as a way to accept all life forms as they are, right here, right now.

It is useful to reinterpret the ideas of the old paradigm as metaphors for rebirth, not the literal end of the world. The idea of resurrection can be viewed as the phoenix rising from the ashes of ignorance into the flight that is guided by our own internal, ethical compass.

We are released from the repercussions of our past, often called karma, by owning our mistakes, recognizing, learning, and incor-

porating the lessons and forgiving others and ourselves. By so doing, the mistakes become valuable lessons to guide us on the next
step of our journey.

Now we can be redeemed, resurrected and forgiven without
needing a priest to do it for us. We will no longer need the paren-
tal/god approval or disapproval as the measure of all things. We
can, as a species, take responsibility for our own actions and every
challenge or mistake becomes an opportunity for growth.

So much of this kind of fear-based judgment has covered over the
innocent, curious, and loving child in us all. Children are shamed
and blamed in ways that make them feel that who they are is inherently wrong. Years of therapy and lessons in self-acceptance are
often needed to recover the childlike spontaneity, joy, and imagination that are hallmarks of a happy childhood and a happy life that
is epitomized in the previous card, The Sun.

This is not meant to be a condemnation of religions. Religions
are a reflection of the different stages of our species evolution. All
religions have core values that emphasize love, truth, and kindness.
The methods of teaching and instilling these values change and
reflect the different ages of humankind.

But to continue to impose parental gods as masters of humanity
is to hold back the growth of the current spiritual movement in the
world today.

For example, the honoring of love as the highest power is helping
us all to accept authentic love in whatever form it wishes to manifest. All over the world there is a growing and unstoppable acknowledgment that love moves without prejudice through all barriers and
confronts all fears on its path. Love between the races, love between
humans of the same sex, love between cultures, ethnic backgrounds
and class categories is burning through a millennia of false and
extremely harmful judgments of what love can do.

In the Realm of Self-Realization we become more and more
aware that we are instruments for love, not the ones who are to determine when love is right or wrong. The beauty of authentic love
is that it has no preconditions and we need to wake up and accept
love's teachings. So much of our great literature and modern movies have been devoted to awakening this consciousness and revealing the tragedy that ensues when we define what qualifies as love.
Romeo and Juliet, Guess Who's Coming to Dinner, and Brokeback
Mountain are a few examples of this motif.

Many of the old separations between people came out of misguided or ignorant fears that individuals who chose a different path
would undermine the existence of cultures or tribes. Science has

XX

♆ TRUMPS The Aeon △

long acknowledged that diversity is in fact the key to the survival
of all species and now that we are becoming a global village, there
is growing acceptance that we are a world family. To celebrate our
differences and our uniqueness helps us widen our horizons and
ultimately our capacity for love.

So now, at the dawning of the Age of Aquarius, with sympathy
and understanding, we can be wise advocates and playful children
as we advance beyond the conflict causing separations of nations,
religions, class, race, and sexual orientation.

Time to replace the Apocalypse with the Apocalypso and dance
on the graves of our past limitations that were rooted in fear and
ignorance of the unfamiliar.

 The perfect sound track would be "It's the End of the World as
We Know It (And I Feel Fine)"by REM.

When you get this card in a reading it would be a great time to
go inside and try to access that child who has been silenced for so
long and just check in. This card in the Thoth deck shows the god
of silence, Hoor-par-Kraat (an aspect of Horus), as a transparent
image of a male child with his finger to his mouth. There are many
ways to employ this symbol.

Each of us has a wounded or silenced part of ourselves from
childhood that languishes unacknowledged in the unconscious. We
can reach out as adults and parent this part of ourselves with compassion, while finding new ways to listen.

Silence is the place we can go to truly find the guidance from our
soul's timeless knowing.

Within the child resides many impulses and joys that we can remember and reinvigorate through activities that will let this inner
child come out and play. Did you love to paint or walk in the woods
as a child? Did you have an imaginary friend who would like to
have a conversation with you again? How about a favorite toy or secret hiding place? An old friend or a favorite book or teacher? This
is especially useful to help you discover what you wanted to be when
you grew up that was set aside or belittled as you became an adult.
To do what we love is to find who we are, as in Joseph Campbell's
idea of following your bliss, articulated in The Power of Myth.

In accessing our deep place of knowing, we often need to stop
asking advice and testing our ideas out on others. To go deep inside
and resurface with a knowing about your next steps in life is a profound gift, but discussing the process with all your misgivings and
doubts often dissipates your power to manifest these steps. This card
signals that you have enough input and now you need to sit with the
possibilities until one arises that you know feels true. To make a fresh

start, it is best to speak of it to others only on a need-to-know basis. Call your travel agent to book the trip; call the lawyer to draw up the contract; come from an unflinching clarity to move forward.

A way of knowing the next step in your life involves the willingness to say to yourself, "I won't regret this no matter what the result." This will keep the ego in its proper place. Instead of measuring the "rightness" of your choice by the rewards or predetermined accept-able validations, you are ready for the adventure, whatever happens.

The I Ching says that we often plant the seeds of disorder along with the seeds of the new order we are establishing. The more we are aware of this, the less we will plant doubts and fears of the ego's reticence about the unknown.

It is time to focus on your relationship with this time on Earth and what your connection is as a midwife of the New Age. This means that you do not want to be limited by any person, by your work, your family, or your home base. Once you have a sense of where you need to be and what you need to be doing, all the aspects of your life, like work, relationships, and location, will fall into place.

The Universe XXI
Planet: Saturn

The Universe means Uni=one Verse=song suggesting we are all here to harmonize our unique voice with the music of the spheres.

In almost all decks we see a woman dancing ecstatically. In the Thoth deck she is partnered with the serpent energy of her own kundalini life force, guided by the vision of the all-knowing eye within a net of stars.

On the four corners we see the symbols of the four fixed signs, Taurus, Leo, Aquarius and Scorpio, creating the structure of the four directions that is seen in some formation in all cultures.

The last time we encountered these four guardians was in the Family row of the archetypes in The Hierophant card. At that time we were neophytes being guided by our religious and secular teachers.

Those images appeared as masks, roles we learned and played out from our upbringing. Now in The Universe card we see them infused with energy pouring through every orifice, alive and reinvigorated with the life force, untamed and unlimited.

Nothing stands between us and everything; and the ecstatic joy of being born into life is enough. It is only through coming into physical form that we can individuate from, and then reunite with, the mystery. The Universe is a woman dancing, she who gave us birth and to whom we return.

My daughter, Celeste Hirschman, who is a sex and intimacy coach, helps people embrace, enjoy, and embody their sexuality. She loves to wear a T-shirt that says "Meet Your Maker," under a subtle image of a woman's torso. This world is feminine in nature, a reality that is confirmed by the fact that every culture, no matter how patriarchal, still calls the Earth "She."

There is an old saying that goddess does not rule the world, she is the world. Attempts to rule the world and all the resultant challenges and failures were experienced in the Realm of Earthly Reality. Now, in the last stage of the Realm of Self-Realization, we see that ruling the world actually separates us from the world we yearn to be one with.

The Fool has danced through the three stages and has now returned full circle back into the arms of the universal life force that

XXI

ħ   **The Universe**   ♄

brought him on the dance floor in the first place. Now we can hear the rhythms and music of the spheres and be fully present in the moment.

Graduating from all the classes and lessons in the school of life, we encounter Saturn who turns out to be the great maestro orchestrating a myriad of circumstances, disciplinary actions and difficult problems to bring us into self-awakening. Although Saturn seemed to be the strict, relentless taskmaster, now The Fool, who has become wise, bows in respect and appreciation.

Saturn embodies the wisdom to guide us in the evolutionary process; offering structures that limit us until we no longer need external forces to command our training and learning. After much practice, hard work, and sweat, under the fatherly firmness of Saturn, we are free to improvise.

When you get this card in a reading

At this final stage, it is key to look at the big picture and contemplate your soul connection with life itself. Try to let all the stories of work and relationship fall away and breathe in the beauty of this eternal moment that you are blessed to be a part of.

As Oscar Wilde so aptly stated, "Be yourself; everyone else is already taken." The gift you have to offer, only you can give.

Saturn is here to tell us to trust in the overall plan of our life and act with confidence in entering into disciplines and agreements that will fulfill this intimation from the divine.

This card draws out in us the expansive experiences of travel that include other cultures and people inviting us to deepen our respect and love of this world in all its permutations. Travels can also be to the inner worlds of dreams and imagination. Both journeys will trigger creative ways to be of service, especially in the realm of deep ecology.

It might also be time to just get out there and dance and sweat your prayers with those you love!

If you are feeling out of sorts when you get this card then Saturn is once again putting on the pressure for you to let go of aspects of your life that have been stagnant and oppressive for too long. Relationships and work that have become intolerable but that you have feared leaving, need to be released. Saturn pops in when there is really nothing else to be done but let the old form go. In truth, it is already over. It's like a snake whose skin is dead but it is too afraid to crawl out of it for fear of being hurt with its sensitive new skin exposed to the world. To allow time for the new skin to acclimate, be kind and firm with yourself and be with those you know love you.

Or paradoxically, it can also be healthy to take yourself away from the familiar so you can remember that you are not only defined by your relationships, your work, or where you live.

There are no beginnings without endings. We have all heard of the "dreaded" Saturn returns that occur roughly every 29 years in our lives. The first one kicks in about a year before we turn 29, the second one about two years before at around 56, and so on. Situations that have lasted 29 years and lost all meaning are really begging to be sacrificed on the altar of truth.

In actuality, our Saturn returns are reminders of the gifts and purpose we came into this life to fulfill. Saturn takes 29 years to circle the earth and as it approaches the position it was in when we were born, the pressure increases to set the template for the next 29 years. It's time to acknowledge lessons learned and let go of anything that has become intolerable. Often relationships and jobs that we were tolerating out of fear or inertia now eat away at our energy level and our ability to experience joy. We are being called to ask the question, does this serve our life purpose in the big picture? Do we want to bring this pattern into the next 29 years of our life? What is the template we are creating for this next Saturn phase?

When we are in our Saturn return we tend to see situations more seriously than most, so try not to be too hard on those close to you.

In the relationship realm we often want to commit to a life partner as well as fulfill the biological clock's urgings to have offspring or adopt. In the work realm we are called to find true purpose and not just satisfy the ego rewards of position, power, and money. In the realm of spiritual growth, we find the need to look at our demons and shadow aspect to go deeper and let go of superficial answers, gurus, or religions that treat us like children. We are ready to face the big questions and sit with the mystery to find a sense of our own understanding and wisdom.

It is not often an easy time but it can be an acceleration of an authentic path if we have already been paying attention to the still, small voice of guidance from within. Being a species of procrastinators, however, we tend to feel it as a pressure cooker until we wake up and acknowledge the messages that are being fired at us from many directions.

It is common for people to experience divorce or the end of a relationship, getting fired, or changing work before the axe falls. But like the Death card, it is a gift in disguise when we can read the signs and leave stagnant situations and trust in our inner Magus and Priestess to show us the way.

Think of the musician who has practiced and studied for years. It is only in the moment of performing that all the work becomes a support of the unique expression that is the musician's gifts to the world. It is not the technical perfection that brings the ecstatic union of audience and player into the now, but rather all that discipline has supported the gift that has always been within the giver.

May we all find the discipline and work that affords us the possibility of uncovering and giving ourselves to the world. Sky clad and freely she dances to the one song and so shall we all in those synchronistic moments of divine reunion!

Note: All the other Saturn-influenced cards in the Thoth deck are either stuck in the past (Eight of Cups), or pushing into the future (Ten of Wands). It is only The Universe card that brings us to the revelation of Saturn's profound message. Life on Earth is limited but if we consciously choose or make structures within which to create, in the moment of creation, in the joy of the dance, all the walls fall away and we are moving with the vibrational music of the spheres.

MINOR ARCANA
COURT CARDS

MINOR ARCANA COURT CARDS

Welcome to the realm of theatre, my friends. Whether you know it or not, you are the director and sixteen characters are vying for the lead role in your play. They are very happy not to have to audition, because try as you might to choose sensibly, your subconscious will place them in their perfect roles to mirror, enhance, or aggravate your life.

When these actors are ill-dignified they will do anything to get your attention. They will appear in the guise of a boyfriend or a boss, a teacher who reminds you of your mother, or any bit part that is open, just to get their feet in the door of your life story. So when you shuffle those cards, make no mistake. They love to gossip and tell all, and they are about to do a little vignette of your current relationships with unabashed honesty.

Every Tarot reader knows that there are basically no holds barred when it comes to the realm of personality. Every deck has a different take on the way these folks look, act, dress, and even what culture or age they live in.

Of course there are some definite parameters that these personalities must stay within or else you would never be able to figure them out or see the common thread that runs between their basic elemental families. The strongest aspect of their nature is defined by the suits they belong to, called Swords, Wands, Cups and Disks. These suits correspond to the elements; Air = Swords, Fire = Wands,

Water = Cups, and Earth = Disks. Air represents the mental plane, Fire the energetic plane, Water the emotional, and Disks the physical realm.

The next defining aspects are the astrological signs that correlate with the cards. There are twelve signs and sixteen cards and this frees up all the princesses to be the primal manifestation of each of the root elements of the four suits. This is similar to the function of the Aces. (See intro to Minor Arcana Numbered Cards on page 217).

Princesses

The following is a brief summary of how the Princesses reveal the essential nature of the different suits/elements.

The Princess of Swords (Air) embodies the essential urging of the mind: fierce and determined, defending the altar of truth at all costs. She will cut through the mental clouds of confusion and ignorance that block our view of the intelligent light of the Sun breaking through behind her. She is raw, young, and inexperienced but she has the courage of her convictions. Hopefully the rest of her Air family will help her be effective in communicating her beliefs and working with others for justice.

The Princess of Wands (Fire) is the center of attention as soon as she comes on the scene. You won't need any logs on the fire when she is present. Her essence is passionate, alive, and ready to dance like a flame for all to see!

The Princess of Cups (Water) comes in like a dream or a gentle wave, offering the gifts of the heart. She is enraptured, in love, and flowing like water into the hearts of all who behold her.

The Princess of Disks (Earth) is wrapped in the warmth of her Mother Earth. A fur coat surrounds her, as she stands strong in her forest home. Sending her own roots down deep, she holds the world in awe and honors the sacred in all she sees.

The rest of the cards are divided among the twelve signs of the zodiac. Golden Dawn Tarot Deck uses the formula shown in the following table.

An even more exact delineation is given in Crowley's deck that assigns the last ten days of one sign and twenty days of the following sign to each Court card. This is pretty complicated and will not really help beginners so I suggest you use the simple version of one sign to each card, and consider exploring the other method later on. In my own experience I have drawn from both these formulas but have not held either as hard and fast rules. For example, the Knight of Cups is assigned to Pisces but in the more complex formula he has Aquarian qualities as well. I have always empha-

GOLDEN DAWN ASTROLOGICAL ATTRIBUTES FOR
──── THE COURT CARDS ────

KNIGHT	Sagittarius	Pisces	Gemini	Virgo
QUEEN	Aries	Cancer	Libra	Capricorn
PRINCE	Leo	Scorpio	Aquarius	Taurus
PRINCESS	Fire	Water	Air	Earth

sized the Aquarian aspects of this card and not felt him to be very Piscean in nature. The charm of Aquarians fits with his uplifting nature and his peacock says he knows how to strut his stuff as a bit of a social butterfly.

His wings represent a flight of the mind offering intelligence to the love he gives in the cup he raises. Aquarius is the water bearer and yet it is an air sign, underpinning my belief that this age's defining quality is intelligent (air element) love (water element).

Also, The Queen of Cups feels like a Pisces compassionate mirror of love and acceptance to me, more than a doting Cancer mother hen. All of us feel differently and characterize people in our own way. It is important not to limit these folks by memorizing their descriptions or keeping them boxed in. These categories are guidelines to help you get to know the characters, not to limit their potential and stifle their aliveness.

I also find that I differ with who is the elder and the younger in a particular suit. In Disks, the Prince seems so much more mature and worldly to me. His hand rests on a globe; he wears no armor, implying that he no longer has to defend or prove himself; and he is surrounded by elements of the Earth that are a deep part of the mystery. Look closely and you will see cell division in its different stages and the seeds and flowers that create new life.

The Knight, on the other hand, is armed in full regalia but he sits on a horse that is grazing in the field while he stares out over a hill that seems to call him on his life path; but he can't seem to move.

I share these impressions to free you up to let go of judging whether you are right or wrong about the defining qualities of a personality card. Saying someone is from Paris and is a farmer would certainly make you draw certain conclusions about the person. But what if he turned out to be the famous farmer who drove his tractor into a MacDonald's to make a political statement about the effect that corporation was having on the agriculture of his country? That is not your typical farmer by any definition!

My main deck has always been the Thoth deck but I have broadened my understanding of any given card by the variations offered in different decks. If you are unable to get a grip on a specific card, looking at the image in another deck may give you the insight you need to weave it into your personal mythology.

Air signs offer the world clear visions, astute analysis, and an incredible ability to focus intention. Their imagination is rife with inventions, plans, and ideas that they articulate through speech and writing. The elders of air can be the eyes in the storm with their ability to stay calm, cool, and collected under great pressure. They have the wherewithal to be objective and see things exactly as they are, so that solutions can be found to even the most difficult problems.

Fire signs express the soul's desire through actions of a spiritual, physical, or emotional nature. Fiery characters are passionate, lively, creative, and in the right mood, incredibly playful! They are initiators and leaders, activating plans and dreams with their enthusiastic and innovative approach.

Water signs bring the pulse of the heart to every situation, letting love and the emotions define their participation. They remind us to always check in with our authentic feelings and know the importance of creating real bonds through honest and heart-based communication.

Earth signs bring into manifestation all the ideas (air), passions (fire) and feelings (water) that are looking for a home in the physical world. They embody the builder, the creatrix, the lover, and all the practical considerations needed to make our dreams real. They represent the needs of the body in the way they relate to the environment, food, commerce, and health.

Seasons, signs, and elements are all further defined in the color palette employed by the Thoth artist, Lady Frieda Harris. Her color choices especially lend themselves to an easy understanding of their implications.

We all innately know the moods and significance of color.

In the Chinese system of Feng Shui, colors are divided into Yin or Yang. Yin is associated with the receptive, moist, feminine principle that brings healing and relaxation. Yang represents the active, dry, masculine principle that brings enthusiasm and energy. Artists have always employed these principles to create the moods of their paintings and when we Feng Shui our homes we can create and enhance healing spaces or activity centers by the colors we employ.

Businesses also use this information to determine what colors to use for their purposes. Spas will invariably use cool blues, greens and neutral tones. Businesses that want fast turnover use oranges and reds to put a fire under people who want to stay too long. A study was done in the 1960s that validated this idea, and that is why almost all fast food restaurants are invariably done in oranges.

When you are getting to know the cards, it is important to allow yourself to be drawn into the mood of the card that is most strongly defined by its colors.

Now let's look at basic color themes for the different suits.

Swords

In the suit of Air, we see the background colors of cool blue, silver, grey and white evoking a feeling of the heavens and the realm of the mind. The sky may be stormy, cloudy, or crystal clear depending on the maturity and refinement of the character. The people are green and yellow to remind us they are of the earth.

Wands

In the suit of Fire, it is easy to guess that we will see golds, oranges, yellows, and reds leaping like flames in the air. Also appearing are coal black and cool blue-green to temper the fire or represent a deeper aspect of the passion seen in embers, coals, and the core of the flames.

Cups

In the suit of Water are clustered all the shades of blue and green, accented with hints of silver, grey, and yellow to create water's reflective qualities, and purple, with hints of pink and white to accent the feminine aspect.

Disks

In the suit of Earth, we find black, green, yellow, and red, similar to the four colors of the earth realm, Malkuth, on the Tree of Life. We also see a lot of brown which is the combination of all these colors and prevalent in animals, plants, and the Earth itself.

The image variations among the different Tarot decks are endless and usually the most challenging part of the deck to learn. Before you jump into the study of these cards through words, I suggest you invite them over for a little social get-together. Meet them like people you want to get to know and understand, so when you run into them later you will know their names and your first impressions. If you are already fairly familiar with the images of a particular Tarot deck you might choose another one you have never explored and start fresh.

Here are some questions to ponder at your party. (Taking notes in a Tarot journal will be extremely useful later on so you can track your ever-changing relationship with the characters.)

Randomly lay out the Court cards and follow these prompts:

• Whom are you immediately attracted to?

- Can you describe why?
- Whom are you repulsed by and why?
- Do some cards leave you cold? Confused? Afraid?
- Do any cards look like or remind you of yourself or someone you know? How?
- What are the surroundings and what do they tell you about the person in the card?
- What symbols or objects in the card help you tell a story about this person?
- What activity would you enjoy doing with the different people?
- Which characters would you rather avoid? Are there cards that puzzle you or leave you flat?
- Can you make couples out of the cards?
- Can you see family relationships?
- What kind of work is this man or woman engaged in?
- What exactly are they doing right now?
- How do the colors play into your responses? Are they cheery and bright? Somber, cool, and serene? Or dark and mysterious?
- Arrange all the older cards in one row and the younger ones in a parallel row (mixing up the suits is fine). Can you describe what makes them more mature or more naïve? Do the elders seem like parents? Do the young ones seem like children of the elders?
- What are the surroundings and what do they tell you about the person in the card?

Don't write anyone off. These responses are exactly what will tell you what they mean to you in your life right now.

Someone who is your perfect soulmate right now may later become a distant friend, or even an enemy and then a friend again.

All of us are many things to many people. Some cards that I love will be scary to someone else. Eventually they all become familiar and they will help you understand this amazing adventure through the social, work, family, and relationship realm of the Court cards.

Just when you think they're predictable and you have a handle on their story, they surprise you by revealing something about themselves you never knew.

For a long time I thought that the Queen of Wands was just too haughty, and so in charge of everything that I just couldn't relate. Turns out I could not see that I was doing the same thing. I was acting out the toxic version of her true nature. I got swept up in the enthusiasm of a scene around an Indian guru and thought I had discovered "the answer." I knew what everyone needed, and I didn't hesitate to tell them so.

Years later when I matured into the healthy aspects of the Queen of Wands, I was able to recognize her and know her again in a new light.

I had become an activist who knew how to articulate with passion and intelligence the issues at hand and my energy was contagious. I became adept at demonstrating leadership as power from within by facilitating meetings that were organized by consensus. Now I know the Queen of Wands to be an experienced, generous, and energetic community worker.

The Tarot characters are also a way to get to know the people of other cultures by meeting them in the Native American, Celtic, Italian, French, and Chinese Tarots.

Now, keeping all this in mind, we are ready to explore the individual cards in their multifaceted personas.

Note: Capitalized signs are the dominant ones for each card and best for beginners to use when starting out. In Crowley's schemata there are ten days for the secondary sign (not capitalized) and twenty days for the primary sign (capitalized).

Queen of Swords
Signs: Virgo/LIBRA

The Queen of Swords shows a woman enthroned in the clouds, a sword in one hand and in the other, the decapitated head of an old man.

This description sounds violent, but she appears totally calm, and the man's face is serene because we are seeing the action in the realm of the mind. This motif appears in many cultures, like the story of Kali and Shiva in Hindu mythology. Kali's archetype is the Lioness, protecting her brood with fierceness; she is utterly fearless of any opponent for she is the mother of us all.

She does not derive from anything. She is That Which Births, and she wears a necklace of skulls to remind us of her universal recycling program, Death itself.

Kali is terrifying to the ego that sees in her face its ultimate demise. In this card she has wielded her sword of truth. The wise old soul, the bearded man, Shiva, has surrendered his head (ego) to her work in defense of the star child shown above her head, symbolic of all that is sacred to the Great Mother.

The Queen of Swords is the calm, clear voice of an experienced wise woman who knows that she can and must speak the truth in service to the heart, to create the changes necessary to move to the next level.

And it is definitely time to move! Not because of duress but because spirit is calling us to take the next step. We are ready to apply what we have learned in the recent past to a new situation that has a higher ceiling for growth, or no ceiling at all. "The sky's the limit!" she calls from her white cloud throne floating through the heavens.

She is often depicted with an owl, which is her totem of vision in the darkness, silence in the hunt, and ability to turn her head 360 degrees to view the past, present, and future.

She does not speak in anger or defensiveness, which is why the face of the severed head is the peaceful face of a wise man. She appeals to the inner Hermit/Crone and does not attack, but rather reveals her perception of the truth as appropriate to those she encounters.

Her season is the autumnal harvest and the Equinox occurs during her reign. This day of perfect balance, when night and day

Queen of Swords

are the same length, is her ritual of justice. She is the personification of the Justice/Adjustment card, where we see Venus girt with the sword of truth exemplifying the principle that truth is only valid when it is in service to love.

She cuts away all that does not need to be preserved through the coming winter. Often referred to as the Snow Queen, the Queen of Swords has the wisdom to take us through the darkening of the Sun. She is relieving us of all that we no longer need to move forward in our lives, and prompts us to be clear about what seeds to store through the winter for the spring planting. These seed ideas and projects are also being mulled over in winter, through meditation or writing, to be ready to burst forth at the proper time.

Shadow

The Queen of Swords, who has forgotten or never discovered her heart's purpose underlying her truth, is instead enamored of her ability to gain power with her mental prowess. An example of this would be the severe schoolteacher who has forgotten to love and care about her students and only demands that they measure up to her standards or else. She then appears cold and detached. Worshipping at the altar of her intellect, she will have wasted her insights by feeling superior to others and, therefore, comes off as arrogant or cruel.

When you get this card in a reading

You are now ready to ascend to the next level of your journey; your expression of that knowing will be graceful and decisive. You may want to write your message in a letter or an article, or work through your thoughts in your journal until you have refined away anything that could be misconstrued.

Let your inner knowing be expressed in ways that the people around you can receive easily. With love, speak to their most authentic self; present your truth as self-evident, not superior or making the other wrong. It is not a time to win points but to awaken acquiescence to the truth you are destined to reveal at this time.

The Queen speaks softly but carries a big sword. One edge gleams with wisdom for all to see, and the other shadowed side keeps her honest with herself, which indirectly keeps her protected by unseen forces.

This is a good time to get a new journal, a sketchpad, or mini-tape recorder. Any of these simple tools will let you carry on an internal dialogue, which is so important as a place to germinate and gestate ideas, and to work through issues during the fall and winter months.

The Queen is a wise herbal healer who gently applies the balm of truth and the good medicine to go with it. She is great at distilling ideas, as well as tinctures. It might be a great time to make some medicines or cordials so nothing is wasted from the harvest.

Virgo is the time that we head into Autumn, so make sure you notice the changing season and start taking an immune booster like a tincture of the powerful Astragalus root, or one of the wonderful mushroom blends. Tinctures let you taste and smell the essence. Try placing the vial over your heart and breathing in its energy before taking it internally. The moments taken to care for ourselves make all the difference to our well-being. We are inherently capable of healing ourselves as well as summoning healing to benefit others.

From her Libra influences, the Queen of Swords knows how to balance mental energy and create harmony in the home. It might be time to use Feng Shui to see how the energy is flowing in your home.

Knight of Swords
Signs: Taurus/GEMINI

This swiftly moving Knight has absolute focus as he charges down from the heavens to make real the idea that possesses him. He has chosen his goal and he has made it short-term and doable. It is imperative that he complete his task, and he trusts that in so doing, the next inspiration and direction will arise spontaneously.

He holds two swords, one to defend and one to attack, metaphorically speaking, for he has sharpened his mind to home in on any obstacles or people who may try to distract him or divert him from his purpose.

He is accompanied by three small birds that symbolize support and approval from the animal realm. These birds show trust in their Knight friend and know that his battle is not a physical one but more a challenge to himself.

Atop his head, propellers attach to his helmet. Look closely and see the words north, east, south, and west written in cursive on the blades. Our Knight knows that his sense of direction must come from within. No maps are available for his journey; he must use his inner compass. He trusts his natural instincts, represented by his tireless and powerful horse, that are synchronized with his sense of purpose.

His green and yellow colors imply that he is of the Earth, but he can get lost in the realm of possibilities and forget that imagination needs manifestation or it becomes fantasy without substance. He is in the process of adding weight and character to his reputation for brilliant ideas, and he will be a better man for it.

Our Knight is most himself when he is intent, awake, alert, and driven.

Shadow

In his shadow aspect, the Knight of Swords only cares about the conquest so he would be particularly cavalier in the arena of love. He may say and do anything to win the object of attraction; he may even believe that he is "in love." But once his lover has surrendered, the thrill of the hunt is gone and the knight is on to the next prey. The same happens in work. He can be ruthless and manipulative while acting like your new best friend, just to make a sale or close

Knight of Swords

a deal. The work has no meaning—just the taste of power and victory gets him high.

Because Taurus is an earth sign of determined embodiment and education, and Gemini is an air sign of brilliant mental prowess, this Knight is only effective when the body and mind are connected in a common purpose.

When you get this card in a reading

It is time to focus on attainable goals and stop trying to figure out what you want to be when you grow up. You may have just come through some unsettling times or the breakup of a relationship, so you need to get hold of your own reins and remember who you are. Do something that you have always known would be beneficial to you. Throw procrastination out the window. Go for it!

Make real at least one of the many impulses your creative mind has offered up, to reignite the flow of creativity by exercising the ability to complete a project. Send a message to your deep self that you are listening and not just toying with possibilities.

Remember that short story you were always going to write, that workshop you were planning to take in woodworking, or that course in CPR you promised your family you were going to learn? What about that trip you were going to take, hiking in the Sierras, photographing the changing of the seasons?

Get rid of the backlog of ideas; choose something and do it. It will change your life. Your heart and soul will sing with the joy of getting that wandering mind to listen and make a plan. Once the floodgate of inertia breaks, new ideas bubble up from the unconscious.

What's most important right now is not what you do but that you complete it. Completion will recharge your whole being and trigger a new sense of confidence. This Knight is will in action. He offers you a ride on the steed of steady determination. Hesitation is not in his vocabulary so it's no use arguing.

Prince of Swords
Signs: Capricorn/AQUARIUS

Our Prince is young and brash. Fascinated by the power and prowess of his brilliant mind, he jumps from one idea to the next, quickly mastering the basics and then, becoming bored, moves on.

In the Thoth image, all this mental gymnastics has the Prince of Swords a bit tied in knots. He loves the challenge of new ideas and is fascinated by fads and the latest guru on the market. But he relishes most his ability to deconstruct and see through any so-called answers; patting himself on the back, he moves on to the next latest thing.

He definitely hones his skills as a devil's advocate and a formidable opponent in any debate, but he is lacking in his own understanding of what makes up his ethical ground. He's the kind of student who can jump into the class discussion without even reading the material and really stir things up. He's a quick study and is more excited about his performance in class or conversation than about actually learning something that may deepen him as a human being. In time he will learn to value his own conscious growth, especially if his mentors and parents encourage him.

Too often this kind of bright child is sent the message that just operating his brain like a well-oiled machine is his greatest asset. Inwardly there is a very lonely child who wants to be loved for who he is, not how smart he is. Children who are prone to mental activities need help balancing this with education in emotional awareness and the joy of embodiment.

As he matures he will find the ability to tame and reign in his mind and humbly see its limitations.

But for now he lives by his wits, using his observations of what he learns as more fodder for reinforcing his arguments. On the other hand, he can be great at brainstorming, coming up with inventive and creative solutions for any problem when he puts aside his inner critic for a while.

His biggest challenge is to use this intelligence in service to his soul purpose by slowing down enough to listen to that still small voice that will not deceive him.

He has learned early on to use his mind to succeed in the world and has received much praise and reward for his prowess on the mental plane. But he will be truly brilliant when he discovers that real satisfaction comes when he pursues projects and pathways that originate from his own inner yearnings. When he finds his way, all his ego-oriented conquests will appear as mere mental gymnastics he has been performing to find status in the world. All his adversarial workouts will definitely serve him now if he uses them to combat his own rationalizations and procrastinations so he doesn't stop short of his true potential.

Shadow

He is prone to cynicism and a condescending attitude when ill-dignified. Like a bird in a tree, he observes what is going on below him and only dives down for sustenance or a tête-à-tête. Detached from his heart, he can still be very charismatic and charming, often teasing his lover with glimpses of his true feelings and then flying back up to his observation spot.

He will tend to get bored easily and jump from fad to fad, or guru to guru, without engaging emotionally.

When you get this card in a reading

Usually people get this card to help them make sound choices that will take them deeper in their personal evolution. After a while, being the best and smartest can become a hollow experience; the adrenalin rush from the latest conquest doesn't last very long.

It's time to rein in the ego's desire to be the smartest, and take time to discover your deepest yearnings within.

A good place to start is to ask, "What do I love to do?" The idea here is to not look for what you would love to do for a career but just what you love doing, whether it be cooking, surfing, eating, or simply taking walks with your dog. If the answer doesn't come easily, then ask what you loved doing as a child. Often what you loved doing had nothing to do with your brain, but because you were best at mental work you were often discouraged or made fun of for doing what you loved. The purpose of this exercise is to reclaim the playful child.

Remember: Your ego is really invested in the smart persona, so it is advisable to take baby steps around it so it doesn't freak out. For example, if you are a very successful businessman, your ego will definitely not want to let you quit your job and go to Hawaii to become a surfer. But if you tell yourself this isn't about changing everything right now, it's just about having some fun, then you could explore your loves without fear of losing anything.

Prince of Swords

Take a trip to Hawaii to surf and let yourself rediscover your excitement and you will have opened a channel to the soul's desire for self-discovery. Other baby steps would be to read a book about a subject you love, take a workshop or class, or do some automatic writing to invite your subconscious to surface.

Princess of Swords
Element: Air

Here we see a young woman fiercely defending her boundaries, her feelings, and the altar of her beliefs. She is striking downward with her sword of truth, trying to ground her words and actions. She has stirred up quite a storm and the clouds are black and grey surrounding her, but the yellow glow of the Sun is trying to break through, symbolizing her yearning to shine forth and be heard and recognized.

Our princess has not yet refined her powers of expression and she often finds herself misunderstood, attacked, or even punished. Inwardly she possesses a real sense of truth and justice and she seeks opportunities to speak out or act on these principles.

She is the young teenage girl in all of us who has found her rebellious desire to individuate and she will find ways to stand out as different no matter what. She will try to provoke others, unwittingly sacrificing her deeper need to be understood.

She may dress differently, get a tattoo on the sly, or use language that is outrageous to declare herself in the world.

As a result she often feels unfairly treated or misunderstood by those around her.

What she needs is the patience and understanding of more mature teachers, mentors, or parents who will be able to see beyond her rebellious actions to the truths underlying them.

People who are reactionary to our Princess will only serve to stoke the fires of her outrage and may actually push her into self-destructive patterns. Until she feels respected and understood, or patiently witnessed, she will not listen. Punishing or judging her will only postpone her awakening to more effective ways to be recognized.

She can best be served by people who are willing to listen and acknowledge where she is coming from and then offer suggestions about how to constructively manifest her sense of justice and express her truth, at the same time commanding respect. Not an easy task.

If a child were angry about being bullied at school it would be best to hear the story, empathize, and possibly take action to correct the situation. Treat your own anger the same way and it will recede naturally, as compassion, love, and understanding soothe this volatile emotion.

Suppression forces it down into our bodies where our internal organs have to deal with it. Often lack of ease, or dis-ease, results.

The Princess wants to be independent, so engaging her in discussions about what boundaries and goals she finds fair can be very effective. If she lives by consequences she has agreed to she will be learning self-governance. If she feels she has an opportunity to be responsible, she will not be as quick to blame others for her misfortune, as she is prone to do if she fails.

This dynamic and courageous spirit can be lost for years in rebellion for the sake of rebellion, so it is key to find healthy outlets instead of laying down arbitrary laws that she does not see as justified.

Many young people found the spirit of the Princess in the rebellious '60s. Some were mentored into greatness while others were lost in addiction, anger, and a refusal to become a part of positive actions to change the world.

Shadow

The Princess's shadow is anger that she enjoys for the reactions and attention it gets. She will tend to identify as the angry victim, wondering why everything and everyone is against her. She is unable to reflect, breathe deeply, and work on understanding her own deeper roots of pain. She can be quite a troublemaker and bridge burner, hurting others with her rash behavior.

When you get this card in a reading

In essence this Princess is the spirit of activism without the wisdom and experience to be as effective as she could be. This Princess may be a part of yourself to which you can apply the same parenting principles. First and foremost, this Princess is about the courage to speak out against injustice so it is a good time to ask some soul-searching questions.

What is it that you feel is worth fighting for in your life? Where do you need to confront injustice? What is sacred to you that is being abused? Whom do you love who needs your advocacy?

All of us want to be heard and understood but too often our issues are really covers for our personal pain. It is time to ask what is at the source of your frustration and anger so you can actually heal yourself.

Many activists spend their lives using the political arena to vent the pain of their upbringing. There can be, and usually is, a real connection between the pain and the chosen cause but if you are not aware of how they are connected you will probably use your time seeking opportunities to vent and be self-righteous instead of becoming a beacon of positive vision and a motivator for others.

Princess of Swords

Queen of Wands
Signs: Pisces/ARIES

This powerful, regal, and authoritative figure often reminds people of the Statue of Liberty. She is fully aware of her ability to direct and rule and will not submit to external domination.

But she was not always so strong and confident. The Piscean clasp holding her cape is a reminder that there were times she was too willing to be subsumed into others' stories and lose her power in emotional dramas.

Now she has found a broader purpose and her history of martyrdom has matured into compassion. By working within community she creates positive social change. When she is doing this work she is untiring and very generous with her time, money, and possessions.

She protects herself from attacks on her character with her mighty wand, but because of her history she often overreacts to criticism and can later regret her biting tongue.

Her hand rests on her familiar, the leopard, who is her constant companion. The leopard's spots also symbolize her darker side and a need to trust her instincts to protect her freedom.

Just like a cat, she cannot be possessed or told what to do, but when trust is established she is an ardent lover and a faithful friend.

Often the initial reaction to such a person is that she is pushy, haughty, and always wants to be in charge. In time she usually reveals that her intentions are for the common good and her initial toughness is really just her determination to keep the project, business, or family successful and vibrant.

She resides on the cusp of Pisces and Aries and is constantly working to balance the compassion of Pisces and the leadership of Aries. This is a rich and wonderful terrain. Pisces alone can be self-sacrificing and Aries alone can be self-centered. The blend is a powerful elixir for a world in need of compassionate, motivated leaders who stay on the pulse of the people.

Shadow

Ill-dignified, the Queen espouses generosity while seeking self-aggrandizement. Pride, haughtiness, and superiority often surface when she forgets her deeper purpose. She has a tendency to

Queen of Wands

give too much and is not able to receive in a balanced way. In the end this is actually very isolating. She can allow others to live off of her. She may become the too-good mother.

When you get this card in a reading

The Queen of Wands calls you to find connection and purpose by giving generously of your energy to help at your children's school, run a non-profit, be the head nurse in a hospital or any other way that you give of yourself to your community that also feeds you.

Be aware that her Achilles heel is criticism. If this card represents you in the reading it is best to count to ten or wait until the next day before responding. Complaints can be gifts in disguise and being such an active person you may be running roughshod over others or being blind to something that you need to change.

If the criticism is unfounded, you will have given yourself time to respond thoughtfully instead of to react out of anger. You could limit your ability to lead if you do not heed this advice and shy away from positions of power for fear of judgment. Or you could burn bridges unnecessarily when your temper gets the best of you.

In love relationships, the Queen often tries to convince herself that someone is right for her. She tells herself that he or she is right because the person is smart, or rich, or educated, or any number of rationales. All she needs to do is listen to her inner self and answer this one simple question: does this person energize or deplete me? In the past, her mistake was to allow others to plug into her energy and feed off it. Even if someone says all the right things and appreciates you verbally, if the dynamic of energy flow is one-sided you are being robbed of your power.

Do not allow your rational mind to talk you into situations that drain you. It is a simple but effective litmus test.

Knight of Wands
Signs: Scorpio/SAGITTARIUS

This brave Knight rises up out of the mysterious waters of Scorpio, leaping into the fierce fires of Sagittarius, confident, inspired, and determined. His dark horse tries to hold a steady path, possessing the deep, transformational wisdom of Scorpio, but this fiery Knight is determined to take a daring leap into the outer worlds as well. His wand is now a torch that has even sparked flames in the mane and tail of his mighty stead.

Synthesizing the changes that are caused by the inner journey of Scorpio, he has done the work of shedding his old skin and now wears a shiny, new reptilian armor to take him through any dangers on his adventure.

He is a confident leader, inspiring, daring, and articulate. From the depth of his soul he has found new energy and has thrown caution to the winds. We see by his hair and the horse's mane that the wind is at his back and retreat is no option.

This part of ourselves is the impetus that pulls us into adventures and projects that come from an inner excitement that cannot be denied. This Knight is carried by vision and the love of the quest. Doubts and warnings are shunted aside. He figures he will have time to reassess later but the opportunity to act is rising now. He trusts his ability to go into the fray and do battle with whatever opposition he encounters. Most likely his biggest obstacles will be his own demons but he would rather face them now as an outer drama than an inner journey.

So our impulsive Knight is on the move. Will he gather forces around him that can aid him on his quest? Will his pride take him down to defeat? Everything about this Knight is unpredictable but full of the charisma that can take us where we have never gone before.

Shadow

Similar to Icarus, there is a danger of flying too close to the Sun where no one can help us. Pride, escapism, and lack of follow-through are other character defects of the Knight. Do you always need to be the leader, lacking the ability to follow? Or the converse can be true, resulting in paralyzing fears and a tendency to be overly cautious all the time.

When you get this card in a reading

More than any other Court cards, this one is the cliffhanger. Will our armored warrior land on all four hooves or will the rider be thrown and have to start again? Has he thought through any alternatives or options if he should stumble or fall? Probably not.

The questions that the image evokes are exactly why this card is both cautionary and encouraging.

When he appears in your reading you can just take the leap and hope for the best. This may be exactly what you need if you tend to always overthink things and never take any risks. We all need adventures, although often what we reap is not what we thought we had sown if we are too reckless. But the experience of leaving our comfort zone is in itself a growth-filled path.

On the other hand, if you tend to be prideful and impulsive and have, therefore, become unstable and unpredictable, it may be time to think twice and try to prepare for some possible outcomes instead of just putting the blinders on.

If this symbolizes someone in your life who is calling you to come along, you might ask if this is an escape from reality. Consider whether they are just saying all the right things without the ability to produce.

If this is you, try not to let your enthusiasm blind you to the possibility that others may be jealous and may want to undermine you; or that you are leaping into success too fast and you might get tripped up by saboteurs or unseen pitfalls.

Knight of Wands

Prince of Wands
Signs: Cancer/LEO

The open-hearted Prince of Wands comes forth with calm authority and has no need of armor. His pose is not one of a warrior ready for battle but of a confident, capable, and wise man who has perseverance and practical knowledge to carry him forward.

Notice that his arms are open and the reins rest lightly over his left wrist. He is not forcing or controlling his familiar, the lion; instead they move as one, with focus and courage.

In his right hand is his wand of power topped with the image of a phoenix, symbolizing his willingness to learn and reinvent himself as necessary. Pride will not blind him or bring him into danger.

The sharp flame-like edges that are everywhere in the picture suggest he has created a power field around him from constant work on himself and he no longer needs his ego or saber rattling to command respect. His face is calm, wise and handsome and he does not seek possessions or power over others. As long as he is doing what he loves and growing as he goes, he is in no hurry to get to some goal or victory to fortify his self-esteem.

The symbol on his chest suggests that his power comes from the heart chakra and he brings all his intention in service to love.

His spirituality is not esoteric or otherworldly. He is embodied and comfortable in the physical world where he excels.

The Prince of Wands is a trustworthy leader because he does not rush off on an impulse but considers the long haul. He will inspire respect and confidence because he is willing to be transparent about his purpose and his plans.

I confess he is my favorite of the male images in the Thoth deck as he emanates confidence, courage, determination, and a down-to-earth approach to life. He can also laugh at himself and rise from the ashes with a healthier ego that does not need center stage to feel powerful.

Shadow

This is not a time to stay with a plan if you are not evolving in the process. Your ego may be attached to position and power without

Prince of Wands

an authentic purpose. Perseverance without pleasure makes a very depressed partner, be it in business or love relationships.

When you get this card in a reading

It is time to consider the long-term plans and commitments in your life. It is an excellent opportunity to enter into an educational or apprenticeship program that could take years to complete.

When this card shows up a few years before a Saturn return, you have a chance to preempt its negative aspects by pleasing Saturn with your commitment to discipline and true life purpose. Then when Saturn comes calling, he will be pleased to enhance your plans with a sense of effortlessness and joy in fulfilling your destiny.

It's time to let go of the ego's desire for instant fame, wealth, or gratification and consider what will help you develop into a better and more experienced human being.

If this represents someone in your life you can be sure this is a loyal friend or partner whom you can depend on.

If you are searching for a relationship, it may be best to cultivate friendships with people who have common interests. You might find the love of your life in an art class or on a bird-watching adventure. By enjoying an activity rather than seeking a mate, you would not be so self-conscious. The next thing you know, some epiphany may find you staring into each other's eyes and realizing friendship just morphed into a strong attraction that cannot be denied.

Concerning health, I tend to look to the suit of Wands for an answer. Since this is about perseverance and the long haul, it is a strong indicator of long life and a healthy constitution.

One last suggestion: Let your sense of humor be a way to express your love or lighten an otherwise tense or negative situation. It will work like a charm!

Princess of Wands
Element: Fire

Ah! The stirrer of the pot has just walked into the party and all eyes are captivated by her vivacious and charming personality. She embodies all her passions without concern for others' opinions. Her fashion statements are cutting edge and suited to accentuate her sensual body. She loves the limelight and entertains all who are drawn to her. Just like moths to a flame, there is no denying the presence of this solar sensation.

She is the essence of fire and waves her solar wand high in the air, proud of her victories and ready for the next challenge. She never loses touch with her animal nature. Cat-like, she can leap as effortlessly as a gymnast from the trampoline to the balance beam. Like the tiger she is linked to, she is curious and fierce and she lets these qualities shine, but with a certain discretion. That is why we see the tiger in a limp, but available, pose.

This young, spirited woman is excited by healthy competition and ready to test her mettle in the world. She wants to shine her light and will not be stopped by others' opinions of her or negative gossip. In fact, she likes to create a bit of a buzz. Her strong, compact body shows she keeps herself in shape and passionately pursues many different outlets. Finding life full of adventure and challenges, she becomes stronger with every skill she masters.

As she grows in maturity, she will hone her skills to make sure that ethical and just behavior is never sacrificed for the sheer joy of winning, but this may take time. The plumes of justice stream from her head, showing her inner will to be in her integrity.

Shadow

The shadow of this card is often manifested as wanting to be the most popular at the expense of others. There is a tendency to want the power and prestige without actually accomplishing or being proficient at anything, like the characters in the movies Mean Girls or Clueless.

If this goes on unchecked, the young woman could spend her whole life social climbing and stepping on others to go up the ladder.

Melodrama is the toxic version of real life drama and in the end is hollow and unfulfilling.

When you unconsciously behave like the princess you may over-react if you feel threatened by someone else's power or talents and try to sabotage them.

When you get this card in a reading

The spirit of youth in all its daring and courage is calling you to action. Do not shy away from letting people see your true self. No need to worry about superficial beauty, the Princess will let you know that we are all beautiful and have charisma when we are un-abashedly ourselves. She calls you to enjoy being in your body and glowing from within.

Try wearing bright and fiery colors and say those things you tend to stifle for fear of what others will think.

When the Princess appears in your reading you know it's in your power to shine in the field of your passion.

If this represents a young woman in your life, it is important to guide her to express her talents in the public arena. If she is shy or introverted, you might help her by having her take private lessons until she gains confidence, and then take a speech, drama, or im-prov class with a kind and enlightened teacher.

Princess of Wands

Queen of Cups
Signs: Gemini/CANCER

Frieda Harris's painting of the Queen in the Thoth deck depicts the image of a woman who is barely visible behind swirling bands of soft light. You must look closely to actually see her face; an even closer examination will reveal her reflection in the water below.

The intention of this illusory image is to make you aware that although she seems hidden, her essential nature is not lost and is, in fact, strong enough to be mirrored. She operates on the psychic and emotional planes and does not desire the spotlight or feel lacking because she is not dramatically in the forefront like the Queen of Wands. Many receive her subtle messages and feel her power. Like the hugging guru, Amma, words are not her primary realm; she is a medium who can transmit and receive. Compare this image with that of The Priestess and you will find a strong resemblance. Note that both cards have a subtle line creating a feeling of reflection between top and bottom.

The Queen of Cups is the loving, compassionate aspect of the mother. She mirrors without judgment and offers reflection and a sounding board rather than advice. She is comfortable in her natural role as a nurturer and has no need to force her opinions or plans on others.

She, however, does not sacrifice herself on the altar of love by losing her own self-worth. Unlike the Princess, she does not give her world away to receive confirmations and compliments from others to validate her existence. She has matured beyond these insecurities.

She simply believes that love is the greatest power in helping others and if she has an opinion or idea she will find ways to help her loved ones explore that possibility without nagging or demanding to be obeyed.

For example, she may ask questions that are on point and rooted in her own life experience to help the beloved explore the issue at hand. But she ultimately trusts in the individual journey that each of us is on and does not to impose her will on others.

She may psychically send her thoughts and encouragement, trusting in the deeper connections of the unseen realms of emotional bonding.

Queen of Cups

Essentially she is a dreamer, and the gestating mother, who brings dreams into reality through patience, nurturing, and the knowledge that all life is sourced in the imagination.

Astrologically speaking, she transmutes the Gemini aspect of herself by sending her visions into the womb of the unconscious to be worked out and allowed to emerge at the perfect time. Like birthing a baby, all creative ideas need the gestation period to precede the actual emergence. She has a peaceful acceptance of life and, like the ocean, she lets the changes pass over her like waves. She trusts that the mysterious moods of the sea are similar to the endlessly changing dynamic of life itself. She tends to see what others would call an emergency as something new that is emerging. Births can be messy and chaotic because there is a new dream taking form that cannot be limited by our ideas of how it "always has been" or how it "should" be.

The Queen of Cups for infancy and the early preschool years to secure the bond of love; the Queen of Wands for the school years to be an active participant in the community; the Queen of Disks, to stay grounded and steady through the teenage years; and the Queen of Swords, whose crystal-clear wisdom becomes a resource as the child steps into the world.

These Queen phases will also change in any given day, week, or year, and they really serve as a guide to remember all the potentials of a truly well-adjusted and conscientious mother.

Shadow

The Queen's shadow self is not able to tell the difference between reality and illusion. Be careful not to get lost in your own separate experience of life. The dream realm is a wonderful place but it is not meant to be an escape from life.

The Queen can also become so passive that she is literally invisible and only acknowledged as an extension of or caregiver to others.

When you get this card in a reading

If this card comes up about how to work with a challenging person in your life, it is usually best to not try to convince this person of anything, or try to change them, but just let your heart stay open and see what arises.

Send your messages silently from the heart and let the truth unfold naturally.

Or you may be pregnant with a child or a new stage in your life and you need to be attentive to your physical needs. Water is your element and friend, so drink a lot, swim, shower and bathe with your favorite oils and sachets of fresh herbs.

Often our younger self falls in love with love, a kind of projection of the inner dream. As we mature we are able to love someone for who they are and not just what we need from them.

If you can be grounded and trust your own emotions you won't need some mental image or description of your "perfect soul mate." Love has its own way of bringing the best lover to you. The person may not be what you imagined but, rather, what you are ready for, to help you grow and learn to become comfortable in your vulnerability.

A new dream wants to surface, possibly this more mature aspect of your yearnings for intimate relationship. Take note of your nightly dreams; if possible, take time before you go to sleep to calm yourself. Ask yourself to remember your dreams upon waking and keep a dream journal to go even deeper into this form of self-exploration.

Note: All the Queens, in a way, are different aspects of the mother, and it would be wise to study all of them to reach a comprehensive sense of the many faces of motherhood. Different aspects are appropriate for different people and circumstances. When we become rigid, we forget that a blending of all the elements makes us whole. Of course, we have personalities that are going to be most like one of the Court Queens, but to limit ourselves to that one image can be stifling. Another way of looking at this would be to see the different queens as different stages of mothering.

Knight of Cups
Signs: Aquarius/PISCES

This character definitely fills the bill as the Knight in shining armor; he is winged like an angel and dressed like a warrior. Depicted leaping through the air on his glorious white stallion, he offers up a golden cup. Who is the lucky one to receive his gift? Could it be his true love, Guinevere, or perhaps his fellow questers? And what is the meaning of the totem crab rising from the goblet? Might it be a reference to the sign of Cancer, symbolizing home? Or is it a more universal spiritual community that he calls us to enter?

Everything about this image is uplifting and full of excitement. This Knight definitely brings hope and promise of a new surge in spiritual awakening. But oddly, we cannot see his face and so it is hard to know whether he can be trusted. Although his horse turns to face us as if to say, "don't doubt my master, we're headed in the right direction," still, one wonders.

Pictured in the foreground is a peacock strutting his stuff, enticing us with yet another totem of masculine virility. He is definitely a charmer and he calls us to join him in high conversation and celebration, and why not? This Aquarian avatar is beckoning us into the New Age with the message that intelligent love is the evolutionary leap symbolized by the water bearer.

There can be no doubt that we are in for a night of revelations and revelry; later there will be time to consider the consequences of an actual alliance with this seductive suitor. Tonight let us only speak of love!

Shadow

When the Knight is ill-dignified, all his charm is just a superficial act that he uses to get what he wants. He is really insecure in his own selfhood and has manufactured a persona to charm his way into the lives of grounded, successful, and practical people.

He will often have serious problems with addictions due to his lack of real self-worth.

When you get this card in a reading

In the realm of relationships, the Knight represents an offering of love. He is loquacious, eloquent, charming, and erudite. The

Knight of Cups

peacock totem suggests he is well-dressed, cares about appearance, and has exquisite taste. He has an easy way and a quick wit, entering into any conversation with grace.

If this is someone you have just met, you can bask in his sparkling wit; but find out more about him before you let yourself be swept off your feet.

If this is you, ask yourself whether you are just enjoying an exciting night out or you actually are sincere in offering the cup of love.

In partnerships and work he will want to share a positive and evolutionary vision for the future and his ideal work will be toward futuristic, technological and spiritual goals.

If you feel this represents you, it is important to consider how you can make your work more meaningful in these ways.

If you are considering this person as a business partner, it is important that his talents are put to work to inspire and catalyze actions. He is not a nuts-and-bolts kind of guy.

If you want to know if you can trust him, find out if he has long-term friendships and good relationships with family members. If he wants you only to himself and says you are the only one who understands him, don't be flattered run.

Prince of Cups
Signs: Libra/SCORPIO

━━━━━━━━━━━━━ ◖ ● ◗ ━━━━━━━━━━━━━

The Prince holds his cards close to his chest and does not let his guard down easily. As we see in the picture he is intensely focused on the serpent rising out of a cup, which represents his will and purpose. He is not concerned with how others feel about him; he must move on his own path no matter what. Although he is definitely driven and seeks power and position, he doesn't care about popularity or social success. He enters into those realms only if it serves his purposes.

The Scorpio influence makes him a very private person who can be ruthless and cold. If he is well rounded he will also listen to the Libra aspect of himself that will keep him in touch with his conscience. This will help him care more about fairness in dealing with others. Since Venus rules Libra she tries to keep him in touch with his heart and help him not be a loner, but with Mars ruling Scorpio we have a bit of an internal battle going on. Mars has the advantage because he rules 20 days of the prince's time while Venus is only allotted 10.

He has a very magnetic and sexy aura and usually makes a fantastic lover, but if the Prince is to go beyond sexual prowess into the realm of intimacy he will need to learn vulnerability, something that his old-fashioned warrior persona considers a weakness.

In truth, it takes a different kind of courage to open the heart and he will do well to practice this, possibly through meditation, where he can explore and confront his own fears without having to deal with others. In the Motherpeace deck image we see a man playing the flute inside an egg-shaped space, suggesting calm music can bring clarity and peace. Using the lotus as the object of his meditation will help him to open, petal by petal, his secret self. Notice how he is so engrossed in the snake that the lotus is drooping downward and unnoticed. If he can look at the roots of his fears that lie in the murky depths, he can connect his lotus flower to source, be aware of his shadow, and grow it up towards the light once again.

In the realm of career he is a super-achiever; his totem, eagle, makes him an excellent hunter, both patient and swift.

The eagle can help him rise above any situation and get the big picture perspective so that he doesn't get lost in the minutiae. This makes him a skilled negotiator, manager, or head of a business.

On the evolutionary path he can be fearless in transforming and reinventing himself, shedding the serpent skin again and again, to come closer to source. Like the god Shiva, he dances willingly on the corpses of the past; he destroys to create.

Shadow

The Prince can be harsh, cold, and cruel to mask the intense passions within. Fearing losing control, he will guard his heart like a bank safe. He can want power, position, and money just for their own sake and, therefore, be very manipulative and cruel. If he doesn't care about the integrity of his lifework or his family, he will hurt those close to him and move on.

When you get this card in a reading

The Prince pulsates with sexual energy so it is a good time to explore your needs, desires, and fantasies. Honor them without judgment and remember this arena is filled with important lessons that can change your whole life. An unconscious relationship with sex can make us feel lonely and others will think of us as cold, or even worse, as predators. But a playful exploration can bring out inner charisma and magnetism that will help us in work as well as relationships.

In the work world it is time to focus, set clear goals, and not let others' doubts or mistrust stop you. You hold the power to move swiftly and accomplish a lot, so don't allow yourself to be distracted.

If the Prince represents your lover or mate, you might try to create an atmosphere of scents, sounds, and tastes that melt away his armor and invite him to open of his own accord. Phrases like "we need to talk" make him fly like an eagle to the highest perch, where he will try to discern your intentions from a safe distance.

If this is you, lighten up and try to ask questions of your partner to better understand him/her instead of making demands. Be willing to laugh at yourself and try not to hold on to old wounds or story loops that keep you locked away in the past.

Prince of Cups

Princess of Cups
Element: Water

Beyond a doubt this Princess is the epitome of the woman in love. She is in a state of rapture, offering her world, symbolized by the tortoise in the shell, without reservation. Her eyes are closed for she does not need to see any more to know that her very existence—her very purpose—has been to come to this moment of bliss!

She lives and breathes in the element of water, swimming in her emotions; possessed by the wonder of feeling complete by the mere existence of her lover. She dances to the vibrations of the music of love and her beloved's voice sends sensations through her body like nothing she has ever felt before. She anxiously awaits a response to her complete surrender, praying her beloved will tell her all she wishes to hear—that she is beauty itself, lovelier than any other, all he/she has ever wanted—all this to keep giving her reason to live. Without appreciation and her lover's guiding step in this dance of romance she could be utterly defeated, without a single reason to go on. Validation from her beloved is the only truth that has meaning at this moment in her life.

All of us have experienced the amazing aura that surrounds lovers as they fall ever deeper into the ecstasy of union. Love is so completely overwhelming because we have found temporary oneness with all of existence. For love to actually develop, grow, and last, it will take more than this initial surrender, but for now every rose is redder and every romantic song is synchronized to our heartbeat. Falling in love is not only emotional but an actual chemical attraction that makes everything more vivid, more alive.

On a spiritual level, falling in love is that which reminds us that we are all interconnected; this realization, in all the myriad forms it can take, is an epiphany for all.

Since she is the Princess or daughter, she is also in the process of individuating. Now her parents are not the center of her world, in fact they are now mere mortals who may apparently lack the ability to understand or accept this phenomenon that is so absolutely undeniable to their child.

Princess of Cups

She has discovered love outside of the childhood experience and now knows exactly what she wants and finds her parents advice overly protective, old-fashioned, and suffocating. Love is her teacher now.

The Princess also loves all things of beauty, especially clothes and decorations for her room and home that enhance her romantic dreams.

She also loves music and dance, exhibiting a gracious flowing presence and losing herself in the vibrations that allow her to explore her feelings in both the lyrics and music that touch her heart and help give expression to her dreams.

Shadow

The Princess can become completely dependent on others for validation. She may spend all her time thinking and doing for others, losing her center. It's like the Fleetwood Mac's lyrics, "I'm over my head but it sure feels nice." If she is not careful, codependency becomes her safety zone.

If you are a mature man or woman you may need to ask, are you regressing into teenage behavior patterns? Are you overly needy, possessive, jealous, or insecure?

When this relates to career, it definitely means you need to love your work or find a way to make it meaningful.

When you get this card in a reading

Depending on the position in the reading, you are dealing with either past, present, or future romantic tales. She epitomizes the power of love to completely submerge us in the desire to please the beloved above all else.

You are either in love or yearning for that more than anything else. Falling in love is one of the greatest gifts this life has to offer and it can be very healthy, freeing, and ecstatic to surrender and let love be your teacher.

It is wonderful to want to offer your love in special and personal ways to others. Think about what would really show your beloved that you see their uniqueness. Generic gifts such as flowers or chocolate are great but they can only say so much.

To not get lost it is important to also find ways to stay centered and involved in activities that give you a sense of self-worth and self-confidence.

Taking lessons in dance or music to help you explore your emotions on your own will also help you be clear in your communication with your beloved.

Or just light some candles in front of a large mirror and dance for yourself.

If this card is your child, she could use very specific appreciations of her uniqueness. You need to go beyond the basic "I love you" and "You're beautiful," to statements or questions that acknowledge her special way of doing things. This applies equally to male children.

Examples: "Your paintings are so colorful, can you tell me why you put that rainbow over the little house?" "I love when you make up your own dances." "Can you tell me another story about your special (imaginary) friend?"

The idea is you are honoring her for who she is and downplaying the often unconscious tendency to treat children like windup dolls, asking them to perform for friends and family the same actions over and over again. This sends a message that what we love about them is not who they are but what they can do that pleases others. The extreme example of this is the overbearing stage mother.

The Queen of Disks
Signs: Sagittarius/CAPRICORN

This classic Capricorn earth mama is completely comfortable in her lush oasis. Having left the desert of her long journey of initiations, she now enjoys the fruits of her labors, and reigns with a wise and worldly demeanor. In the image she holds the whole world in her hands and her totem, the goat, stands guard on his own globe of animal instinct.

She is very sensual in nature and loves to luxuriate in the best of the earthly delights. She is adept at practical and financial matters and never buys into the lie of scarcity. Abundance is her natural state and she is often referred to as the money queen.

From her helmet rises the horns of the markhor, symbolizing her ability to tune into influences both near and far, as well as to attract and magnetize people to serve her will. Like her companion the goat, she loves high, wild places.

She is traditionally a fertility symbol and loves to create a home that is full of family pictures, heirlooms and rich warm colors. Delicious aromas greet all who enter her realm. Her house is where everyone hangs out and she loves to have feasts and parties where wine, laughter, and great conversations fill the air. She cares very much about healthy foods and is very knowledgeable about herbs and remedies that she often makes herself. Just mention an ailment and she will be quick to offer you the perfect antidote.

The influence of Sagittarius keeps her from becoming too much of the serious and overly responsible person often associated with Capricorn. Pan and the centaur are both part animal and part human and so, in a way, is our Queen.

Shadow

She can become dull, overbearing, and demanding. Thinking she knows best how everything should be done, she cannot share responsibilities and then complains about having to do everything herself.

Her sensuality can go too far and end up in the realm of addiction.

She can become obsessed with money and spend all her time shopping and acquiring possessions. Her house can turn into the cluttered mess of a pack rat. She can also feel the weight of the

Queen of Disks

world on her shoulders and feel like she is always the one holding the bag. This tendency to be overly responsible can kill her natural Pan-like nature and make her a real party pooper. Sometimes, if no one else will do something, maybe it just doesn't need to be done right now.

When you get this card in a reading

Enjoy the sensual pleasures of life, stock up on all your special treats, buy things for the home and functional items for your work. Be generous and hold gatherings to bring together your family and friends. Bonds can be deepened as you celebrate and appreciate your bounty.

It is a good time to get centered in your home and put business matters in order as well. Imagine drawing energy and resources to you or call for support or workers who will do repairs or improve your environment.

It is not a good time to travel; not because of danger but because you need to hold down the fort, so to speak.

If your question is about fertility, this is a definite yes! And also if you see the Queen of Cups, The Empress, or any of the Threes (except the Three of Swords,) it adds weight to a prediction of pregnancy.

The Queen is a confident, devoted mother and a loving wife. But she will be a stern disciplinarian if things start to get out of hand.

In the business realm she runs a tight ship and can carry her weight and even help her fellow workers whom she will tend to mother as well.

No need to worry about money, just don't spend your time running after schemes; get grounded in a plan and follow through step by step. The Queen of Disks symbolizes tenacity and perseverance as well as an optimistic sense that all will turn out well.

Knight of Disks
Signs: Leo/VIRGO

Here we see a soldier in full armor astride a mighty steed, but he is motionless in a field and his horse is grazing while he stares out into the distance. This image draws varied and often contradictory reactions.

Some see him as resting to prepare for the next battle; others sense that he is done with war and wants to find a new direction but he is so defensive, he doesn't know how to move on. The way you see him will tell you a lot about your direction in the area of career.

He always seeks purposeful, practical work because he is a gallant servant to his people. His helmet, crowned with the head of a buck, is thrown back as he imagines what life would be like over that hill. The buck signals us that he possesses knowledge of the animal kingdom, and hints at a hidden shamanic aspect to his nature, for the deer is often considered a gateway to the other realms.

This stocky, sturdy character feels trustworthy and solid. Although he learns new skills slowly, once he masters anything it is integrated deeply into his being.

The Knight reigns as the lion for the last ten days of Leo so leadership is not foreign to him, but his nature is much more defined by the earthy sign of Virgo. The fire of Leo, tamed by Virgo, becomes the slow, smoldering fire of growth.

He is practical, a capable craftsman, excellent with agricultural concerns, but the influence of Mercury also adds an intellectual side to his potential. His thoughts are not of the abstract or philosophical type.

He is a critical thinker, concerned with physical manifestation, be it harvesting a crop or reaping the benefits of a carefully thought-out financial transaction. Able to analyze and dissect any problem, he truly enjoys finding answers. That is why he also makes an excellent scientist or physician.

Shadow

When ill-dignified, the Knight becomes dull, lazy, and unwilling to learn anything new. He becomes dogmatic and defensive about his beliefs and is unwilling to consider other points of view. He will be stingy, selfish, and surly, and still believe he is in the right.

When you get this card in a reading

It is important for you to examine your lifework without being defensive. Are you holding on to a job for financial security, when you know there is more to life? Is your supervisor dissatisfied with your work? You might need to be more open to constructive criticism.

If you are a father, physical activities are a great way for you to bond with your child. Playing sports without a competitive edge, gardening, or just regular walks and talks can be a perfect way to connect. Try lightening up on the criticism of your children, focusing instead on drawing out and encouraging their uniqueness. You will tend to want them to find a career for financial security and reject artistic tendencies as impractical, so you might want to help them find ways to be down-to-earth about their artistic endeavors.

Concerning relationships, you would do well to be a good listener and ask questions. You will probably be the quieter one in the relationship but if you let yourself, you could really enjoy a vivacious, outgoing, spontaneous partner who helps you push the envelope.

If this represents a male love interest he will make a very loyal and caring partner, although his expressions of love will be more by doing than saying. He will be slow to warm up but loyal and steadfast once he makes a commitment. As a lover, he will be very attentive to your needs.

Knight of Disks

Prince of Disks
Signs: Aries/TAURUS

This man of the world has already proven himself in his profession and is now more interested in his work as a way to understand the meaning and mysteries of life.

We see him without any armor, for he seeks no confrontations and is not defensive. His demeanor and charisma declare his confidence and power wherever he goes.

His hand rests on the world because he is well-traveled and erudite. His chariot is made of circles suggesting his well-rounded nature; he lets his instincts and determination draw him forward, symbolized by his totem, the Taurean bull. Because he straddles the cusp of Aries the Initiator and Taurus the Manifester, he usually has a lot of projects going at once that he will eventually complete.

Behind him, the grapes of Bacchus let you know he loves the raucous, bawdy, and sensuous celebration of life. He will eat more, drink more, and laugh harder than anyone at the party.

The most fascinating part of this painting is the intricate pattern of the background. Filled with seeds, spores, flowers, and cell division, it tells us he is fascinated by the very origins of life. His work takes him into a deepening of his understanding of life itself.

Having mastered the skills of his profession, he is an excellent mentor and teacher.

He is a connoisseur of the world of food and wine and often has an amazing garden where he experiments with growing the best and most delicious delicacies.

Shadow

Stubbornness, arrogance, alcoholism, obesity, greed, and sexual addiction show up when the Prince has not really found meaning in his work. He only wants to acquire more things to indulge his every whim, trying to fill the vacuum of his lack of purpose.

When you get this card in a reading

Your lust for life calls you to work hard and play hard.

In the field of work, you can accomplish your most challenging feats right now, so don't shy away from chances to show your stuff.

Prince of Disks

Awards, bonuses, and expanding opportunities will be coming your way. It is imperative that your work be a gateway to your understanding of life. Whether you are a gardener or a businessman, you need to go beyond mere efficiency and success toward discoveries that take you to the next level of awareness and expertise.

Your sense of fun is heightened, so let the good times roll with sensual pleasures. It is a time of sexual fulfillment; get creative setting the stage for romantic trysts, trips, and tasty treats.

Be careful of your tendency to run roughshod over others. Whether you know it or not, your personality can be very intimidating. If you can relax into your power from within and let go of a need to dominate, you will actually have more fun and people will like you more. Instead of paying lip service to your formidable presence, people will open up to you in new and refreshing ways.

Although you love to give your children gifts, the gift of your authentic interest in their lives, thoughts, and dreams will mean so much more. Remember to do both.

Princess of Disks
Element: Earth

The Princess of Disks glows from within as if she holds a secret that allows her to be totally comfortable in the world. She has found the wisdom and happiness that comes from being grounded in the great mother. Her power emanates from deep within. Her shield, the Taoist yin/yang circle, symbolizes the fact that her protection is non-reaction. She is the divine witness, aware and responsive to impulses that come from knowing when to act and when to be still. The eastern traditions of self-defense are in truth the ability to move with the flow of energy, by knowing that any threat has within it the seed of its own destruction if it is sourced in fear and anger.

She is earth of Earth, surrounded by the ancient wisdom of the trees. Even the roots are exposed, showing that she lives in the earth, not on it.

Her long fur wraps around her, letting us know she is loved by all her relations; her horned headdress keeps her receptive and tuned in to the intuitive and instinctual arts of awareness.

Her scepter is pointed downward for she has no need to rule; she is calm wisdom personified. The diamond on the end was formed under pressure in the deepest recesses of the earth. This reminds her to listen in silence for guidance from the depths of the unseen forces that continue to shape our lives. The voice of the soul is what moves and breathes when stillness allows.

Shadow

Are you always seeking greener pastures and external approval and rewards? Have you lost your center? Are you unable to feel that peace and solitude can be your allies? If so, slow down and listen to your body; follow your breath and know you are just where you need to be.

When you get this card in a reading

It is time to ground yourself in your body and in the natural world. This Princess represents wisdom and happiness that comes from the realization that we are interconnected with all of life and the universe itself. She is not concerned with material wealth; instead she wants to be comfortable in work that serves.

If you are thinking about applying for a job, at some point when you are on site, reverse in your mind the application process and imagine they are applying to you. When you have a moment, close your eyes and feel if you belong there. Can you actually see yourself being in this space?

It is a time to act only when you feel, like an actress in a play, that you just got your cue. When you are with family and friends, try to listen and witness more. People will seek out your ideas and advice if you hold back and wait for a natural opening in the conversation.

You are discovering a deeper trust in your own sense of knowing. This is not a time to leap impulsively, but to trust that if the timing is right you will find action effortless. This is a time to trust the old adage, "To thine own self be true."

Princess of Disks

MINOR ARCANA
NUMBERED CARDS

NUMBERS, NUMBERS, NUMBERS!

Believe it or not, you probably know a lot more about the nature of numbers than you realize. We are always using the symbolic meaning of numbers to describe our lives. The following sentences will demonstrate this very simply.

The union was divided about how to create a dynamic structure that was flexible enough to accommodate the changing times, while still reflecting the original principles.

- Union = one
- Divided = two
- Dynamic/create = three
- Structure = four
- Changing = five
- Reflection of original principles = six

The union needs to grow by communicating a clear message of its core values and the tools that can be used to manifest the will of the workers, strengthening the foundation in the process.

- Grow (growth) = seven
- Communication (communication) = eight
- Foundation = nine
- Manifest (manifestation) = ten

When you think of numbers as a natural part of our language, they do not get delegated to the "I Hate Math!" ghetto, but instead reveal themselves to be the basic building blocks of life.

To create anything, we must go through the natural progression of numbers.

It is not something that we are always conscious of, but the rhythm of numbers runs through our language constantly.

In becoming conscious of this we can see them as building blocks that are being inserted into language to make things happen. Prioritizing, planning, measuring, analyzing, can all be happening without a single number being mentioned and yet the nature of numbers is present all the time.

Music, something that we most often think of as a medium of emotion, is all structured through mathematics.

When we learn to notice this, and study and apply it in our lives, synchronicities, theories, and formulas can show up anywhere.

Numerology and the Kabala are just another language we use to describe and understand the world.

In fact, the failure to fully acknowledge the significance and function of natural progression will result in a faulty project. In retrospect, we can usually analyze the stages that were skipped, avoided, or done in a sloppy manner.

The I Ching states that the seeds of disorder are often planted in the beginning of any endeavor, so a clear, strong, and uncomplicated beginning will bode well for a successful completion.

Note: The significance and meaning of all the Minors, Aces through Tens, can always be further understood by meditating on the same numbered card in the Majors realm; for example, Magician I for Aces; Priestess II for Twos.

This same idea can be related to the astrological applications of any given card. Example: Mars rules the Two of Wands in the sign of Aries. Reading the descriptions and meditating on The Tower (Mars) and The Emperor (Aries) will deepen the understanding and interpretation of the card. The archetype can offer more insights, stories, and depth to the significance of the Minor.

Experiment: Pick a Minor card, read the astrological notations. Then find the Major that represents the planet on the Minor card, the Major that represents the sign on the Minor card, and the Minor card you picked. Place all three cards in front of you and let your imagination tell a story.

In this way the Majors and Minors flesh out each other's mythic implications.

ACES

ARCHETYPE: THE MAGUS I

KABALA: KETHER, THE CROWN

Wholeness, state of union, seed of new beginnings.

From acorn to oak tree, baby to adult, caterpillar to butterfly, all "seeds" contain the blueprint to grow into their full potential.

Note: Even ages of earthly existence have seeds that contain the vision of that particular evolutionary period. For example, we are coming out of the time of the sacrificed god called the Age of Pisces where we have witnessed the best and the brightest martyred to awaken the rest of humanity. Jesus, Joan of Arc, Martin Luther King, Jr., and all the wise women called "witches" who were killed in the burning times.

We are now transitioning into the Aquarian Age of intelligent love where we can heal and evolve out of the toxic version of possessive love into a time when our love serves the freedom and growth of each other's souls.

When Aces appear in your reading, it is a sign that a new time, stage, move, or event is occurring. If we cannot revive our current situation, then the Aces are calling us to make a fresh start, with clarity and a full release of the past.

It is traditional that when asking a specific question of the cards, Aces mean YES!

Astrological Note: The Aces or ones are seeds of elements, not specific signs, and relate to Air (Swords), Fire (Wands), Water (Cups) and Earth (Disks). All other Minor Arcana have specific planets and signs assigned to them.

Kabala: All Aces occupy the sephira or station called Kether, or the Crown. It may be helpful to understand this symbol by relating it to the crowning of a child's head, its first appearance in the world.

Ace of Swords
Element: Air

Air is the realm of thought, vision, inspiration and awareness, so dust off your double-edged sword of truth and be unabashedly honest with yourself, while using the other edge to send your truth out into the world.

When the Ace of Swords appears, it calls us to awaken to a new idea or follow through on one that has been waiting in the ethers for a long time.

The Ace of Swords is often depicted as a sword in the clouds and a hand grasping the hilt.

Take hold of your vision; face your procrastinations, even if you can only begin with baby steps at the start of the process. Dream Big! What happens can only expand as far as you can dream it.

Write your new idea down, or tell it to one trusted friend, or send it in a prayer and call for a path to open before you.

In the Thoth deck we see a sword crowned with the twenty-two rays of cosmic blessing. Twenty-two is the number of pathways on the Tree of Life, the number of letters in the Hebrew alphabet, and the number of archetypes in the Major Arcana.

This implies that the universal forces are willing to aid you in your creative process; ask and it will be given.

Native Americans use cornmeal to open the way. As you walk out the door into the world with your new idea, sprinkle some cornmeal in front of you as you walk, saying, "May the path always open before me." Repeat this three times.

When you focus your intention and embody your will by speaking it aloud, amazing miracles can come your way.

Shadow

Using this sword to attack, blame, and try to prove that others are the root of your problem is a strategy that allows you to rationalize and procrastinate about personal challenges instead of owning your own evolutionary process.

This sword is not a weapon but a symbolic image that will help cut through the lies, resistance and rationalizations to see things as they actually are.

1

Ace of Swords

Ace of Wands
Element: Fire

Fire is the realm of spirit, action, passion, will, and desire, so this Ace is definitely a call to get moving! When you hold this card next to a diagram of the Kabala, or Tree of Life, you can see how it shows the igniting of every sephira or station. It shows the entire schemata of the energy field awakened and alive! Energy is moving free and unobstructed, and we are ready to go, go, go!

You have moved from the vision of the Ace of Swords into the first stage of the manifestation of will.

Your desire is strong and your excitement palpable. Hesitation has been cast to the winds and motion becomes its own delight.

In the Motherpeace deck we see a baby bursting out of an eggshell, fully formed and ready to experience this new life.

All creatures that break out of their shells or cocoons need to find the strength to emerge all by themselves. Any attempt to help will actually disable the being, because without making this first entrance solo, the life force will not be fully surging with the strength and vigor needed to survive.

The butterfly, the bird, or the snake all need to muster their own will to be. It is the same with us; we must pull on our core resources to be able to successfully thrive in the world.

This card indicates you are ready to activate your ideas and move through your current circumstances with courage and flexibility.

Shadow

When this energy bursts forth, you need to be aware of your effect on others around you and refrain from trying to force them to do your will.

This force is best channeled as an inspiration to those who you desire to help you on your journey. If you inspire instead of grasp for control, you will attract freely offered support that has the most potential for success.

Note: the diagram of the Kabala can also be seen in the Ten of Cups and the Ten of Disks.

Ace of Wands

Ace of Cups
Element: Water

◖●◗

The Ace of Cups shows a beautiful image of the grail emerging out of the lotus, as west meets east in defining this card. You seek the grail or reward of your quest for life's deeper meaning through the unfolding of consciousness symbolized by the lotus.

This card symbolizes a joie de vivre, a love of life that is universal and not limited to or defined by any external being or thing.

It also signals a readiness to open to new beginnings in the arena of relationships. You have cleared old stories by learning the lessons they offered and are once again in the present moment. The heart wants no restrictions at this time, just the freedom to enjoy the journey. You are open, ready, and not afraid to be vulnerable.

If you are already in a committed relationship, it can also signify that there is a need to renew the original intent. Sometimes we get lost in the forward motion of our lives and we need to revisit what set us on this path in the first place. What was the heartfelt intent at the onset of the love affair, creative endeavor, or enterprise? It may be time to review and renew your vows, commitments, hopes, and dreams.

For work, it may mean a new job or a time to evaluate whether or not you are being fulfilled in the way you originally envisioned, and if not, why not? It also suggests that it is your emotional relationship to work, not just the practical considerations, that needs to be re-examined.

Shadow
You may have a false sense that everything is light and perfect while pushing down or not acknowledging your fears about intimacy. Be careful not to mask loneliness with manufactured optimism.

1

Ace of Cups

Ace of Disks
Element: Earth

The Ace of Disks is the seed of new beginnings in the element of earth. Earth is the realm of manifestation, governing the body, work, possessions, and physical accomplishments.

The image of the intersection of the wings of heaven with the trees of earth echoes The Magician's theme of "as above so below." The trees are symbolized by the cross section of a trunk to give us a sense of the passage of time that is needed to grow anything in the space-time continuum.

It is time to plant the seed of your vision in the physical world.

It can also mean the seed is already there and starting to grow. Either way, it is important to water and tend the seed to bring it to maturity.

Shadow

It is important when you get this card to make sure you are planting your idea in fertile ground that has been prepared through careful planning.

Just like a seed of a flower, there are specific seasons and conditions that must be considered if the seed is to survive.

It is only a seed and does not have the power to grow if it is neglected. It needs water (loving attention) until its roots go deep enough to be able to find its own source of nourishment, so stay focused and attentive to bring your seeds to fruition.

1

Ace of Disks

T W O S
ARCHETYPE: THE PRIESTESS II
KABALA: CHOKMAH, WISDOM

Twos represent change, polarization, opposites, or paradoxically, complementary natures, a sense of balance, equality, and the magnetic connection between things.

Twos represent the first division in the creative process, the first separation that makes one thing distinct from its opposite.

All twos are connected to The Priestess and therefore, have the added meaning of being a reflection of the one. Just like the Moon reflects the Sun in the heavens, The Priestess transmits the message of The Magician across the unknown toward manifestation.

Two of Swords
Astrological Aspect: Moon in Libra

The Moon finds acceptance and balance in the sign of Libra. It is the first attempt by the Ace of Swords, your new vision, to find a receptive counterpart in the realm of ideas.

The Two of Swords is called Peace in the Crowley deck, and shows two swords crossed through the rose of Binah, the great mother who contains the womb of all life.

This card is very useful in exploring our relationship to motherhood. All its aspects are feminine in nature. It is ruled by the Moon that regulates the menstrual cycles, in the sign of Libra that is ruled by the planet Venus. Thus it asks us to explore the following questions, as appropriate:

- Are you at peace with your biological mother?
- Are you at peace with yourself as a mother?
- Are you at peace about your desire for having children or your decision to not procreate?

For a man this card would also be peace with your mother, wife, or your own ability to be a nurturer, especially for single and gay dads.

Beyond the gender aspects it is also about being at peace with one's self and suggests a time to slow down enough to reflect and let the answers come. As the Beatles said, "Mother Mary (Moon) comes to me, speaking words of wisdom (Chokmah) let it be."

There is wisdom in inaction; await an impulse that cannot be denied.

Slow down and find your center. If you have already found peace, let yourself enjoy it.

Shadow

Be careful about rash decisions or influences from others, or you will find later on that you did not act from a place of inner balance.

2

SWORDS **Peace**

Two of Wands
Astrological Aspect: Mars in Aries

This is the life force that we all feel as the thunderstorms of spring call us to let go of our old winter skins, like old clothes, and join the dance, anew!

Fire has ignited the world again, and like thunder that is followed by lightning, so the vibration precedes the illumination.

The Two of Wands presents the image of a Tibetan dorje and it is called Dominion. In Tibetan teachings, thunder sends our egos scurrying for shelter from the awesome powers of nature. It is in these moments of awe that we are able to release the insignificant limitations of ego fears and reconsider where our true domain is in our lives and in the world.

This card is an awakening, an epiphany, that sends a shock wave through the false structures that hold you back from opportunities to reinvent yourself. The change is internal as an old persona is shed to let the soul's journey continue. It is similar to the idea of the phoenix rising from the ashes and taking flight.

When you feel you are truly in your domain, your place of power, then the ego will reform itself around the soul's desire.

This card says that events are happening to catapult you out of inertia into your next becoming. These events can be shocking and very unsettling. How you perceive and respond to them will determine the outcome. You can view shocking events as "emergencies" or find your breath and your inner ground and see what is "emerging."

When you find your core purpose again, then you will no longer want people to hold you to their image of you in the past.

Sometimes it will mean moving away from negative influences and toward people and situations that will meet you on this new plane.

Shadow

This is not a call to burn bridges and create a ripple effect of confusion and mistrust by those around you. Let the transformation happen from within first and then the changes you make externally will be able to be supported by outside forces.

Dominion

Two of Cups
Astrological Aspect: Venus in Cancer

——————————————◗ ● ◗——————————————

This card is connected to the ocean; it is the dance of Venus/Aphrodite, foam-born goddess of love, dancing in the sign of Cancer, the crab. Another way of saying it: love (Venus) has found a home (Cancer) in your heart.

In every deck I have ever seen this card is about falling in love. The lotus flower that we saw in the Ace is feeding the two cups.

Two dolphins are entwined around the cups to evoke divine marriage. Dolphins have long exemplified true love. They are loyal, humorous, intelligent, and playful. They treat each other as equals. These are great qualities to aspire to and remember as you get swept up into nature's most excellent way to experience union.

The chemistry that takes over when opposites attract is truly a force to be reckoned with!

Alexandra Genetti's deck, The Wheel of Change Tarot, shows a beautiful lace tablecloth underneath two bubbling champagne glasses, suggesting the celebration of the union that may result.

In the Motherpeace deck it shows a merman and a mermaid toasting under a full moon at the ocean's shore.

Since it is the goddess of Love in the sign of the home it could also be pointing to the need for more love in the home. Or, if it is in the environment position it could be a home you may be considering moving to. It would suggest that the home should be chosen only if there is a true emotional connection. This card is not about the practical or financial. In fact, those considerations tend to fly out the window when love blows in.

The Two of Cups is calling you to surrender now and dance before the song is over and you've missed your chance. When love calls, answer!

Shadow

This card can also come up in a reading when the luster has rubbed off your current affair and, instead of doing the work to go deeper, you are ready to run. If you want the relationship to go beyond the initial attraction, one of these days you're going to have to move through the turbulent waters that inevitably arise and learn respectful and embodied ways of communicating.

Ask yourself if you are avoiding the challenges of true intimacy.

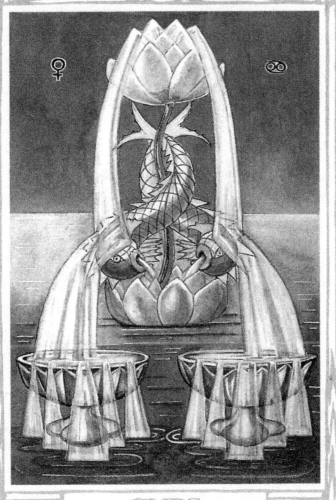

2

Love

CUPS

Two of Disks
Astrological Aspect: Jupiter in Capricorn
———————————— ◑ ● ◐ ————————————

Jupiter offers a chance to expand your potential in work by emphasizing the creative aspects and letting go of limitations. Capricorn's tenacity will see you through.

Usually this indicates a job change. It could be a new job, or reinvigorating the current work with creativity. Or it might be a whole new career.

The Two of Disks is called Change in the Thoth deck, reminding us that the only constant in the universe is change. Crowley put forth the equation change = stability as a simple way to remember this principle. Too often we fear change and grasp for false security in stagnant situations.

The image in the card is of a snake called the ouroborus that takes the shape of the infinity symbol. The snake is eating its own tail, showing us life's infinite ability to feed on and reinvent itself out of the old form.

An actual snake appears to be dead as it sheds the skin of its past and comes forth sensitive and new. All your past is compost to nourish your future becomings.

Let the kundalini life force rise and expand, grounded in the practicality and responsibility of Capricorn. Jupiter lends a hand by expanding your realm of possibilities for creative rebirth.

Shadow

The god, Pan, can also be a capricious trickster, so be careful of jumping from one hilltop to the next without truly learning the territory. Jupiter can dazzle you with opportunities that are not in line with your true nature, but the money or the elevated position may be hard for the ego to resist.

If you tend to want change just for its own sake and have yet to find meaningful work, then just changing jobs will not satisfy the true intention of this card.

All action needs to be rooted in the willingness to work hard to bring creativity and imagination to whatever situation you are in.

2

Change

THREES
ARCHETYPE: THE EMPRESS / GAIA III
KABALA: BINAH, WOMB OF CREATION

Threes represent the dynamics of birth. The Great Mother has become pregnant with future possibilities of life forms and ideas.

It is the number of synthesis, presenting the idea that the result of the union of opposites is informed by both and yet is a unique entity in and of itself.

This mystery goes beyond the mere cloning of already existing forms, and demonstrates the infinite possibilities of life on earth.

Three of Swords
Astrological Aspect: Saturn in Libra

Breaking through old man Saturn's limitations of past psychological influences, try to find the internal mental equilibrium of harmonious Libra.

The image of a sword piercing the rose of Binah shows the sometimes-painful process of psychological self-examination that is needed to discover what is unconsciously stopping you from giving birth to ideas or projects that will fulfill your destiny.

Saturn's ultimate purpose is to help you find ways to create your own structures and discipline that are self-motivated. But when you resist the pressure and refuse to probe your ingrained self-denial, you will not experience the joy that comes from offering your unique gifts. This process often needs the encouragement and insights of qualified professionals who will help you work through your blocks and enter the dance.

When Saturn calls, he is asking you to listen to your own drummer and find the rhythm of your own creative process. Then self-discipline becomes the tool you need to fulfill your hidden dreams.

Sometimes this card will mean that your own physical mother is the source of some of the painful truths you need to face.

This does not suggest you judge your mother as the source of your dysfunction; instead, find a way to be an evolution and not merely a rejection of her.

Sometimes our own mothers were unable to be who they wanted to be, because of the cultural judgments of their generation. I have heard endless stories of mothers who really wanted to be businesswomen or artists and instead had children and always carried a feeling of loss and sacrifice. This is very wounding to the child, but it can be overcome.

Shadow

Often when we blame our mothers and reject them without understanding, we will actually become like them.

This card may show a tendency to define oneself as a victim and become a therapy junkie, seeking counselors and teachers who will "cure" us.

3

SWORDS **Sorrow**

When I first went to therapy, my counselor told me that it was my journey and she would support and guide me on my path, but would in no way take the lead.

If you seek someone to tell you what you have to do, you will be like the caterpillar being pulled from its cocoon, unprepared to have the strength to fly solo. Or you may be unconsciously seeking the mother you always wanted. Ultimately every teacher or guide can only help you identify your challenges and give you tools to overcome them. You still need to do the work.

Saturn refuses to let us off easy. But when we learn to dance to our own rhythm, we will find the whole universe is dancing with us and vice versa.

Competition and comparing ourselves with others is a shadow aspect of this card as well.

Three of Wands
Astrological Aspect: Sun in Aries

The Sun has engendered the world with spring (Aries) and you are "pregnant" and gestating with new life! Here we see contained energy; the awakening and breakout of the Ace and Two of Wands has now resulted in fertilization and it is time to nurture and care for yourself as your own patient mother.

The Three of Wands is a strong indicator of actual pregnancy, as all threes are connected to the divine mother, The Empress, whose number is also three.

Literally, the Sun has engendered the Great Mother with the Mars (yang) energy from the two, so this can also suggest a male child.

The three flowers are known as the roses of Isis, the Great Mother of Egypt. If you want to become pregnant, you might ask Isis for some help. Divinities are aspects of creation that respond to our sincere intentions.

Often this card represents being pregnant with one's self. If that is the case, it is important to really pay attention to diet and exercise and to engage in activities that feed the body and soul. Massage, meditation, long walks, acquiring beautiful clothes and objects for the home, will all send a message of self-love that is paramount during times when we don't actually know what is next in our lives. It is a time to trust in the process. Whether it is about actual pregnancy or the gestation of the next stage in our lives, patience and perseverance are the "virtues" we need to hold to. In the Thoth deck this card is called Virtue.

In terms of timing, I use the nine-month-to-a-year period as a measure of how long you will need to let the flowering take place.

In order not to "miscarry," either literally or figuratively, your well-being must be first on your list.

Shadow

Wanting to force a new start or bring into the world a project that is not well-developed shows impatience and the inability to allow the mystery to unfold. Be careful to decide mentally about feelings that are just stirring; let them simmer on the back burner for a while and see what bubbles to the surface.

Being in the unknown can feel frustrating, yet it is really an opportunity to go deeper.

When you are asked what you are doing with your life, the ego wants to jump up and declare its purpose. Impatience will create many false starts, much like false labor.

Note: These more exact interpretations come with practice. Readers develop a recognition of certain feelings that accompany valid guidance, and over time learn to trust and act on these intimations, strengthening the power of the intuitive.

3

WANDS **Virtue**

Three of Cups
Astrological Aspect: Mercury in Cancer

Time to revitalize communication (Mercury), that celebrates the joys of home and hearth (Cancer). This card often appears when we have forgotten to make our home feel vibrant and alive with social and family gatherings.

It's time to turn the TV off, clear away the junk, bring in some fresh flowers, and invite folks over for a meaningful gathering.

In this modern world we tend to become very isolated and forget that our primary relationships become more dynamic and fun when we have others to interact with. Maybe you've become a bit bored with your marriage or can't think of anything new to do with the children. How about having a feast or a potluck and warm the home with good company.

Mercury's influence in this card calls us to add depth and meaning to our gathering by focusing the energy in a conscious way. This can be done in numerous ways. For example, how about asking each person to respond to a simple question:

- What event or person most influenced your life?
- What was the highest, lowest and most awkward moment in your day or week?
- What is your greatest dream for the future?
- Let your imagination run wild in thinking of new ways to bring the celebration of your life home.
- A simple game of charades or a theme party are always fun.

Theme party ideas

Come as your favorite celebrity, superhero, bad guy/gal, or historical figure.

Come as an animal, vegetable, or mineral.

For the daring, do an "anything but clothes" party! We had some great costumes for that one, ranging from bubble wrap to coconut shells and a grass skirt!

Too often we surrender the world of entertainment to mass media. How about a music jam, or our all-time favorite, the no-talent talent show that tends to bring some really cool creativity out of the closet!

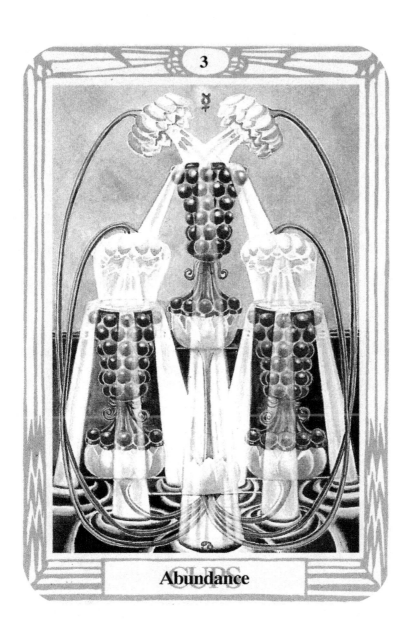

3

Abundance

The next day your home will glow with the feelings of being filled with love and laughter. Some of our sweetest moments come in the afterglow of a celebration.

In the end, our relationships give us the greatest joy, so bring it on home and revel in magic!

Often depicted in this card are the three graces dancing and toasting to life. Invite them into your home; you won't be disappointed!

Shadow

Sometimes we become too isolated and focused on our primary relationship, expecting it to fulfill all our emotional needs. That's when jealousy, based on fear of loss, can raise its ugly head.

Love cannot be possessed and likely will move on or just dry up if it is damned up and trapped.

When this card shows up, it's time to trust love to guide the course of the relationship. This choice to relinquish control brings us into the present, unobstructed by expectations.

I associate this card with a six-month period in which all discussion of the ultimate direction will be tabled. Time to go with the flow and restrain the ego's desires for answers and commitments.

Real commitment can be voiced in words, but words will not create that commitment.

Watch out for those conversations in which you both agree on everything you want in a relationship. Best to demonstrate the ability to show up in the moment and work through difficulties to strengthen the relationship.

Three of Disks
Astrological Aspect: Mars in Capricorn

The fierce determination of Mars is welcomed in the Capricorn sign of tenacity, practicality, structure, and responsible action.

In the Thoth deck we are viewing the pyramid from above, implying that we have the opportunity to create a real structure that is linked to, and inspired by, our higher purpose.

The pyramid is the most stable form we can build. Look how long the pyramids in Egypt and Latin America have lasted. This form allows the winds of change to blow around its apex while it remains fully grounded on the earth.

Mars will give you the resourcefulness to take action to bring into the world ideas that may have been floating in the imagination for some time.

This card is a good reminder to get practical about your visions and anchor them in the world.

In the Motherpeace deck there are three women building the temple of the goddess, another structure that is physical but rooted in the spiritual realm. The three women suggest that working cooperatively with two other people will be dynamic and advantageous. It is a good time to be sure that job divisions are defined according to the unique skills of the individuals to avoid overlap and misunderstandings.

This card appears, especially in the past, indicator, or subconscious positions, to give confirmation that you have accomplished an aspect of your lifework. You are no longer dependent on another's approval or a particular institution or job to feel secure; you now carry within yourself this pyramid of experience and accomplishment.

This can also suggest that you need to free yourself from the limitations of structures that are not honoring your level of accomplishment.

Could be time to become a freelance consultant or start your own business in your field of expertise.

It can also mean that since you have proven yourself in one vocation, it is the perfect time to bring another dream into reality. Given the knowledge that the first career will always be something you can fall back on, there is less fear of striking out anew.

Or you could let the established career serve as a bridge to gradually fade into the background as the new one becomes a reality.

Shadow

It is important when this card appears to reexamine what your higher purpose is in your work. You may have forgotten or lost connection with the original intent.

To only take on the weight of responsibility so often linked to Capricorn would be to forget that this is also the sign of the playful goat that loves and delights in creativity.

Any job can be infused with conscious effort. I once heard a story of a bus driver who chose to make every one of his riders feel respected. He even helped an elderly woman find a restaurant where her friends were giving her a birthday dinner. He learned she was dying of cancer and this would probably be her last celebration. She only knew the street and he went into every place on the block until he found her friends. When the driver's daughter heard this story from her father through the program StoryCorps.org, she said he was the best dad in the whole world.

Many of us have been raised to believe that work is meant to be hard, boring, repetitive, and a sacrifice for the sake of acquiring money. Mars wants to be passionately engaged and challenged, not fearfully fighting for mere survival. Ask yourself, "How can I give meaning to my work?" If you cannot find an answer, consider exploring new possibilities.

Remember, responsibility really means the ability to respond honestly to any situation.

3

Works

FOURS

Fours represent structure, order, law, and government. Fours are associated with stability, the status quo and the many ways humans organize themselves to manifest a certain plan or idea.

Structures can either function to serve the community or they can become an exclusive or dominant force that can become hierarchal, rigid and restrictive.

When form follows function then structures, be they physical or organizational, can give us places to gather and ways to work together for the highest good of all.

If they are in service to the community as a whole, they are functioning in a healthy way.

If they are designed to keep certain people out and use others as slaves to the few on the top, they are oppressive and dysfunctional.

The ability to organize and build is a great asset. It is necessary to have limitations within which to accomplish things. A community center or an artist's studio are positive examples; corporate factories that exploit foreign labor are negative ones.

Four of Swords
Astrological Aspect: Jupiter in Libra

The Four of Swords is called Truce in the Thoth deck, and indicates a temporary compromise to maintain harmony until a larger shift can happen.

One situation connected to this idea is a job that you no longer want but cannot leave yet due to financial dependency. Another is a young person who is being supported by parents while attending college. You may need to go along with the parental rules until you are really independent.

It can also relate to compromises in a divorce that would avert a battle that could be emotionally damaging for the children.

Jupiter teaches us to save our energy for the opportunity we really want and to tolerate the current limitations, knowing we will soon be released. Libra is the sign of Justice, but sometimes the fight is not worth it. If the present circumstances can help in the long run, hang in there until the change can be permanent.

It is not suggesting a compromise of principles, just going with the status quo and maintaining a harmonious relationship so your focus can be on the next stage.

When this card shows up in a reading, it may be a good time to seek a third party to help mediate a disagreement.

It is definitely an indicator that challenging existing structures and authority figures will probably be unsuccessful at this time. Choose your fights carefully. If you must initiate a challenge to defend your integrity, this might be a good time to build your case and wait until you know you have the will and the wherewithal to follow through.

Shadow

Sometimes the influence of Libra can encourage us to give too much, for too long, just for the sake of harmony.

Staying in a bad job or dysfunctional marriage in which we sacrifice our dignity is not advised.

I tend to associate this card with a six-month period. Much longer than that and there is probably an underlying tendency to feel that validation is something others give you instead of something you can give yourself. You do not want to spend your life keeping everyone else happy while your deeper purpose is sublimated.

SWORDS **Truce**

Four of Wands
Astrological Aspect: Venus in Aries

The Four of Wands is a card of springtime and Venus is asking us for Completion of relationships and situations that are no longer growing after the experience of a stagnant winter.

For example, when you are in a relationship in which you keep experiencing the same challenges and you both respond in the same old ways, then you are going around in circles like the image in the Thoth deck. Venus's desire is to open new doors so you may feel stimulated and enlivened by love once again. Often it is difficult to make closure when there is the lingering feeling that the true potential has not been reached.

There is a desire to continue to hope for change even when the patterns in the past have not evolved into a deepening of communication and joy.

Wintertime offers a testing period in which you can go inward and clear away blocks to prepare for the coming spring. When the Sun shines its light in the season of beginnings and everywhere love is in the air, you will be ready.

If attempts have been made to communicate in new ways through some form of therapy without success, or there is no willingness to do so, then it is time to let go. It is often easier to imagine leaving a very dysfunctional relationship then one that is just stuck. There may be another turn of the wheel in the future, but staying in inertia is not going to help.

In applying this card to projects, it is time to stop overextending the scope of the plan and complete what has already been set in motion. Then it will be easy to see where to go next and what challenges are left to be faced. Otherwise the energy that was released at the birth of the idea may just dissipate and be lost altogether.

Another facet of this card that is very useful is the idea that was developed by Vicki Noble and Karen Vogel in The Motherpeace Four of Wands card.

The image depicts four young girls celebrating menarche, the onset of menstruation.

This is a very significant stage and it is too often not honored. In fact, it can often be a humiliating experience. What would you

4

WANDS

Completion

have wanted to happen to celebrate this initiation into sexuality? Create a gathering or a personal ritual that acknowledges your true self. It is never too late to celebrate that fiery and exciting time and many women have taken my suggestion and created a gathering with their friends, or just taken time to journal and remember. Heal and honor that young woman who holds much of our power to manifest our will in the world.

There is a movement alive in the world today, exemplified by the magazine New Moon for young girls. It is a venue for conscious discussion and bonding around this topic, which is still considered taboo for most young women.

This concept can also be applied to men who felt lost or unable to understand or enjoy the onset of puberty. This stage can be particularly painful for gay and transgender youth. If you have teens, try to let them know you accept them for who they are, however they want to express their love and desires.

The Tarot does not give a lot of opportunities to explore this stage of growing up, so this card opens a window by bringing fresh air to a time of confusion. Our older selves can nurture and bring to life that dynamic power that was treated in a dysfunctional way.

Thank you Vicki and Karen for giving us the gift of this insight! The Motherpeace deck offers a refreshing perspective on the Her-story of our planet and is a wonderful deck to give to a young woman celebrating menarche so she can understand her story in a woman-identified way.

Shadow

You can become limited inside a safe and apparently harmonious relationship, using coping mechanisms instead of authentic communication to keep the ship afloat.

Also, be careful not to rush to complete a project just to be done with it so you can move on. The project may be sent out into the world without being refined to its greatest potential.

Four of Cups
Astrological Aspect: Moon in Cancer

————◐ ● ◑————

Now the suit of water has reached the height of romantic fantasy. The days of wine and roses are in full swing and we are enjoying the luxury of the high tide of love! The Moon has lured us into the dreamy state of bliss that makes everything in our life pale by comparison.

If you are not currently experiencing an actual relationship like the one I have just described, it may be that you need to invite in your lighthearted desire to entertain romance without the heaviness of measuring each potential lover against the standard of what you ultimately want in a life partner.

Maybe it's time for a lighthearted fling or just allowing your fantasies to surface. It would be a wonderful time to take an ocean voyage or a trip to a sensuous spa with all the self-indulgent perks, to tell yourself you deserve to luxuriate and imagine romance.

Removing yourself from the same old routine and spending some of that hard-earned money just for the pleasure of it can liberate your romantic self from the practical, linear workaholic who forgets to go with the flow.

The pink lily on the top of the card wants to lure you out of the mud from which it grows and let you open to the Sun. This card can be great fun if you stay lighted-hearted.

Shadow

This card often shows up in the past, indicating that you have been unable or unwilling to take relationships past the romantic fantasy stage. This may have resulted in a long string of superficial love affairs, like those of the playboy/playgirl archetype often portrayed in movies.

If you are in a long-term relationship it can mean one of two things: Whenever real problems and conflicts arise (like what appear in the Five of Cups), instead of sitting in the fire, hearing and acknowledging the issues and trying to find ways to build bridges of communication, you will attempt to recapture the sweetness of romance. Eventually this results in instability because one day when a make-or-break situation arises, there will be no tools of practiced and authentic communication to help you weather the storm.

Or you have already begun to fantasize about past or future lovers who are easily idealized since they don't exist in the everyday.

Although fours are about stability, water is a very fluid medium and any attempt to hold it in a solid configuration will be challenged. The folly of this card is to be delusional and falsely lulled into a sense of security.

It is wonderful to allow our dream lover to emerge and enjoy the calm before the storm. But when the storm hits, or we hit the iceberg, the Titanic will sink and there won't be a lifeboat to get you to shore together if you don't prepare by facing the smaller challenges along the way.

Luxury

Four of Disks
Astrological Aspect: Sun in Capricorn

———————————— ◐ ● ◑ ————————————

This card is the epitome of stability. We have the ever-constant Sun in the hard-working, responsible, and down-to-earth sign of Capricorn, within the number four archetype of practical form and function.

Pictured in the Thoth deck is the view of a castle as if we were hovering above it. We see the symbols for the four elements atop the towers on the four corners. The castle is protected by a moat and the only entrance is a drawbridge.

The card is aptly called Power. Everything is in order. We see a well-protected stronghold that would be very difficult to undermine or penetrate.

This usually indicates that you have established a strong foundation in work by building over time a trusted reputation in your chosen vocation.

It also indicates a clear understanding of good boundaries; lower the bridge to the inner sanctum only to those who offer support and respect.

Many times this turns up in a reading where a person, or couple, is considering buying a home, often for the first time.

This would be a very positive affirmation to go ahead.

Shadow

There is a lack of awareness about the need for good boundaries, especially in keeping chaotic forces out of your home and work environment.

When the question is about buying or building a home, often latent issues surface and challenge the individual or relationship to rise to the occasion by addressing power dynamics, commitments, and special needs.

This decision to deepen the obligation to one another can make or break a relationship. Often issues around home and family from childhood surface.

- Did you move around a lot?
- Are you trying to create the home you never had?
- Are your partner's issues or desires different than yours?

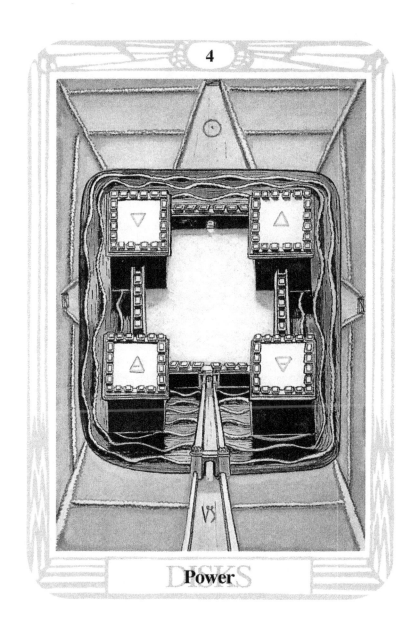

Power

If you recognize these issues and use this potential for a new home as a way to deepen your connection through honest acknowledgement of each other's wants, fears, and past patterns, then the decision you make can create a stronger foundation.

It is best not to compromise and hide your needs, otherwise they will seethe as resentments and surface later.

FIVES

ARCHETYPE: THE HIEROPHANT V

KABALAH: GEBURAH, SEVERITY

Fives are the position on the Tree of Life that represents movement and revolutionary change. It is the most challenging number because it means taking an idea and turning the gears to set it into motion. Therefore, all the fives demand action by naming the obstacle or inertia blocking movement.

The energy is unstable so there is a need to make constant adjustments to stay on course. Mars is unpredictable but determined and must traverse the path ruled by Venus in Major Arcana VIII, called Adjustment or Justice. When the combination of Mars and Venus is at its height, loving, courageous action is called for. May it be so!

Five of Swords
Astrological Aspect: Venus in Aquarius

Venus is weakened in the sign of Aquarius; she has no foothold to ground her visions in reality and can become lost in fantasies.

Often when we pick this card we find ourselves indulging in ideas and dreams that feel pleasurable because they are safely out of reach of the test of time and reality. To take your dreams into manifestation could mean Defeat. As long as your ideas stay in the realm of the possible they can be embellished and indulged and the ego can feel important without having to actually do anything at all.

Some people live their whole lives talking a good game about what could be and miss the gift of learning the lessons of growth that come from actually trying to make them real.

It is not the victory or defeat that make us great but the willingness to try. The process never ends; there is no final defeat or victory, only the joy of diving in and learning to swim. You will be glad you did!

In the realm of relationship, the Five of Swords suggests we need to go past the threshold of fear and risk vulnerability, but the mind is quick to detect signs that are often misinterpreted as rejection. It is important not to make assumptions too quickly, so try to stay open. The heart knows that to become soft and receptive is risky. But it's the only path to intimacy, so the mind's protective measures must be held in check. Say an aspiration to yourself such as, "May I stay open and trust in the power of love to remove obstacles."

Try to stay present and breathe. If you are concerned about something, wait until you are calm to address the situation with the one you are attracted to.

I remember a comedian once saying, "This is love: Here's my heart, here's a knife, please don't kill me!"

All love relationships must and will have pain involved and it is often the moments that hurt the most that take us deeper.

Concerning career, this card signifies our fear of failure because others might be better than we are. If we reflect on the meta-level accessed through the Aquarian Star card, we are reminded that each of us has a unique way to express ourself in any field of endeavor.

5

SWORDS **Defeat**

Instead of succumbing to the unconscious fear of inferiority, focus on what is unique about your approach and be reassured that no one else but you can bring your gift to the world. Once my friend Jill came to my house just before she was going to sign a lease on a storefront to open a business called "Milk and Honey." At first it was disturbing for her to see the card called Defeat but then we considered that she would not really be competing with others because there wasn't another women-centered, goddess-based store in the whole county, and fives always come up when you are about to take a risk into something new.

She did not allow superstition to sway her but held to the deeper meaning of offering her unique gift and went ahead and signed the lease. Her store was very successful and unique.

Shadow

In relationships, we often secretly withdraw without admitting it to our beloved, but energetically others feel our retreat. We will go so far as to say nothing is wrong even when asked, "Are you okay?"

Ironically, since so much of our communication is actually non-verbal, this unspoken defense mechanism may eventually cause the very result that is most feared—loss of love and attention.

At this point it is valuable to practice transparency. Answer by admitting your fear. "Usually when I feel like this I just run away, but I care so much about you that I don't want to repeat this same pattern over and over again."

If the person truly cares about you, your willingness to be vulnerable will touch him or her deeply and open both of you to the next level.

Five of Wands
Astrological Aspect: Saturn in Leo

In the image we see the harsh rule of Saturn has weakened the fiery, passionate power wands of Isis and Osiris, the divine couple of Egyptian mythology. The immature aspects of the child Horus are limiting the natural freewheeling spark of Leo.

In the realm of sexuality, old patterns of stimulation, probably from adolescence, have reasserted themselves. The initial chemistry that appeared to be fresh has devolved into boring patterns. Now, repetition of what is known to "work" to bring climax, dominates.

It is time to open the space for imaginative role play, conversations, and surprises that actually reveal the naked beauty of the participants. This will lighten up and refresh the relationship through discovering one another again. Instead of mutual masturbation, allowing the vulnerable expressions of fantasy can bring true intimacy back.

The Saturn influence implies that time and money pressures have usurped the realm of pleasure. This can stem from being a workaholic or fear of intimacy itself.

In the realm of work, a certain drudgery and boredom has crept in. It's definitely time to brainstorm ways that will awaken inspiration.

If this is tried to no avail, or the work situation is too rigid and there is no opening for change, then start exploring other options.

All the fives, and Saturn as well, tend to put pressure on us from the negative, asking us to consider how much more we can take until we break free.

Remember, Leo is the sign of courage and leadership, and to enhance these qualities you need to use the discipline of Saturn to make your own structures that, by their very nature, encourage creative growth to manifest.

The concept of drudgery may also be rooted in generational beliefs passed down through our family that tell us work is not supposed to be meaningful, creative, or fun.

If this is the case, it might be time to review these old stories and, without blame, become aware of your upbringing and see the pressures that forced these beliefs on your parents as well.

Shadow

Sometimes we wait until our body is screaming for help before we heed Saturn's message. Since Saturn is connected to bone structure, an aching back or other physical difficulties may be the only way to get us to finally surrender to change. In the modern world this can be connected to carpal tunnel syndrome or any repetitive motion that is not balanced with purpose and restorative movement.

The highest aspect of Saturn is shown in The Universe card, where a woman dances freely with her own life force, represented in this card by the passion of Leo.

5

WANDS **Strife**

Five of Cups
Astrological Aspect: Mars in Scorpio

There is something very striking about this intense image; can you see what's missing? It's the only card in the suit of water in which there is no water.

The reactive and angry aspect of Mars has completely evaporated all the waters in the deep Scorpio well; the pentagram is inverted, symbolizing the victory of matter over spirit. Mars is on the warpath, gathering all his past heartaches and using them to prove once again that love is false and can't be trusted.

What are you to do? If a moment of reflection is allowed, you will find that it is actually the desperate need for giving and receiving love that has sent you into a downward spiral. Instead of lashing out and escalating the situation, it is time to realize that pain and hurt feelings need tenderness and clarity to be healed.

This card is like the point in all those Hollywood love stories when the inevitable conflict arises. We have seen the protagonist fall in love in the preceding Cups cards: birds are singing, the whole world seems to have offered itself. Then a lie is exposed, or someone misinterprets a situation as unfaithfulness. You know the story; we've seen it a thousand times. It is really the point at which vulnerability is at its height precisely because we have completely given ourselves over to love. Now the ego, fearing pain and hating itself for trusting once again, has found a way to prove love wrong.

Are you willing to sit in the fire and stay present to find out what's really going on or will you run, strike back, give up? All these options and many more are told in the great love stories of the world.

When we watch them in a movie or read them in a novel, we can hardly wait to see how our lovers find their way back to each other. In real life they don't always live happily ever after, but always there's a chance to grow and deepen our experience of the mystery called love.

A hidden aspect of this story is that often love tests our integrity and it may not just be in the relationship arena either. Love has a way of exposing our contradictions in all aspects of our lives.

Love often exposes and heals prejudice or injustice, overcomes obstacles, and gives us the courage to become truly great in ways we could

Disappointment

not have imagined without the urgency of our desire to be with our beloved or save her or protect him.

Love is the evolutionary awakening force in all our lives and when this card shows up you are close to a truth that will profoundly change your life. Whether you are reunited with your loved one or you must move on, remember the greatest aspect of the warrior is the courage to see things through. Don't let your Mars yang energy stay steamed up too long or you may have deep regrets that will take a lot of forgiveness to heal.

Shadow

When you get this card, it's time to look in the mirror and with the tenderness of a caring mother listen to yourself and try to uncover the source of your intense reactions. Otherwise you will just be feeding the demon of your own loneliness while blaming others for everything that hurts you.

When anger at the lack of love takes over, its potential for danger, violence, and pain truly knows no limits.

Many people believe that humans are just innately cruel, but I would argue that it is actually our softness, vulnerability, and need to be loved that is our essential nature.

Violence and cruelty do not come out of nowhere. They are born of abuse and pain that can easily be traced through an individual's personal history. One of Scorpio's strongest shadows is its inability to let go of past offenses. It's like being a human time bomb just waiting for the next event that will trigger the memories of pain that simmer just below the surface.

Our jails are full of hurt little children who were not loved and cared for and grew up destined to repeat the patterns of violence and abuse that were inflicted on them.

To end this cycle, punishment is futile. All living beings respond to love and respect. The encouragement to find purpose and fulfillment in life can be awakened only through this approach to rehabilitation.

We are usually unaware that the disappointment in a current relationship can trigger all the old, painful memories. Thus the situation gets blown way out of proportion. The person you love may feel blamed for everything that has happened to you in the past that hurt you.

Another aspect of this card is the unconscious tendency to make possessions more important than caring, symbolized by the inverted pentagram. For example, a workaholic father who spends his whole life earning money to buy the best for his family cannot understand when his loved ones don't appreciate him and actually feel he is not there for them.

Money cannot substitute for engaged interest and participation.

Five of Disks
Astrological Aspect: Mercury in Taurus

This card is called Worry in the Thoth deck. A wise woman named Sedonia Cahill once said that worrying is praying for what you don't want to happen. This simple truth will help you get a grip when you are overwhelmed with worry.

As Mark Twain so aptly stated, "My life has been filled with terrible misfortunes, most of which never happened." Instead of letting your mind endlessly imagine all the possible disasters that could be unfolding, send out a positive aspiration.

For example: "May I trust my daughter to find her way through her present challenges." "May my friend who has cancer find the courage he needs to face his fears and find a way to heal." Intention, prayer and ritual are ways to transform worries into waves of love that can cross all barriers of time and space.

Mercury, our great communicator, stimulated by our fears, has tricked us into letting our mind research and present all the bad outcomes it can remember from similar past experiences. What Mercury is really seeking is to be re-inspired and released from the stubborn inertia aspect of Taurus.

When this card is related to work, it means you are bored and stuck. This calls for a re-invocation of purpose. This can happen by learning something new about your work or talking with your fellow workers to find a way to bring purpose and shared vision back to the environment.

This can also be accomplished through bringing in a trained facilitator or taking a class at the local community college.

If you are certain that there is no worthwhile way to shift the energy in the workplace, then it's time you considered finding other work.

This card frequently appears when we have been in a job for a long time and are too lazy or stubborn to recognize the need to change. What is familiar feels safe even when it's boring. Use the determined Taurus energy to learn something new instead of digging in your heels.

Shadow

The shadow aspect of this card seeks to blame outside forces. Why is life so boring? Why doesn't anything exciting ever happen to me? These are questions the ego asks when it doesn't want to face the harder question of how it can change the current circumstances. When we are uninspired, the mind often fills the void with worries. This can happen to parents during the empty nest syndrome. Instead of finding new activities, the parent stays fixated on the child's life in worrisome and unhelpful ways.

5

Worry

SIXES
ARCHETYPE: THE LOVERS VI
KABALA: TIPHERETH, BEAUTY

Six holds the central position on the Tree of Life, representing the radiating solar energy of harmony, peace, and beauty. After moving through the difficult challenges of the fives, we have arrived at a conscious awareness of the creative process that originally emanated from Kether the number one position on the Tree of Life.

On the Tree, the six is a reflection of the one, but now we have gone through the stages of manifestation that bring us to an understanding of how creation happens.

Six is universally a harmonious number as shown in the yantra of the east, an image of ascending and descending triangles. It is used as a mandala or meditative tool to bring clarity and peace.

The symbol of an ascending triangle represents fire and a descending triangle, water, echoing the mixing of fire and water in the hands of the alchemist in the Major, Art XIV.

The Merkaba, also called the Star of David, is yet another example of the deep resonance this symbolizes in so many cultures. Merkaba, loosely translated, means the chariot of the light body.

In nature we find the hexagon as the basic building block of our friends and allies in the bee world.

Six is therefore a number of integration and wholeness, not hierarchy.

Six of Swords
Astrological Aspect: Mercury in Aquarius

The name of this card is Science and it represents a new interpretation of that word. Mercury has discovered a holistic approach to the study and understanding of life by being placed in relation to the visionary sign of Aquarius, representing the application of loving intelligence.

This new science offers us a release from the narrow, isolated, and sterile world of the laboratory and opens the way to apply our heart/mind to seeing the interrelatedness of all life. The fields of deep ecology and bio-mimicry are being born in this time to pull science out of the lab and into a compassionate relationship with our Mother Earth.

Mind, heart, and body need to be centered like the six swords pointing to the central rose and cross. If you look closely, you will also see a circle contained in a square.

Although some may see the cross as religious in its significance, the deeper meaning is that the cross, folded up, becomes a cube holding the unfolding rose of the natural world. This signifies that our man-made structures and concepts are ethical when the rose of life is still at the core of our values.

Outside is the chaos of mind, sharp-edged and cruel, randomly thrusting ideas forth without regard for the heart or the effects these ideas have on life.

Aquarius is also the sign of electric energy and, therefore, technology. If you are working in the field of science and technology it would be beneficial to ask if what you are doing is serving the world. Are you in your integrity? Are the results of your work doing harm to the web of life?

Since Mercury and his caduceus symbolize the medical world, this card also represents healing.

If you are a nurse or doctor you may want to expand your approach by learning about integrated medicine that focuses on wellness and preventive medicine as opposed to the treating of symptoms.

In some parts of China, you have regular checkups and pay the doctor when you are well. He takes no pay when you are sick!

6

SWORDS **Science**

If you are suffering from illness, it is time to consider healing all levels of your being and trying to understand the underlying causes and lessons. Disease is a great teacher and love is the greatest healer, but too often, especially in Western medicine, all the focus is on the symptom, not the cause.

Other modalities to be considered include spiritual and psychological counseling, energy work, massage, exercise, and a healthy and pleasurable diet. Going into the natural world of trees and sky and sea are also deeply healing. Studies show that tree hugging actually boosts your immune system.

In the realm of relationships this card calls you to consider whether or not you are acting in an ethical way. It often appears when we are being manipulative, deceptive, or unfaithful.

Are you acting out of love or possessiveness? Are you deciding what is best for your loved ones without considering how they might feel?

The mind is a beautiful and creative tool when it is grounded in love and not on fixed agendas of right and wrong. Try being in the other person's place before making plans to fix things the way you think will be best for everyone.

Shadow

Science has become a god that supersedes and overrules all other approaches to understanding situations and solutions. Be careful or your mind may become a weapon instead of a tool.

Have you become so isolated in your work that you have lost touch with what effects your work is having on other life forms or environments?

If you are ill, have you become angry with your body and judgmental of yourself and others, blaming, instead of claiming your innate power to heal and forgive?

Many parents and communities have lost the courage and integrity to guide their children in the use of all the new technologies that we are being bombarded with. These products have come out into the world without any discussion or guidelines beforehand. Time to have a parent circle and see if you can find ways to help your children deal with this onslaught.

A PRAYER FOR OUR CHILDREN

I pray we will let our young ones
lie in tall grass completely serene,
Free to dream of adventures beyond the machines.

Now I walk through hallways of houses
that used to be homes,
And see that our young ones are sitting alone,

In darkened rooms with curtains drawn,
yawning and pale and glued to the screen
Playing a game called Death by Degrees.

They do not see me or their mother at all;
not even a nod, a smile, or hello.
Just a sideways glance that says please go!

Do we know what they're feeling?
Do we know what they want?
Do we have any power to turn this around?

Beep, Click, Ringtone, Alarm;
The language of linear wiring and sound,
Techno babies, techno girls and boys
Where is the music in all this noise?

By Magick

Six of Wands
Astrological Aspect: Jupiter in Leo

Bursting with energy, light, and power, this card says you're on your way! Jupiter has been your teacher and trainer and now you are rewarded with a sense of accomplishment, victory, and independence!

The six wands are topped with the symbols for Isis, Osiris, and Horus. The Isis rose is for love and birth, phoenix for regeneration and the winged orb of Horus to take flight into the world. They represent the skills in these arenas that you have mastered thus far in your life.

All your powers are active and you burn with the light of passionate enthusiasm. This card is very similar to the Major card, The Sun.

Inwardly there is a sense of freedom and aliveness that brings honor, pleasure and financial reward from without. Jupiter is proud of his excellent student and will offer you more opportunities to share and show your gifts to the world.

This is a great card to receive when you are engaged in sports events or other competitive situations. Just remember, it is your passion for what you do and your need to share it that will give grace and longevity to your work. The word compete, comes from the Latin, com, with and pete, strive; so to strive together makes everyone greater. Keep your ego in check when it seeks to have victory just to win or to seek revenge. Jupiter's offerings may suddenly evaporate because you will have lost the core purpose of your pursuit.

For young adults, this indicates a time to let go of dependency and realize that standing on your own, even though challenging and often difficult, lets you shine as an individual, out of the shadow of your parents and their influence.

All of us are interdependent but we must learn to carry our own weight and often take on the mantle of leadership so others can depend on us. For women, it is time to feel good about yourself even if you are not in a relationship. Own and honor yourself for being self-sufficient. Maybe it is time to buy that house you always wanted and stop waiting for a man to do it for you. Then you might

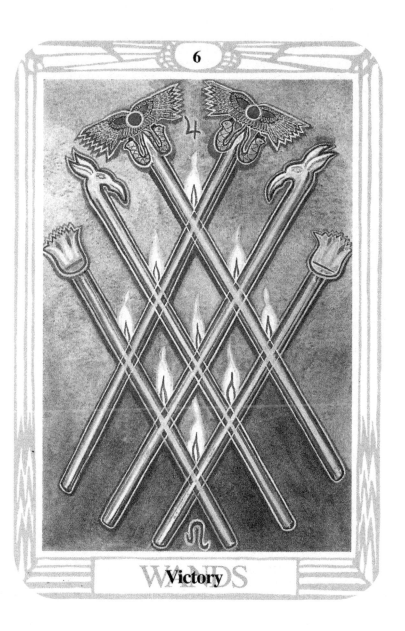

Victory

attract someone who can be your equal in relationship, instead of someone whose role is to provide for you.

It is a great card for starting your own business or becoming an independent consultant. Leo is calling on you to have courage and let your wild mane fly in the wind! It is a time to be the leader of you, or of many; the field is wide open.

On the physical plane, your sexual energy is free, open, and rising. Let yourself express this ecstasy and it will feed all aspects of your life. Go to the local sensuality shop for a treat or buy an erotic book and some body lotion you love and touch, touch, touch!

Shadow

You are stuck in a feeling of dependence and fear and can't find your inner passion. Everyone else seems to have all of Jupiter's luck and you are secretly jealous and feel inferior.

Try doing simple things you love to awaken your childlike playfulness.

For now, don't try to figure out what you need to change in a big way. Do something daring and cutting edge, it will bring you completely into the present moment.

Be careful not to judge yourself in relation to others. Get into your body and let those juices flow; deeper inspirations will be released by these small acts. Trust.

Whether solo or with someone, your body deserves to be heard. This is no time to wallow in self-pity if you can't feel your libido. Love yourself in simple ways, like taking a sensual bath, getting a massage, or just taking the time to hug yourself and give yourself appreciation.

Six of Cups
Astrological Aspect: Sun in Scorpio

In the Five of Cups, you hit the rocky bottom of the Scorpion sea. Now it is time to push off from there to soar up higher than before. You have dared to face disappointment, anger, and fear, to swim more deeply in the waters of love. Now pleasures that you didn't know were possible are bubbling to the surface.

The shadows in the Scorpion's cave, when exposed to the sunlight, vanish. The heart becomes light and joyous. Now the initial feeling of falling in love is renewed and has more power to endure. Bridges of communication have been built that can be traversed when difficulties arise in the future.

The more we are willing to shed light (Sun) on problems, to take a deep breath and not give in to our fears, the more we can experience the joy of lasting relationships.

A level of maturity has been reached that in the end is more gratifying than looking for the next big flash of love (Two of Cups) or the luxury of an unstable illusion (Four of Cups).

We can also feel more comfortable in exploring the mystery when we trust the hand we hold.

If you are not in a relationship at present, it means you have looked closely at your history and now know how to enter into love with your eyes open. Now you have a briefcase of lessons learned instead of carrying heavy baggage that's just waiting to be unpacked the next time love comes calling. Now, more than ever, you know what you truly need to have healthy interactions and you are ready to invite the next experience. You are confident in your ability to maintain your inner equilibrium.

Within the family it is time to forego problems and practical concerns and take time to enjoy the love that underlies these lifelong bonds.

In terms of work, try to be more kind and cooperative with your fellow workers by bringing empathy into the environment. It is a time to listen and reflect so that you can mirror the best of what others have to offer.

Shadow

You are carrying an underlying cynicism about your ability to experience love. Time to seek out a therapist who can help you understand the source of this lack of faith.

Today there are also somatic therapists who help you listen to what your body has to say about what hurts, what helps, and what you carry from the past.

It is also a good time to notice what your body is telling you about interactions with different people and social situations.

When your stomach aches or your chest feels restricted, your body is trying to tell you what is going on. The body always lives in the present moment and it doesn't lie.

In the family and the workplace, the suit of Cups is always about feelings; but be careful not to slip into gossiping and undermining others.

Pleasure

Six of Disks
Astrological Aspect: Moon in Taurus

Lady Frieda Harris, the artist of the Thoth deck, created such a unique glow in the center of this card that just meditating on it brings lightness and serenity to the viewer.

Take a moment and experience the opening of the lotus and the many layers and circles as the unfolding of your own higher consciousness in the crown chakra (top of the head). Now breathe in this light and ask yourself what dream (Moon) you want to experience next in the physical world (Taurus).

This card is called Success, but it is not about resting on your laurels. In fact, it is calling you to take the next journey of initiation into unknown areas that will enhance your life path and career.

This can be done through education, travel, writing, or devising a new discipline or method to your work.

In each of the orbs is a planetary influence so you have all the help you need to move forward. These influences may take the form of knowledgeable and helpful people in your life or different aspects of yourself.

Mars = courage, determination
Saturn = discipline, thoroughness
Jupiter = opportunity, luck
Venus = love of work, service
Moon = instincts, imagination
Mercury = inspiration, synchronicity

Look to the other cards surrounding the six and their planetary influences for what is propitious in the moment or the near future. These allies and opportunities come and go, so it is best to not wait when success calls you out.

One thing is definite. Taurus, the bull, wants you to work with all your might to bring the next level of expertise and accomplishment into your life.

The Moon offers an initiatory process that may be fraught with challenges but she is exalted in Taurus, which means she gives pleasure and insight to those who risk going beyond their comfort zone

6

DISKS **Success**

to keep growing. After all, Taurus is the garden party of the zodiac, so feast on all levels—mind, heart, body, and soul.

All the sixes are good omens and this one offers visible results in the world of manifestation, especially work.

People will notice you now and reward your determination and dedication. Don't worry about making mistakes, just take them in as lessons and keep going. Fellow workers, teachers, and project managers will appreciate this as well.

Shadow

Are you feeling successful in terms of financial compensation, possessions, and position but empty inside? Taurus loves "to have" and can get lost in seeking possessions and power. Try looking at "having" on a more spiritual level by asking different kinds of questions like:

- Do I have deep purpose in my work?
- Do I have loving and meaningful relationships with the people I work with?
- Do I have peace of mind?

One shadow aspect of Taurus is stubbornness. Are you refusing to change even though your body is tired of working 70-hour weeks to get to the top?

Ask yourself what success really means. At the end of your life, how do you imagine you will define success for yourself?

SEVENS

ARCHETYPE: THE CHARIOT VII

KABALA: NETZACH, VICTORY

Seven is a number of growth. After the integration of the six there is a push to grow into the next stage of development. Seven stands at the opposite side of the five on the Tree and like the fives, is full of challenges. Here we see that only in the suit of action and spirit, called Wands, is there the power to continue on the journey.

After the difficulties in the fives there is recognition that growth is possible when there is flexibility, passion, and courage.

On a spiritual level this is an integration of the three and the four, the feminine, Empress III and the masculine, Emperor IV. It is a mystical number in many ways. It is full of the vibrations of creation manifested in the number of colors in the rainbow and the number of notes in a scale of music, restarting at the octave or eight.

Seven of Swords
Astrological Aspect: Moon in Aquarius

The influence of the Moon from its dark side is very present in this card. In fact, all the planets that were aiding us in the Six of Disks are now showing their shadow.

Hesitating to act on the original impulse of the Ace and work things out as you go along has lead to the ego/mind insinuating itself into the plan. Now all the fears of the past are gathering and chipping away at the central sword that was glowing and radiant before.

Take the Ace of Swords out of the deck and remember the central truth, plan, or vision that you are trying to keep in focus.

Looking at the Six of Swords as well will help you find the strength of your convictions.

On the Tree of Life the combination of one, six, and seven is a powerful vision of new growth that combines the initiatory pathways of the Priestess and Death. The unknown cannot be avoided but it can be encountered with courage, wisdom, and curiosity.

In the Six, the disturbing and sharp edges have been held in the background by the integrity and wholeness of the circle in a square. Now they have snuck in again and are like nightmare monsters that appear larger than life.

This card often appears when we have succumbed to the late-night worries that create insomnia. If that is the case it is important to prepare for sleep in a peaceful way.

Make a cup of chamomile tea or turmeric and warm milk and sip it while listening to some nature, chanting, or meditative music. Or just sit in silence and follow your breath. When the negative thoughts begin to gather like dark clouds, ask yourself two questions. Do I actually know that what I am concerned about is true? Is there anything I can do about it now?

Almost always the answer is no to both questions.

If this logical approach doesn't work for you, write out an aspiration and read it and repeat it many times until it becomes a mantra in your mind. Example: "May all obstacles be removed on my new path."

When you compose aspirations, it is important to read them over a few times and see if they flow easily. If your mind sticks on certain

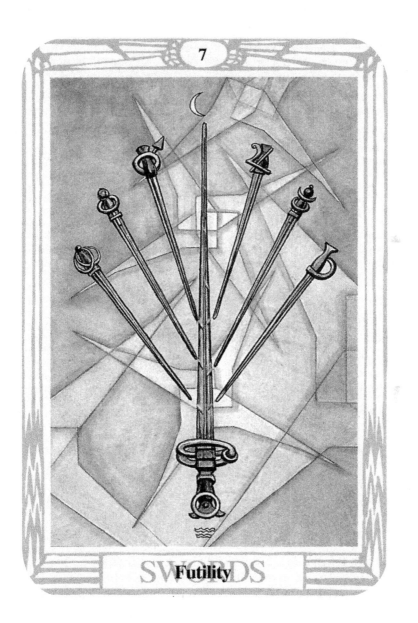

7

SWORDS

Futility

words, try again and simplify if necessary.

As a poet, I have discovered that when I read something out loud I can feel if it works.

If you respond to sensory stimulation better, use aromatherapy with a sachet or incense; or put a few drops of your favorite calming essential oil in the water of your diffuser.

Ask yourself to dream about the positive unfolding of your vision just before you go to sleep.

If necessary, take some Valerian and let the earthy taste of this magical root drop you down into the arms of Mother Earth.

When we wait too long to move ideas out of the suit of Swords into the motion of fire and water, the mind becomes its own worst enemy and starts sending up validation for our unconscious fears in the guise of logic. Do not be fooled!

All things are possible. In the light of day, these thoughts will scatter and clarity will return.

Futility is really just giving up and has nothing to do with what the challenges or obstacles are. Even if all the negative things you can imagine do present themselves, then they are the problems you need to solve to complete the project and grow as an innovative problem solver.

Every shadow has its true form that it follows around. The Moon and all those planets will once again give you the gifts you need if you don't give up. The following paragraph incorporates all the planets that appear on the swords:

Expanding opportunities abound to bring your dream into reality. Have the courage to send your message out and be ready to share your passion and determination to make it real.

Jupiter = Expanding opportunities
Neptune = dream
Mars = courage
Mercury = message
Venus = passion
Saturn = determination

They say that every poison has its antidote nearby; inherent in every problem is the solution. So it is in the yin/yang world of shadow and light.

"Have you ever seen your mother, baby, standing in the shadow?" is a line from an old Rolling Stones song. Sometimes our mom is a sexy, mature woman, not a just a nurturer. Shadow dancing can bring out our sensual side and get us out of our minds.

The caring Mother Earth aspect of yourself will dance without fear, patiently waiting for you to accept her skills in birthing ideas. For it is She who knows all light is born in the dark of the womb.

Keep breathing, keep dancing, keep dreaming. Futility itself is an illusion. Pull in Leo, the complementary sign of Aquarius who is the mama lioness; let her tend your visions and dreams. Teaching you, like a cub, how to fight for your nourishment and how to hunt down your dreams, playfully and with humor.

Shadow

"Nothing matters." "I always fail at everything I try." "It's no use, why even bother?" These negative reinforcements do actually set up roadblocks on our path through life.

The fearful mind left to wander on its own can take us on detours and into dangerous places. Remember times when you refused to ask for directions even though you didn't really know where you were going?

Directions and aid are always available within us or in the world. The Tarot itself is such a map. Quiet yourself and guidance will come.

Note: Neptune, Venus, Mars, Jupiter, Mercury, Saturn are the symbols on the hilts of the swords.

Seven of Wands
Astrological Aspect: Mars in Leo

The message in the card is extremely important for the times we are living in. Mars in his destructive, dominant, and violent aspect is wreaking havoc all over the planet. The Seven of Wands offers suggestions about how each of us can help the ethical Mars aspect of ourselves wake up and be of service to the world. Together we can reclaim the glory of the Martian archetype. It will not help to try to defeat the greatest warrior of all. Remember, you cannot dismantle the master's house with the master's tools.

We need to open a new field of action to this tired and tyrannical god.

All of us need the drive and determination of Mars as well as the courage to face all of the challenges of life.

Mars, after all, rules the birthing sign of Aries and the dying sign of Scorpio. He has the undaunted fierceness to face these twin towers at the borders of existence. The evolved Mars will never give up because he is in service to the heart, his Venus.

Life without Mars would be life without adventure, discovery, valor, and the strength and resourcefulness to create, invent, and accomplish great feats.

Making friends with the evolving persona of the hero is the path to discovering the shamanic warrior that has always existed throughout time. He is not ruled nor is he a ruler. Since this card is designated Mars in Leo, another aspect of leadership is emphasized. Leo is the big-hearted, dramatic, and powerful sign of courage. The combination is dynamite! When Mars hears the passionate call of his lion heart he uses all his skills and tools to tackle the task at hand.

The six wands of power in this card represent all those tools we already have. We have used these wands to achieve the victory of the six, but all the sevens demand that we keep going and keep growing.

The seventh wand calls us to create new tools that are needed to meet the challenges of today.

Will we lay down our sword and shield and create a new relationship to power?

Valour

Or will we perish by repeating the patterns of the past where revenge and greedy wars were respected, honored, and rewarded?

Each of us must make this choice. When you receive this card in a reading it is time to burn with the fiery passion of your purpose in this life. Go with all your might to clear the field of action that will allow you to present your highest self and your highest gift. Give it now to this world that aches for the authentic warrior. Be courageous and peaceful, brilliant and humble and use your intelligence in service to the heart.

You already have six wands of power but how will you shape the seventh that can take you beyond your limitations? If visceral reminders work best for you, then find a wooden branch like the one shown in the card and create your own wand of power that can be used as a walking stick or a ritual tool, or both. You can use beads, leather, feathers and/or carve into the actual wood. Just make it your own.

The lion, tiger, and all cats, implied by the Leo influence, are never meant to be tamed and controlled. To break the spirit of the wildcat is tragic and heartbreaking as you can see in the face of animals in our zoos and circuses.

Have you tamed the wild cat in yourself to the point that it has forgotten what it feels like to be free? Have you forgotten the thrill of pursuit?

Of all the sevens, this is the only one that gives us a way through; all the others show us the obstacles, temptations, and pitfalls.

Shadow

Your ego has gotten the best of you and you are no longer asking what is right. Power is an end in itself and conquest is your greatest thrill.

In your worst aspect, violence can bring a rush of adrenalin that can become addictive.

Most of us don't go that far, but when we play with the lust for power, the potential for such extreme behavior lies dangerously close to the surface.

Ask yourself: Are you reacting without thinking? Are you starting to believe your own lies, thinking that you know better than anyone and that might makes right?

We all have within us the tendency to fight, even physically, when threatened, insulted, or angry. It takes real valor to take a deep breath and ask how to use your power for the highest good of all, and that includes your "enemy."

Seven of Cups
Astrological Aspect: Venus in Scorpio

It is said that Venus loses her dignity in Scorpio. The goddess of Love becomes objectified and used only for the fleeting pleasures she can bring. When we do not love ourselves, we treat our body as a set of orifices that is meant to gratify our every whim. This will only pull us deeper into the stagnant, unhealthy swamp of addiction. In this paradigm other people and, in fact, the entire world, become only a resource for our reckless, selfish desires. My Indian teacher, Ciranjiva, wrote in a poem, "Desire moments fetter time through space, path blazed by desires in flame, journey awakes to its joyous game, guided in darkness, now in light, motion becomes its own delight!"

This does not mean that we have to deny the pleasures of this world. In fact quite the opposite, when motion becomes its own delight, every meal, every sensation, is just another joyous experience of an embodied, conscious being in this beautiful and mysterious world.

Sadly, the pursuit of pleasure to fill a void can never fully satisfy. Love, as represented by Venus, is not a temporary sensation to soothe our loneliness.

Love is the experience of oneness, wholeness, and compassion that reminds us of the interconnectedness of all life. Love is joyous because we can lose our lonely, personal hell by surrendering our demanding needs and sacrificing our ego on this most sacred altar.

We truly love when we are overcome by awe, gratitude, and appreciation for ourselves, other humans, and other life forms of the sea, the sky, and the earth. Unconditional love is an aspiration we will work on our whole lives and some of the qualities are desire for the beloved's happiness and wellbeing, gratitude, and non-attachment. To place the beloved's happiness and free will above what we want is a truly enlightened act.

All of us possess the shadow of addiction, but when it possesses us we have lost the will to be a loving servant for the betterment of our community. We are now a parasite and our disease cannot be cured until we go inward and discover what is truly lacking.

A unique aspect of this card is that it shows up in almost all teenage girls' readings.

To give Scorpio a break, it must be said that all teenagers want to explore the mystery of sexuality, as exemplified by this sign, and it is a force of nature that can be ecstatic. Sex can charge our whole being with the essential life force that is often referred to as kundalini or chi. But it is a sad commentary on our society that most young women end up experiencing their introduction to sex in ways that are demeaning and painful. It can take years or even a lifetime to heal.

If you are a young woman and this card comes up in a reading, ask for guidance from your parents or other family members. If there is abuse in your family, seek out peer groups, mentors, Planned Parenthood, or counseling that will help you learn how to stay in your power while creating safe and conscious ways to enjoy the newly discovered pleasures of your amazing body.

Peer pressure to do things you do not want to do, or are not ready for, is hard to resist, but the irony is that social cliques push you over the edge and once you've fallen you are alone, scared, and hurt.

If you are a young man and get this card in a reading, I suggest you do the same. Although boys are told not to admit it, sexual encounters that are unconsciously enacted under the influence of drugs and alcohol cause scars in your psyche as well. Nothing superficial and ego-centered will satisfy your aching heart. Whether you are the oppressed or the oppressor, you are still devoid of the joy of consensual, respectful, and knowledgeable sexual exploration.

Shadow

There is a lack of awareness that what you need is hidden in your heart. You have chosen to use other means for temporary gratification such as shopping, alcohol, drugs, pornography, video games, the Internet, TV, and unhealthy foods.

Addiction can take a myriad of forms. Although positive in nature, even work, the gym, or reading can become a way to avoid your soul's desire.

If you are suffering from this disease, this lack of ease, it is time to explore ways to love yourself and find healthy forms of self-expression.

If you are dealing with a loved one who is in denial, an intervention may be necessary. It is worth it to try to break through, although it is also important to know when you have done all you can externally. Then it is time to just hold a space in your heart for that person to change on her/his own, send them loving intentions and release your judgments. It is called letting go, and letting love. The Scorpio Major Arcana, called Death, is also called Letting Go in some decks. We have many chances to experience its benefits before the final release of physical death itself.

CUPS

Debauch

Seven of Disks
Astrological Aspect: Saturn in Taurus

Since the card is called Failure and the image is somewhat depressing, the initial response is usually negative. Alexandra Genetti, the creator of the colorful and richly pagan deck, The Wheel of Change Tarot, finds the naming of the Minors upsetting and she uses her magic marker and just crosses them out. I can certainly respect that approach.

Sometimes these names can be very limiting but I have also gleaned much meaning from these labels.

This dark image following on the heels of success makes us wonder what went wrong.

Did we fail to actually heed the advice of the six and go deeper on our journey and now we are paying the piper? Was it time to leave that line of work completely and we just made some superficial changes? Did the stubborn attachment to material reward hold us prisoner?

Or is it something further under the surface like our early training that pleasing others is the only way to feel a sense of accomplishment?

It is key to remember that even negative images are meant to show us the way out. Right or wrong, good or bad judgments don't change anything so we need to ask, what is really going on here?

The coins in the image do not feel like any kind of reward since they are held in a spider-like web, meaning we could get trapped trying to extricate them. The unusual black background and lack of any light shows us what happens when inspiration has flown the coop and only the stubbornness and greed of Taurus and the demands of others, signified by Saturn, keep us pushing along.

In the Book of Thoth it says that the seven Disks represent the bottom seven sephiroth on the Tree of Life. This means we have lost connection with one, two and three that represented the original inspiration, the yang wisdom, and the yin understanding, respectively. Now we are only submitting to the demands of our boss, the public's image of us, or the need for financial reward.

Failure does not have to mean we are inept. In fact, it often is the slave driver or the overachiever who receives this card. This is usually rooted in an early experience of being programmed to perform

7

Failure

for family or in school by doing what pleases others.

The converse meaning of this card is that we have felt invisible in school or at home. We have been given the message we are stupid or a troublemaker with no potential.

The Major Arcana of the sign of Taurus is often called the Teacher. But teachers can be compassionate and inspiring, or judgmental and hurtful. Young and developing minds are profoundly shaped by the mentors they encounter.

If you have had this experience in your upbringing, now is the time to heal. Find a class in something you have always wanted to learn about and then promise your inner child that if the teacher is not respectful, inspiring, and kind to you, you will leave on the spot. Your inner child has probably decided to never go into a classroom again, but as an adult you can leave if you want to. Your younger self does not know there is freedom to choose.

All of us want to keep learning all our lives so take a class in surfing, or hieroglyphics, knitting, or astronomy. Just learn about what you love in a healthy environment and new worlds will unfold before you. This is your chance to embark on a journey of defining your own education and releasing the tyranny of the "should" voice from your upbringing.

Although this card usually deals with work, it does show up frequently, especially for women, around "failed" relationships.

In our culture women are much more defined by their relationships. When it is time to leave a marriage, it is often the fear of having failed, combined with the fear of being judged as a failure, that keeps women entrenched in negative or abusive situations.

You are not your relationships and when you are unhappy, and nothing has worked to change that, true success comes when you have the courage to move on. If there are children involved they need to see happy, self-actualized parents, whether they are together or apart.

To some people, the card looks like owl eyes or spider webs. Both of these totems represent the wise woman in each of us. You would do well to heed her voice and ask what truly holds your spider web together and what owl dreams you have let fall by the wayside.

Shadow

There is a loss of purpose and a sense that pressure from without is ever-present. You can't even remember how you got to this place in your life and it seems as though there is no way out. As Ricky Nelson sang in his song, The Garden Party, "Ya can't please everyone, so you got to please yourself."

EIGHTS
ARCHETYPE: ADJUSTMENT / JUSTICE VIII
KABALA: HOD, SPLENDOR

Now that we have moved through the growth of the sevens, and Mars has dared and succeeded, we come to the eights and are ready to power on, inspired and activated by Mercury, the Messenger (the planet that rules this sephira). The path of Mars, The Tower, connects seven and eight. So if we don't get stuck building castles in the sand, we will have blasted through limitations and will be on the path of success.

Mercury is ready to tell everyone inspirational news and will not let us wallow in old stories. Eight is also a number of balance that is achieved by fine tuning and re-adjusting to circumstances to stay in our center.

Turned on its side, eight becomes the lemniscate, the symbol of infinity, reminding us that all life is interconnected and ever-changing. The lemniscate is traditionally shown on the hat of The Magician, the Major Arcana Mercury card.

Eight of Swords
Astrological Aspect: Jupiter in Gemini

As with the Seven, we see mental chaos in the background. Two large swords are pointed downwards, suggesting they are ineffectual. There are six other swords trapped behind them.

There is a total lack of clarity and focus, but ironically, life feels full and rife with options.

The mind is divided and possibilities come to the fore and recede from one minute to the next.

It is like a board of directors in your mind, with all the voices chattering away and bickering about what is best for you. They probably include your parents, siblings, teachers, employer, friends, and competitors who have taken over your ability to know what is right for you.

The ego is searching for the next opportunity to show them all how great you are. Right now you are very vulnerable to these influences that are in your mind, as well as those manifesting in schemes from external forces.

Time to regroup. One of the simplest ways to do this is, first of all, to avoid all major decisions right now and try to find your own rhythm again in your daily life.

Jupiter is playing the trickster, throwing all kinds of possibilities your way, and roaming in the house of Gemini. From one minute to the next, any one of them can sparkle like the golden ring of success.

Try to re-establish a schedule that prioritizes what you already know is important in your life, including special time just for yourself.

Notice when you are being distracted or overwhelmed by other people's demands and politely but firmly get back on track.

Otherwise you are like a moon that has lost its orbit around its planet. Your "moon" dreams need to be reconnected to your real-time earth body to be able to manifest plans that are soul-driven. Time to re-establish your schedule and keep to it.

A divided and confused mind is very susceptible to influences and accidents, so it's time to get out of the whirlwind.

Often Jupiter, in the guise of family, friends, or business associates, has the best of intentions but that does not mean what they are

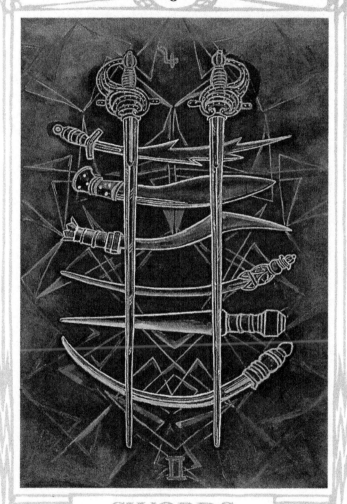

Interference

offering is what your journey is really about at this time.

Mom may offer a job at her business, a friend may suggest a trip to South America, and your employer may offer you a promotion. These are probably their well-intended ideas about what is best for you, but do they match your inner drive or not?

The meta-level of the card is called Adjustment and it's time to do just that to come back into balance. You are wobbling like a spinning top. Before you topple, stop and listen to that still small voice within.

Shadow

You are so busy there is hardly a moment to spare. It's as if you want to keep busy just to avoid looking at yourself in the mirror.

You show your love for others by running yourself ragged, but now you are starting to wonder why, especially since they expect you to continue in this pattern.

Or you want to get ahead in the world and if you could just make a fast buck then everything would fall in to place.

Be wary of investments or job options that do not match your real purpose. The quick fix is just that. Over the long term, no steps can really be avoided.

Eight of Wands
Astrological Aspect: Mercury in Sagittarius

The excitement emanating from this card is palpable. Eight lightning bolts are being sent out in all directions, full of the electricity of inspired ideas and actions.

The rainbow overhead symbolizes diversity of all kinds. It is time to explore different cultures, groups, classes, and environments with people who are dynamic and vibrant, with visions and plans for what is possible.

You are ready to be swept up in excitement, or you may actually be the one in the center, inspiring others.

Crowley says the combination of Mercury and Sagittarius creates electric dynamic speech.

It is very important to work and play in cooperation with others. Don't be afraid to be with people of different backgrounds or ways of thinking. You need to be awakened and have your horizon of possibilities broadened.

Communications can ignite positive projects that will affect your life for years to come if you can stay present.

If you are looking for work or ways to reinvent your present occupation, now is the time.

Rewrite your resume and send it out to at least eight places and don't worry about who doesn't respond. Just follow the pulse of receptivity.

Have a meeting of your fellow teammates and brainstorm about new approaches to the work at hand. Leave the inner critic at home and let new ideas bubble up. It is amazing what people will come up with when they are not inhibited by fear of rejection or judgment.

If you are an activist, or always wanted to get involved in a cause that concerns you, it will be much easier right now than you thought, and very rewarding.

If you are more shy and need to take baby steps, that's okay, too. How about taking a class at the local community college? Make sure to spend time going to some of the multicultural activities on campus, as well.

If you are in a healthy, happy relationship, share your joy with others by throwing a party or going out socially with friends. It will keep your love life full of vitality.

If you and your partner are not getting along, it's time to take the lead and start doing what you want to do. Move out into the world more. If your partner wants you, they'll just have to try to keep up! If they get lost in the dust of your fast turning wheels, that's probably what needed to happen anyway.

If you are single, consider dating someone out of your social, cultural, or racial strata.

Everything about this card says to broaden your horizons. Travel, learning, and meeting new people are all on the agenda.

Shadow

You are full of ideas, hopes, and dreams, but your fears of being judged or making mistakes are keeping you in a "safe" place.

But that safety zone is starting to feel awfully lonely and boring. Most of the time, your fear of judgment is rooted in being judged in the past and now you are the one unconsciously sitting back and judging others while life passes you by.

Or maybe you spend your time fixated on the lives of famous actors, politicians, or strong personalities in your immediate circle. A thousand times you have thought what you would do in their shoes, but it is time to take a Fool's leap of faith and test your own mettle in the world.

If you have always been afraid to speak your mind, it's a good time to take a speech class or singing lessons. If you want to finally throw caution to the wind, how about an improv class?

The willingness to learn is probably the single most enlivening thing that people can do to stay young at heart.

8

WANDS Swiftness

Eight of Cups
Astrological Aspect: Saturn in Pisces

The leaden skies of Saturn weigh heavy over the Piscean sea. We could pray for rain, thunder, a cloudburst to relieve quiet brooding; or we could just hope the dark clouds move on.

But nothing has changed for a while, and the longer this goes on, the lonelier you feel.

If you are in a relationship, this card indicates a point of comfortable stagnation, where nobody wants to rock the boat. Yet both parties know something isn't right.

Pisceans are notorious for letting things sink into malaise without wanting to admit it, even when everyone around them knows what's happening. They will still pretend all is well.

But Saturn is not going to let up until something changes. The default patterns that have developed are built on unspoken words and missed chances to say truths that could threaten to change everything. But some lightning might just crack open a place for the light to get in if we trust love enough to admit that something is amiss.

It is often more difficult to change when two people have become comfortably bored and inert, than when they are fighting and the problems are flying around.

Either way, the key is in the Hod sephira ruled by Mercury, where all the eights reside. He is the master communicator, trickster, and healer; all three are needed to awaken our lazy lovers.

Time to take a holiday, do some therapy, or have some mystery dates to spark the passion once again. A mystery date is when one person plans a surprise event and only tells their lover what they need to bring or wear; and off they go!

Usually these lovers have a good chance to dance and play again, but the energy and excitement are not going to come back magically on their own.

Effort shows caring and the willingness to become vulnerable and listen to each other to find out what's really going on. Even if the ego smarts or feelings are hurt, it's time to check in and find out when and how a lackluster routine has slipped in and become the norm.

Indolence

At this point the relationship is not really threatened. But if it's allowed to wallow too long, trouble awaits. Trying to keep things safe may be just what pushes the situation into the danger zone.

Excitement and distractions of some sort will be showing up soon, and they may take you away from the one you love, catching you unawares but vulnerable for a change that turns your lights on.

A good cry and honest grieving about your loneliness, then some self-love as you would give a child who is sad, is the first step toward clearing the air. Then dry your inner child's eyes and take him or her for a walk to find that "somewhere over the rainbow" hopefulness awaits you once again. Love is always available if we put ourselves out there.

One time I was in Mexico and feeling lonely. Instead of staying in my room, I went for a swim by myself. Within minutes, two Mayan children came down for a swim and started chatting and laughing with me as children do.

All of a sudden, the little girl just swam over and threw her arms around my neck, with the sweetest smile on her face!

I thought, here I am a thousand miles from home and the universe gave me love in the sparkling eyes of a 5-year-old cherub who just wanted to play.

"No matter how lonely you are, the universe is always offering itself to your imagination," says nature poet, Mary Oliver.

Shadow

If you are not in a relationship, chances are you have given up and resigned yourself to the "fact" that the Universe doesn't care about you. You don't bother going out for fun anymore or seeking opportunities to meet a partner. After all, if the universe wanted you to be happy it would send a lover to you. But that is not usually how it works. If you are walking around with the Eeyore dark cloud over your head, no one is really going to find that very attractive. But if someone saw you dancing in the rain, well, that's another story altogether!

This is a card of exhaustion that cannot always be cured by rest. Sometimes the only way to get recharged is to get moving. Try brisk walks, a dance class, or a trip to experience a new environment.

Eight of Disks
Astrological Aspect: Sun in Virgo

The image of a beautiful tree graces this card and brings to mind stability, gradual growth, careful planning, and balance. In the realm of work, it calls you to do some long-term planning to ensure a future for you and your family. The name Prudence, implies a need to be conservative in the realm of finances as well as to make sure all paperwork is in order and your checkbook is balanced. Virgo loves order, discipline, and attention to details. If these are in place, it allows the Virgo mind to do what it does best, serve.

If you have not established your career, it is time to consider what your skill set is best suited for. It is a good time to make a business plan and stay within your budget to finance a new enterprise; or work for someone as an apprentice until you can strike out on your own.

If this is about relocating, then make sure you want to stay a long time in the place you choose. And choose carefully, not impulsively.

Since this is an aspect of the Libra card of balance, Adjustment VIII, it literally means that being in nature, especially in a forest, will help you to slow down and find your center. You can also find a tree in your backyard or the local park and make a special effort to visit on a regular basis. Sit with your back against the trunk, then close your eyes and send down your roots with the roots of the tree and imagine you are drawing up the nourishment you need.

This card often shows up to encourage you to continue in your craft and enjoy the perfection and beauty that you create. If the income is sufficient, then be grateful for meaningful work. Like trees, anything that takes a long time to form has the potential to last a very long time.

Shadow

Be careful of allowing impatience to insinuate itself into your consciousness. This card is about slow growth and gradual progress. Do not allow yourself to be caught up in money-making schemes; just find practical ways to improve your business.

Being prudent is not the same as being stingy. Generosity can take many forms that aren't expensive. Since crafts are a favorite Virgo pastime, you might consider making a present or writing a poem or song as a way of giving to others.

Prudence

NINES

ARCHETYPE: THE HERMIT / CRONE IX

KABALA: YESOD, THE FOUNDATION

Nine is the final primary digit in the decimal system and therefore represents completion. All other whole numbers are a combination of zero through nine.

On the Tree of Life it is the lunar center, Yesod, nine, directly below and reflecting the solar center of Tiphereth, six. It is referred to as the foundation and is a very good number for an address of a business or home. (Add all the numbers together until they can't be reduced any further.)

Nine of Swords
Astrological Aspect: Mars in Gemini

The Rider-Waite deck shows a woman sitting in bed with her head in her hands and nine swords on the wall behind her. The implication is that she has just woken up from a bad dream and is despairing, sad, and fearful.

This nightmare is not new. The internal battle zone is rife with old stories of being disrespected or even abused. Now this criticism has been internalized and the mind is obsessed with replaying negative self-talk.

Mars is residing in the dualistic sign of Gemini, ricocheting back and forth between anger about painful memories and anger at oneself for perpetuating the suffering. Mars is so caught up in the internal battle that there is very little energy for external movement. Everything feels like a chore.

It is a difficult pattern to break because it is internalized and is usually below the surface of conscious awareness. Nothing is necessarily wrong in the external world, but there is a lack of martial energy and will to create because of the internal chatter, asking why everything is so hard, so painful.

Questions arise like "What is wrong with me?" "Why doesn't anyone love me?" and "How come what I want doesn't matter?"

This card has an uncanny tendency to appear most often in the subconscious position in a reading. This invariably means the dream realm has taken on the role of creating scenarios to reveal this internal dialogue, but too often there is no memory upon waking.

It is valuable to work on remembering dreams so that the internal storyteller can serve as a vehicle for healing and change.

Ask yourself before sleep to remember your dreams. Make sure you give yourself time to become quiet and peaceful before sleep. Keep a dream journal next to your bed and write down anything you remember without interpretation.

In time anyone can learn to become a conscious participant in the dream realm. Dreams are rich in symbols and help us understand our personal mythology. It's not about right or wrong, but about listening to and feeling the emotions that take on a myriad of forms and faces.

9

SWORDS **Cruelty**

For example, if you keep being chased it is possible to decide to turn and confront the pursuer. All the characters on some level are aspects of you. This is not the realm of ethics but the realm of the soul. Let them speak to you without judgment.

Another tool is to retell the dream using "I" for all the characters and objects. "I was a table covered with a feast and then I (your father) broke the table and then I (your mother) screamed." Explore all the manifestations of your imagination from the different perspectives of each character and element. These stories will serve to reveal your wounds, your ability to be kind and present for yourself and eventually give you an understanding of how to bring this awareness into daily life.

Shadow

The dark side of this card is the tendency to be a martyr and identify with sacrificing oneself at work and in relationships. If The Hanged Man also appears in the reading, it is even more apparent and there needs to be some deep work with therapy, dreamwork, journaling, or shamanic work to shift this pattern.

We are leaving the Piscean Age of the sacrificed god and coming into the Aquarian Age of intelligent love. Love applied to the self enriches all other expressions of love to others.

Note: Marijuana inhibits the ability to remember dreams.

Nine of Wands
Astrological Aspect: Moon in Sagittarius

The Sagittarius symbol is an arrow and almost everything about this sign is expansive and directed outward and upward. The ruling planet is Jupiter so this comes as no surprise, but here we see the Moon stepping in to mitigate this movement by bringing that dynamic energy into the internal system of the body.

The Moon suggests that after all the stages of development in this suit, we have now reached a level of experience and wisdom that calls for containment. Note that all the arrows are tipped with moons and the feathers are moons as well.

Since this is an aspect of the Hermit/Crone IX, it is time to honor this stage of development by running energy that magnetizes people to come and be warmed by your fire.

In the realm of work you have established a record of dependability, optimism, congeniality, and trust. People know they can count on you to get the job done or to delegate in respectful and appreciative ways. If there's problem solving to be done you will be flexible and creative, making the process enjoyable and fruitful at the same time.

In the realm of intimacy you have reached a level of maturity that exudes confidence and sexiness. If you walk into a room, just let yourself be and watch how people naturally gather around.

In family life you tend to be the strength and center of your clan and your calm authority serves as reassurance that everything will be all right.

Shadow

Don't let the ego lead when this card arises. There can be a tendency to be so happy to have arrived at this level of confidence and energy that you will seek out compliments and cheap thrills. There will be an urge to burn through the storehouse of energy you have accumulated.

Just stay in your center and act as an antenna; the right people will come to help you manifest the lunar dreams. When you get too excited about how good you feel, use the classic Buddhist response, "No Big Deal."

Often we seek the thrill and not the steady ride.
Stay grounded.

Note: To deepen your understanding of this card see story about The Voyager Deck, page 377.

9

Strength

Nine of Cups
Astrological Aspect: Jupiter in Pisces

One of the most optimistic cards in the whole deck, it is traditionally considered the wish fulfillment card. Send your wish out into the world and be ready to receive. Jupiter, the god of Fortune, would love to bless you with the fulfillment of your heart's desire if you let The Fool in and take a leap of faith and trust.

This card is called Happiness, and promises a time of joy and deep satisfaction.

Having gone through the many stages of emotional growth, from falling in love to finding the heights of ecstasy, you are ripe for reward. Not only have there been the experiences of pleasure, but also the hard work of dealing with conflict. When all seemed lost, the willingness to be vulnerable and transparent allowed you to build bridges over troubled waters. Now there is a foundation of true wisdom and happiness. The soul's yearnings have not been brushed aside for the momentary pleasures.

The Motherpeace card shows a group of women relishing the joy of an outdoor spa and celebrating the moment, naked and free. It might be time to make this image a reality and indulge in the simple deliciousness of water, breezes, and balmy days!

If you are not in a relationship and this card appears in the past, it would be helpful to reflect on stable, happy times in your life. Are you comparing everything that shows up to that past ideal? It would be more useful to see this card as a sign that you have learned what happiness feels like and can offer gratitude and be open to how love chooses to present itself now.

Shadow

If you haven't experienced any stable, loving, and respectful relationships in your life then it is time to look at what strategies you are using to avoid or ignore this painful truth. Many people become workaholics or alcoholics; either way, what they really want is love.

It is time to go to the meta-level of this card, The Hermit/Crone IX, and do some introspective work, through therapy or a retreat, that takes you out of the rush of daily life. There are answers and wisdom deep within that can be tapped, if you will slow down to

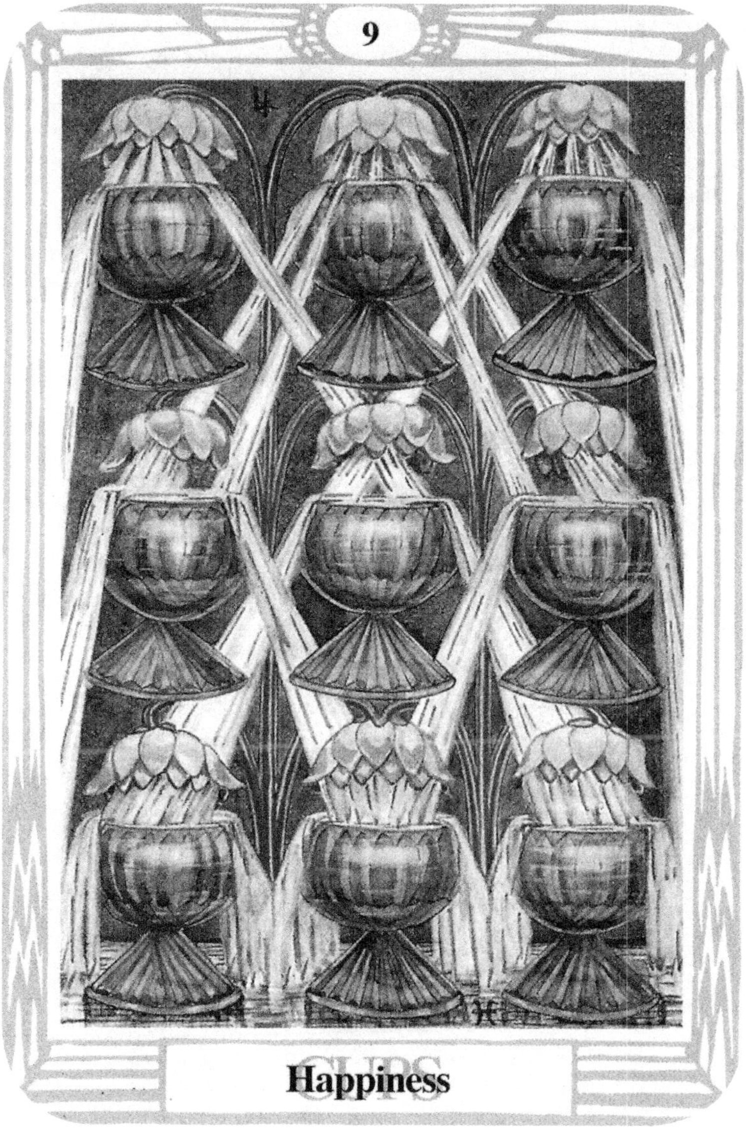
9
Happiness
CUPS

the pace of receiving guidance.

The other all-too-common shadow of this card is the inability to receive. The Universe may want to give you blessings but if you are always the giver and doer, where is the space or the pace to receive? People who always care for everyone else are usually hiding deep wounds and a lack of self-esteem. A child who never experienced being loved for being itself learns to do things for others just to be liked. If this grown child is angry about the past, life will be a string of rebellious acts sending the message that, "Nobody loves me, so nothing matters anyway."

Most the time if even one person sees your true self, the process of healing can begin.

Often we become identified with the giver because it has proven to be a way to be loved and accepted. Ask yourself what your inner self truly aspires to be.

Nine of Disks
Astrological Aspect: Venus in Virgo

When the Nine of Disks appears in your reading, Venus is rewarding you with the respect of your community for your dedication to meaningful work. You have created a stable foundation after applying the Virgo qualities of critical thinking, service, and attention to detail.

Venus in Virgo literally means love of service. The Six of Disks is called Success and the Ten of Disks is called Wealth, but we can have these accolades without really experiencing fulfillment. This card is called Gain because it represents work done to grow and evolve and give your gifts to the world, not solely for external reward.

Financial practicality is also a Virgo trait so this is not a card of the starving artist; but the deeper purpose is always the primary motivation.

The Motherpeace card shows a woman in deep concentration as she creates a sand painting. This ancient meditative art allows us to experience the reality that everything is transitory. Knowing it will be taken by the winds of change, the true artist will still give everything to the work.

In the Thoth deck we see that the three circles that formed the foundation of the pyramid in the Three of Disks have now interlaced. A deeper integration and mastery has taken place after patient dedication.

The work in this card is not limited to the creative arts; any work can be imbued with the qualities of service and perfection. All paths offer fulfillment when we are in service and authentic at the same time.

Shadow

The qualities of Virgo can take perfection to an extreme. When the details become more important than the original intention to create, the outcome can feel soulless. All of us have experienced hearing music or seeing art that technically excels and yet we are not moved.

Be careful not to lose the feeling for your work by trying to achieve a level of perfection. There is an Arab tradition of error in the making of designs, such as in the art of rug-making in which the weaver intentionally makes a mistake; this acknowledges that there is no ultimate perfection in this world and it is best to humbly bow to this truth rather than play "God."

In fact, there's an old Persian proverb that says, "A Persian Rug is Perfectly Imperfect, and Precisely Imprecise."

9

DISKS **Gain**

TENS

ARCHETYPE: FORTUNE / THE WHEEL OF FORTUNE X
KABALA: MALKUTH, THE KINGDOM

Ten represents the end of a cycle and the beginning of another. The seed that was planted in Kether has now moved through all the stages of development and arrived in the sephiroth called Malkuth. This is the only station on the Tree of Life that represents the actual physical plane of existence.

The key words tied to the number ten are manifestation and conclusion. Now that the journey is complete, it is time to return to the one, or unity, again. There is nothing more to be done and to linger is to deny the basic truth of existence, that there is no permanence.

It is believed that the decimal system is derived from the ten fingers of the human hand. Note that the word manifestation is rooted in the word "manus," which means hand, and "festi" which means to fasten. Without our hands we could not make all the art and structures that now exist in the world.

Ten of Swords
Astrological Aspect: Sun in Gemini

In the Thoth image we see ten swords pointed inward and therefore ineffectual. The sword in the center with a heart is broken, symbolizing the mind's inability to listen and act from love.

Thought is caught in a web of fear and yet the mind obsessively pursues a plan, an answer, anything to find a way to fix the situation. When fear is the emotion being reinforced by the mind, nothing positive can arise. And yet, the mind refuses to relinquish control. Every plan has a very short life span as other fearful thoughts topple the last set of false conclusions.

There is a feeling that nothing will work, nothing can help, and desperation, isolation, and madness ensue. In reality, the isolation and preoccupation of the mind is blocking the way through this difficult time.

The ideas can even border on mania and a belief that only you know the truth or only you have ever felt what you are feeling right now.

In a Tarot session this card appeared as the indicator for the reading. The client had tried in every way to come up with an answer and nothing was working. I suggested he had reached his wits' end and even though his mind was doing everything it could, it had reached its limits. The mind only knows what it has already learned and experienced and the heart yearned for growth and new beginnings.

I offered that at times like this the antidote is our dear friend The Fool, who doesn't pretend to know the answers, he just trusts that everything is possible at any given moment and it's time to take a leap of faith out of the tortured chambers of the mind and into the world.

To our delight, I turned over the next card and there was our fearless Fool surrounded by all the symbols of endless possibilities!

This demonstrates that within the Tarot the challenges and gifts are always coexisting. So it is in life. If there is a problem, the solution is inherent in that moment, but the logical cause and effect approach can often leave us bereft of an answer. There are countless stories of "Aha" revelations that come at the point where we give up in utter frustration and just let go. At that point, without realizing it, we are actually ready to receive from the Universe, having

10

SWORDS **Ruin**

dethroned the god of our limited human mind. Then, voilà! The clouds break and a light shines on the way through the problem that had seemed insurmountable.

Another way to deal with this dilemma in the early stages, before you are so entrenched, is to tell others what you are experiencing; you will probably find that others have felt or are feeling the same thing.

If this has become an actual mental disease, then professional help should be sought immediately.

The heart needs understanding, the body needs touch, and the mind needs a long deserved rest.

Shadow

This card is called Ruin and implies that no matter what you do there is no way out. This is only true if you continue to try to figure it out, fix it, or find the perfect plan. Then, out of the depression there will be manic phases of false elation and clarity that will slam you to the ground again and again.

When we turn the situation over to the "sage" as the I Ching advises, then a positive shift can happen. But when we distrust the "sage" no help can come. This book of wisdom posits the idea that the Universe moves in a zigzag fashion and just when there seems to be no hope, the impossible happens. It is like a river moving underground that suddenly surfaces and bathes us in the refreshing waters of life and love once again.

Ten of Wands
Astrological Aspect: Saturn in Sagittarius

Saturn has thwarted every attempt by Sagittarius to change the situation and the attitudes of the people involved. You are now trapped and suffocated and it is time to accept the reality that no amount of cheerleading is going to bring the team to victory. The structure (Saturn) itself must be changed so it is time to revamp, retreat, be patient, or leave.

The card is called Oppression and shows eight wands that were active in the past trapped behind two large wands that look like the bars of a prison cell. These same bars appeared as crossed Tibetan daggers in the Two of Wands where another past limitation of the ego had been blasted from the throne of power. Now a new wall is blocking progress but the strategy-confident Sagittarius refuses to step back. This is exhausting, frustrating, and definitely ineffective.

There are a number of ways to work with this situation that can be experienced as great life lessons. Often when there is blockage, the path of least resistance is the way to go. If you keep butting your head against a wall maybe you need to stand back and use the aspect of Sagittarius that can see the full spectrum of options by taking in the big picture.

One time I was at a demonstration during the Occupy movement and we had been forcefully removed from our camp. We had returned to reclaim the commons and were facing down a line of cops.

I looked to my ally, Brad, and saw a mischievous twinkle in his eyes. He said, "Let's slip around the sides of the line." When we did this, all of a sudden the police were surrounded with free spirits smiling and leaping around them. The power dynamic shifted. For quite a while the police continued using their rigid approach for crowd control. Every time they formed a diagonal or a straight line we slipped playfully around them, weaving creative chaos while the police were caught in the limitations of hierarchy.

When nothing is working, doing nothing may be the antidote. Regroup and release goal orientation to clearly see the situation at hand. A way through may then arise from within.

Remember the containment and magnetism represented by the Nine of Wands, and recharge.

In the realm of relationship, a need to acknowledge your shadow is necessary. Are you angry? Are you possessive? Do you think your partner needs to change?

Within this shadow energy you can explore what authentic needs lie behind these demanding desires.

Shadow

When there is an attempt to force change externally it often results in exhaustion, judgment, and even depletion of the chi. Retreat, regroup, and remember to review your original intent.

If you are actually ignoring warning signals from your body you need to slow down and stay healthy.

Living in Northern California, I have read for folks who grow marijuana. This card can indicate that you have blinders on and are not reading the signs that legal troubles are lurking around the bend. Those "prison" bars can become a reality if you are not careful.

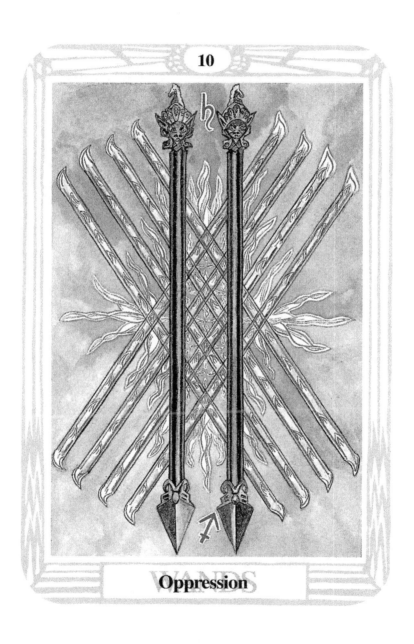

10

Oppression

Ten of Cups
Astrological Aspect: Mars in Pisces

In this card called Satiety, we see the diagram of the Tree of Life superimposed with ten cups filled to the brim. One interpretation is that the dreams and desires of love's intention started in the Ace have reached fulfillment. When this happens, we need to trust that at this point the cups need to empty so that the cycle can start again.

Too often, though, long-term partners are unaware that they are not really sharing a vision of the future. The original dreams that brought them together have either been fulfilled or left by the wayside.

For example, the children have grown up, the house is bought, the work is serving to maintain a lifestyle, and the thrill is gone. Everyday communication has become lackluster and boring. You can continue to put a band-aid on the problem and pretend that small adjustments will make things okay, but in reality this is just a stopgap measure. It is time to assess and appreciate what has been manifested and release what has not.

Take time to be together and dream again. Let go of the practical reasons why something can or cannot happen and let the possibilities spill forth. Celebrate what you have manifested and imagine what you could see in a bright and playful future. Call on The Fool in you that fell in love in the first place and give him or her free reign to dream anew!

Shadow

If you have just met someone and this card appears, it takes on a different meaning. This is a warning that you have forgone the natural stages of love's growth and become deluded by a romantic fantasy. You are convinced this person is The One and that you will be together forever. The potential for two people to experience perfect synchronicity and cosmic connection is always present. It is intoxicating to feel this "soulmate" vibration. This is usually how love casts its spell.

But when this playful dance turns into future planning, trouble usually lies ahead. Yes, there are those rare moments when this experience carries through the rest of our lives, but it still takes work on communication to make it real and lasting. Usually what hap-

10

Satiety

pens is that you have found someone who fulfills in words and gestures all you have asked for, but you actually have no idea if you can become intimate and communicate honestly when the relationship is challenged by real life events.

It is best to enjoy the flash of union and then just stay present with love as your guide and not your mind's idea of happily ever after.

When we jump in with everything we've got, move in together or quit a job and move just to be with this person, we may ignore red flags along the way.

I once wrote in a poem, "Damn love that it shows the potential and then you have to live with the reality."

This person has filled in the "application form" you have created in your mind and everything matches up. But do we really know what kind of lover we need to grow and love and stay true to ourselves at the same time? It's a process, not a goal that can be reached in weeks or months.

Be grateful for the wonderful feelings of oneness with another and then stay in your power and dignity.

Mars, the igniting fire of our autonomous will, can really get swamped by the Piscean illusions and blend with the beloved to the point of drowning. Even your friends and family who see you losing it cannot get through to you. Only you can rescue yourself.

Take a few days to regroup and remember who you are and what your path is. There is no need to rationally destroy this budding romance by pulling up the roots. Keep watering and tending the relationship and yourself.

People who have loved you all your life are good guides at this point in the dance. You don't have to ask their advice, just bring your lover around and see how the interactions unfold. This will help give you a much-needed perspective.

Try not to judge your friends' and family's reactions, just stay aware.

As the Rolling Stones put it, "You can't always get what you want, but if you try, sometimes you just might find you get what you need."

Ten of Disks
Astrological Aspect: Mercury in Virgo

Here we see once again the image of the Kabala, or Tree of Life, as we did in the Ten of Cups. All the symbols on the Disks are different icons for the god/planet, Mercury, who rules Virgo. This is the culmination of the original intent of the Ace of Disks. In the Ace, the seed was planted. Here it has come to full fruition. The template within the seed has been transmitted by Mercury from the crown/Kether to the actual physical manifestation in the final station/sephiroth, Malkuth.

Traditionally, this has literally meant money coming your way; on a mundane level that still holds true. But in the Motherpeace deck we see its meaning on a deeper level. In that image we see a circle of people drumming and holding space to support the birth of a baby. The implication is that true wealth is found in community. In these trying times, it is important to remember that it is a loving community that will be our safety net as financial systems continue to destabilize. When there is generosity and giving, we all benefit and feel we belong and are cared for.

I remember a couple who came to me for a reading. Close to retirement age, they were parents of four adult children whom they loved dearly. The husband received the reading and he wanted to know if he should keep working and make some investments to ensure they did not become a burden on their children. He had recently suffered a heart attack and was concerned about his health.

In the position of hopes and fears, Death appeared. This was not a prediction of death but rather the confirmation of the reality that he was afraid that he might not live that much longer. The Lust/Strength card was also present and implied that it was time to live each moment to the fullest.

The outcome was the Prince of Disks that is strongly associated with the idea that one no longer needs to prove anything to the world in terms of work. This is symbolized by his hand resting on the globe, and the fact that he wears no armor, meaning nothing to defend. The Ten of Disks was in his inner self in the future and it was suggesting that true wealth is within us and with those we hold in our hearts. Death, in its aspect as hope, was suggesting he wanted to let go of work and live fully. Both of them began to weep and felt relieved that it was time to release into the arms of those who love them and let go of money as the safety net.

The root of the word wealth is "weal," which means wellbeing, happiness and health. So many of our words have been perverted to serve economic systems when their roots are in our relationships. The word economics itself is from "oikonomos," which means management of the household.

Shadow

True wealth is not found in isolation and hoarding and yet so many of us today try to secure our future with money and possessions. Hoarding rooted in fear will eat away at our "weal" or health over time. We hold onto things until we die and then will them to our family. But since this shadow is selfish, often the family ends up continuing the hoarding and fighting over the terms of the inheritance. Then the inheritance turns out to be the ugliness of greed and no one benefits. It is best to be generous in life and not hold the strings of material power until the bitter end.

Another aspect of the shadow is the lack of trust that our family, community, and the Universe will provide for us. Mistrust breeds mistrust, selfishness breeds selfishness.

Parents, family members, and friends can lend or give money with strings attached, to hold power over others. This breeds dependency and resentment. Money always has its limitations but its best function is as a vehicle of energy exchange to be given freely with no attachment to outcome.

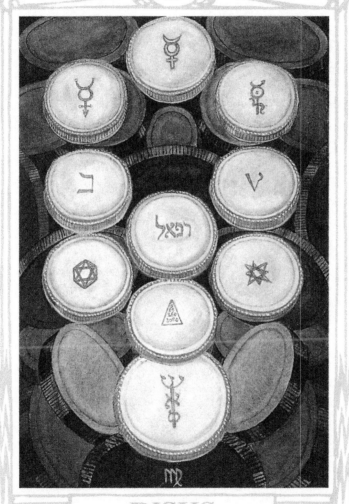

10

Wealth

How To Do
A Reading

CREATE THE SPACE

First of all you need to create a sacred space for your reading. Lay out a special cloth and place your deck in the center. I put an amethyst on my deck to create a sense of containment. Purple represents the highest vibration and amethyst has long been associated with psychic attunement. My particular stone was given to me by a client as appreciation for my work so it holds a positive message for me every time I use it.

When I first started doing readings, I was outside at Fisherman's Wharf in San Francisco, and the wind soon informed me of my need to keep the cards from blowing away. Being a resourceful Virgo, I walked down to the beach to find some shells and stones. One shell in particular I still have in my collection. People began asking me the significance of the stones and I realized that they epitomized perfectly the basic principle of a grounded spiritual practice. As above, so below. In other words, when we use an object, it should have a practical and magical purpose. My stones hold my cards in place and grace the reading with a wonderful vibration. I sometimes like to have stones of all the colors of the rainbow represented, to give me a full spectrum of energy.

So gather your magical shells, stones, figurines—anything that has power that you have collected over the years—and bring them in to play. All that energy was just waiting to be actualized! Now arrange them with intention, burn some incense, light a candle, add a vase of fresh flowers if you like. Take a moment and breathe in this beautiful space you have created.

When we take time to create a beautiful space, we send a message to our inner being and enter an altered state in which we become a channel. This entire process is very important. Your whole being will respond. I have noticed in the many years I have done this that I can always open the channel as long as I repeat this simple ritual. I always do the same things. It is like placing a key in a door to a special room where magic transpires. It unlocks my connection to my inner wisdom and the wisdom of the ages.

When I do readings in my home, I let different figurines or stones speak to me and I bring them into my sacred space. I just walk through the house and respond to my "in house magicians." I will feel them "saying" they want to participate. This process will also enliven all the powerful objects in your home and it's great fun when your client notices a particular statue and comments on their connection to it. Ah! The joys of synchronicity!

Now bring in the kitchen witches and put the kettle on for tea. It is always important to offer comfort for the body as well as the soul, creating a sense of welcoming and sharing that puts your client at ease and feeling cared for. If they don't want any tea make sure you at least provide them with a glass of water. It has been customary throughout time to offer sustenance to all who enter your home and to fail to do so often keeps us distanced and disconnected without knowing why. We are all one under the skin and this is a simple and unspoken namaste to your fellow traveler.

The final step in your preparation is to ground yourself. Sit down, relax, and close your eyes. Take a few deep breaths and exhale all your concerns of the day, releasing them down your body into the earth, drawing up renewing energy with each inhale. Feel the power of Gaia enter you and know that she will nourish you and keep you flowing as you do your work. You are not alone. The Tarot is an ancient tool, linked to the collective unconscious, and you are tapping into, not taking, that knowledge.

Remember, you are in service to the highest good of all and the autonomy of each person you serve.

Take note: If you are stressed or feeling burdened by your own problems, it is best to bathe or at least smudge with some sage before beginning this whole process. All the preparations have a cleansing effect and bring you very much into the present moment.

Now it is time to do a silent meditation and focus your intention of service. I do a Sanskrit chant (see chant Om Hrdaya Namah, page 389) and then I call in the goddess: "She changes everything she touches and everything she touches changes." Next I utter, "Do what thou wilt, and harm no one, Loving is the Law." That's my ritual, developed out of my spiritual history; you will need to create your own. You can chant, tone, sing, state an affirmation, or do whatever has spiritual significance and meaning for you. It's good both to be silent and to invoke the archetypal powers or divinities you align with so that you activate both aspects of the conversation that is about to take place. Then you are ready and willing to be receptive and listen to the individual as well as speak with clarity as a channel for this divine oracle.

Over the years many people have suggested ways to glamorize my set-up, but I just have these stones and cloth and I keep it really simple. It isn't a show so I don't want my ego getting all excited about what it's doing. My ego knows its place. You will find what works for you, but the underlying intention must be to serve the Tarot in a respectful way. I believe this ritual is a signal to my soul to come forth and channel the truth that the cards are about to reveal. The ego is relegated to its proper role as a satellite of the soul and is relieved of the desire to fix, judge, control, or direct someone else's life. The ego can relish being a capable, caring, serving, and positive expression that will draw people to you and make them feel welcomed and comfortable.

Learning the next lesson took me a bit of time but without it I would've probably quit a long time ago.

It is imperative that you prevent people from dumping their life's problems in your lap. You are not a spiritual mechanic. Everyone fantasizes about someone else fixing their lives and answering all their questions, but, ultimately, this is only the desire of ego. The soul's journey is unique and self-motivated, and oracles are meant to be reflections not remakes. If you give your clients an inkling that you are willing to judge and fix then you are dealing ego to ego, and they will probably take you up on it. When this happens, your energy will probably drop and the words will stop flowing. Ironically, it is much harder and very draining to try to play "God" than to just let spirit work through you.

A reading is meant to offer the information, revelations, confirmation, and tools the individual needs to evolve and grow. All spiritual modalities are available to us as mirrors, not mandates. Trust the unfolding, and do your work accordingly.

To begin the Reading

To begin, pick up the cards and shuffle the deck. This will serve two purposes: one, to clear the energy from the past reading and, two, to reconnect you to the cards. Then ask your client or friend to shuffle the cards. I use the large edition of the deck of Thoth for my readings and it feels very awkward the first time you hold them so I always suggest a few ways to mix them. For example, hold them sideways instead of lengthwise like we usually do with playing cards, and proceed as usual. Or hold them lengthwise in one hand, resting them on the palm of the other hand, and shuffle. If you sense that the person is still uncomfortable with the cards ask them to mix them face down on the table like go-fish, or pile them in stacks, or play with them in any way that is easy for them. This may seem like I am belaboring a point, but clients create their reading by doing this so it is essential that they are connecting in a relaxed way with the deck.

Some readers don't have the other person shuffle the deck; in fact, there is an old superstition that no one should touch your deck but yourself. I am not a superstitious person and I find there are numerous advantages to having the other person shuffle. You are not responsible for the cards that appear; they create the order with their own hands. Also, I find it very revealing to watch someone shuffle cards. You can tell a lot about a person by the way they handle an object. Sometimes cards fly out of the deck and I take note of them for future reference. It is especially significant if the cards end up in the final reading. Sometimes I peek and notice what cards are on the bottom or moving through their fingers as they talk about specific aspects of their life.

Which brings us to the next step. While they are shuffling the cards, you will start asking them questions. At this point, really re-lax and listen to the person, observe them like the great Sherlock Holmes, take them in, drink them in. Notice what they are wearing, how they hold their body, observe their jewelry. I have often sur-prised people by knowing they are married or what sign they are. They will look amazed and ask, how did I know that. I am not a mind reader but I do recognize a wedding ring on the left hand or a Scorpio necklace. Just as the attire and accoutrement in a Tarot court card informs us about the character of the card, individuals are always revealing themselves to you and we are always reading each other. If these powers of observation are heightened and en-hanced by the language of symbolism, we are well on our way to knowing a whole lot about this person. Also, your instincts will take notice and be attracted to, say, a bracelet or a pin on a lapel or the slogan on a tee shirt. I might make a comment that will inspire the person to reveal a fascinating anecdote about their life. You are get-ting to know them, but with a heightened sense of intention.

Example: Once a client was wearing a t-shirt with a heart in chains and I asked her if that is how she felt. She had indeed consciously chosen the shirt as she was going to have a serious discussion with her partner about continuing their relationship. I suggested she take the shirt off before they met. She laughed and agreed.

I always shake hands with my clients to make a physical connection. Although I already know their name from this first intro, when they are shuffling the cards I ask for their full name and write it down on a piece of paper. (I often use a template with a pre-printed layout and my contact information for the client to take with them. When they come across it again they might call for another reading. Check page 360 for template.)

I find names and the origin of names fascinating and will often learn a lot from inquiring about how they got their name. Most names are given at birth and connect to family history and some names are taken for spiritual or other reasons that will enrich your understanding, not only for the reading at hand but for use in future readings. Take the name Veronica. It is derived from "veros icon," which means true image and comes from a story about Jesus. As he is carrying the cross, a young woman steps forward out of the crowd to wipe his brow and an image of Jesus appears on the handkerchief, to the amazement of the throng. From then on she is called Veronica. This could be a stepping-off point for the reading. Is she presenting her true image to the world? Is she compassionate? Names are powerful and deeply connected to our destiny.

Lately, I have been asking for my client's middle name as well. Some people use their middle name for their first name and therein lies another story. Also, the way they pronounce their name tells you whether they like it or not. These are all clues for Sherlock's deductions.

I do not want to imply that you should be some kind of scientific observer. Very often the person will immediately start telling you a very emotional, sad, or difficult story and naturally your empathy will become the central focus of the way you are listening and holding space. To gain a heightened sense of awareness of the client on all levels is to serve in the highest capacity. Notice your own reaction to the person and, at the same time, try to refrain from judgment.

First I ask for the client's birthdate. Next I ask what kind of work they are involved in, possibly adding questions about how long they have done the work and where. I also inquire if the person is currently in a relationship and if so, what is the partner's name and birth date. If the person has children I will also request their birth dates. All these dates give me the information to calculate what their life cards are and what year they are in currently (see page 370 for formula). Also, this numerology can be used to understand the nature of the day a certain event took place, for example a wedding, an accident, start of a new job, or even the death of a loved one. This number can relate to the day of death or the year the individual died in. For numbers involving death, I have found that when the Hermit/Crone comes up, there is a sense of resolution of the life course. First, because nine is the number of completion; second, because the card is about deep inner wisdom of the soul, which hopefully means they learned what they needed to know this time around. I do not ever imply I know this for a fact; I only offer it as food for thought.

Some of the happiest marriages I've seen are ones where the wedding took place on a Justice day (in the Thoth deck, Major Arcana VIII), or on one of the Equinoxes, March 21 or Sept 21, because this implies an invocation of equality. This information also tells me if they are in their Saturn return, which occurs around your 29th, 58th, and 87th, birthdays. Saturn takes 29 years to orbit the Sun so it doesn't return to the position of your birth until these years. Saturn is the planet of structure, form, discipline, and responsibility; therefore it puts pressure on us to fulfill our lifework. From my experience, it usually starts to be felt one year before the 29th birthday and about 2 years before the 58th. The choices we make at these crucial junctures set the template for the next 29 years. This is a point at which we do a lot of soul-searching about our lifework, desire for family, love and marriage, all the deep issues of life. Things that were stagnant and tolerable become stifling and oppressive. I relocated and divorced in my first Saturn return. On the other hand, a career that is exciting and loved can skyrocket.

The final question I ask is what their intention is for the reading; what do they want feedback on; do they have any specific questions. They may need help in framing the question. If they ask, "When will I meet the love of my life," it would be more self-empowering to ask, "How could I invite a healthy relationship into my life?"

If they ask a yes or no question like, "Should I take this job?" it would be more useful to ask, "What do I need to know about this job, that would help me make a decision?" It is important to help them reframe the question so the answers offer tools and food for thought. Remember, it is not a reader's job to be the authority over someone's life. Make sure to let the person know that asking a question will not limit the reading to one topic but instead will give it a focus.

By now you may be thinking that this is too much to deal with. Of course, all these details are not necessary to doing a reading, especially if you are doing a short reading or you are just a beginner. But as you grow in your knowledge, you will find that these layers of information offer a wealth of insight. Revisit this chapter from time to time and see if there is a new tool you want to add to your toolbox. If you are new to the Tarot, but familiar with Astrology, just knowing someone's sign is a good starting point.

It is possible with the Tarot to deal with any question at all. I find that oracles love to respond to very specific questions and the cards will amaze you by how exact they can be.

My favorite story illustrating this principle took place several years ago when a client informed me that she was about to have an operation on two discs in her spine. The first card was—what else—the Two of Disks! This is a card of transformation, shedding of the skin, and a release of new creative energy. I also had her throw the I Ching for guidance and the Hexagram was #52, Keeping Still, which focuses on the stilling of the spine, staying calm, not going out into the world, really meditating on inner peace. The woman felt she was given the guidance she needed to let go of her fears and go through with the surgery with a sense of confidence and inner clarity. She returned a few weeks later to tell me the operation was a success and she was grateful for the grounding advice I had given her.

It is always a relief to do a reading for a client who is aware of the true purpose of the Tarot, but clarification is often necessary because of the prevalent Hollywood perspective about the cards. Over the years I have developed different ways to introduce the Tarot to newcomers.

When I am asked questions such as "Isn't it scary?" or "I don't want to know," or "Isn't there a Death Card?" I need to dispel the fear that is the source of all these questions. I reassure them that it is not scary and that I am not about to tell them about Mr. tall-dark-and-handsome or predict the exact events of their future. What I intend to do is tell a story of their life through the lens of the Tarot. If a client can see himself or herself, which they always do, this outer confirmation helps them to trust that inner voice.

I do not want to discount the powerful predictive powers of the Tarot, but prophecy needs to be put into a larger context or else it can be very dangerous. I have heard so many horror stories about people being told when they or their loved ones are going to die, or that they'll never find love or they will get cancer in two years. One reader even told a man that he was her executioner in a past life! We are not meant to plant these seeds in people's minds. People are so open and vulnerable during a reading and then they are haunted for years by these thoughts. Never claim to know the exact facts of someone else's life. You are misusing and misrepresenting the cards if you do.

Now, you are ready to begin the reading. Remember, every card has many meanings, in fact, an unlimited potential of expressions. The aspects you choose to emphasize will be influenced by the individual, their circumstances, questions, age, history, the current moment and, of course, your intuition. A diamond has many facets but it is still one stone. The Tarot cards are living archetypes of the collective unconscious; they are not arbitrary symbols of the human mind. Crowley liked to call them "seventy-eight debutantes at a coming-out ball." Well, Crowley was always a bit extravagant, but you get the point. They are like people who don't want to be stereotyped, seen as two-dimensional, or judged as good or bad. The cards are just facets of how life works. They are characters in the play (Court cards), or cues for the next action (Minor Arcana), or a divine force manifesting in your daily events (Major Arcana).

The cards are exactly what you need to encounter at this moment to become aware of the conscious unfolding of this stage of your life. As they say, "The cards never lie." Trust the cards and relieve your ego of the responsibility of knowing everything.

Let your intuition flow and say the first thing that comes to your mind when you turn over the cards.

I only turn one card over at a time. I find this is very important because it is almost impossible not to "read" ahead to the end of the "story" to see the outcome and that will color your ability to spontaneously tell the story as it unfolds before your eyes. If you know the outcome, you will contrive to arrive there. This way you stay spontaneous and improvisational; in other words, in the moment and real. You will naturally build the story and stay fluid with each new card you encounter.

Sometimes I start the reading by asking the person what they see in the card before I say anything. Assure your friend or client that there are no right or wrong answers. The Tarot cards are meant, by the pictures alone, to tell us where we're at without any mental extrapolation. Symbols do a brain bypass and go straight to the soul if we let them. The cards are a gallery of art. At an art show, people have their unique tastes and reactions and they are as valid as our interpretation. We, like a docent in a museum, can fill in the history and symbolism that has been accumulated about the card, but that is not meant to challenge the client's own reflections. If the person is reticent to say anything, ask some questions to prompt them. "Are you attracted to the card? Is it scary, exciting, confusing?

What stands out, what calls to you? Can you tell me a story about what is happening?" Listen carefully to what they say and try to weave it into the context of the reading as you go.

Stay focused on the client's reactions so you can sense if they are with you. The first four cards in the basic Celtic Cross layout all represent the present. After I have completed this section I usually check in and ask for feedback. "Do you have any questions so far? Is it clear? Are you with me?" If they are totally with you and say that's exactly what's going on, which will happen most of the time, then just keep going. But if they are puzzled, it is very important to reexamine the cards. You may offer further clarification or suggest a different angle to consider. For example, sometimes a Court Card is really about the client and not someone else in their life. You might have been projecting the image outside and they want to bring the image back home. The cards are always right but our perception can be skewed and there is nothing wrong with reworking an interpretation.

On the other hand, if the individual is sitting back in a judgmental stance and telling you, "Well, this card is right but you are wrong about that one," it is important to reframe the conversation so you are not passing some test. You are not doing this to be the great Houdini and impress them with your magic tricks; you are here to help them receive the profound teachings of a vast accumulation of human experience of which you are a knowledgeable and devoted servant. I tell my clients that my readings are interactive and the more they participate the more they will receive. Now let's look at the basic Celtic Cross layout.

CELTIC CROSS DIAGRAM

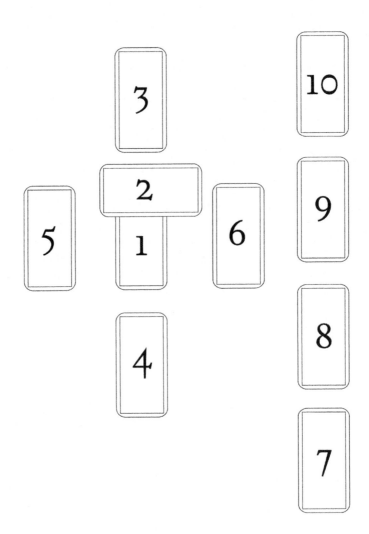

THE READING

PRESENT

1.THE INDICATOR/SIGNIFICATOR

This card represents the focus and essence of the entire reading. It can be what you need to work on, or possibly what you want to create. Is this card challenging or an asset? In a way, the other nine cards are an extrapolation of the first. There are ten cards in a reading because this is a natural human number of manifestation. "Manu" means hand, of which there are ten fingers. This is the biological origin of the decimal system. So when an idea has gone from conception to materialization, it is natural to return to one and begin again. Written mathematically, $10=1+0=1$. It is all one, once again. Perhaps that is why hands are held together as one in prayer, to recognize and honor a moment out of the realm of making or doing and, instead, to just be.

This card sets the focus of the reading, so it is necessary to relate anything pertinent to it as the other cards arise. The indicator is what is happening now, the present state of things. If it is a Court Card, it signifies the personality that is expressing a particular motivation. The Princess of Cups is very often considered the woman in love, whereas the Knight of Wands shows an inspired urge to take action on an idea. A Court Card often represents another person in their lives but when it is the indicator it is also a reflection of their own self, otherwise it would seem the whole reading was about the other person. It is useful for the client to know that this person is also representative of part of themselves. If it is a Major Arcana, then focus on a principle that is at the root of the card as opposed to the people or events that will present themselves in the Minor Arcana. For this section, let's assume the first card is The Emperor.

The Emperor wants to know how we relate to power, symbolized by the ruler/father figure. How are we dealing with our own power? What is our relationship to people in power like a boss, competitor, or actual father? What about our relationship to hierarchal institutions like the government? Do we avoid, condemn, embrace, or compete with people whom we see as powerful? These are questions The Emperor raises in a reading. Each archetype raises its own questions and asks us to look at life through that lens.

2. MOVING THROUGH

This card creates a bridge between the past and future and asks us to consciously be aware of what we wish to leave behind and what momentum is carrying us forward. It suggests a situation, person, feeling, or guiding principle that needs to be integrated or released. The nature of the card will make this pretty clear.

Traditionally this is called the Crossing card, the energy that is opposing the indicator. I do not like to assume that the two cards are in opposition but if this is the case then proceed accordingly. For example, let's say The Emperor was crossed by The Fool. You would first reveal the power issue and follow up with The Fool seeking freedom and new opportunities. The Fool would love to put us in his knapsack and take a leap of faith off the cliff of all our securities. But to integrate The Emperor and The Fool, we are looking for a balance between order and chaos or, in more human terms, spontaneity and structure. Some people actually have these as their life cards, The Fool being the personality card and The Emperor, the card of the soul.

3. THE CONSCIOUS MIND

This position represents what is foremost in the client's mind. If the first two cards and the intended focus are around work and then the Princess of Cups shows up, it might indicate that a relationship has taken precedence over the issues at work. On the other hand, it may indicate that there is an emotional need to be appreciated for the gifts and talents being offered at work. A third option could be that there is someone at their job whom they are attracted to.

Each of these options is plausible and it is only practice and experience that will teach you what feels right for that reading. After a while you will sense when your true inner Priestess/Magician is speaking and how different that feels from your judgmental ego voice. People are always asking me if I am psychic and I answer that we all are but we must trust that voice and act on it. If we constantly deny and suppress this inner knowing, after a while it doesn't surface very easily. An apt analogy is that we are all potentially strong and muscular, but not if we don't work out.

4. THE SUBCONSCIOUS MIND

This will reveal the underlying dreams, desires, regrets, fears, blocks, or old hang-ups that need to be brought to light. Sometimes everything outwardly is aligning for us and yet we are unable to progress. There is a strong connection between the previous card and this one because we often sublimate past problems and they sit like a dragon guarding our fears and making us immobile. Let's say this card is the Five of Cups, called Disappointment, and the card in the past position is The Tower. Both of these cards are ruled by Mars, the fearless and flexible creative energy that activates our passionate drives, or the shadow urge for "power over" that leads to fighting, anger, and destruction.

The client has carried this anger and disappointment into the unconscious; when that feeling of lack of recognition arises again, the reaction could be overblown because there is so much emotional history that comes into play.

Since The Emperor is the first card, this would be a good time to ask the client if there has been a conflict with his father (or other authority figures) and to suggest that is why this whole situation is more emotional than logical. Maybe the client was always trying to prove himself to his father and was never seen for what he was. The Fool could offer a whole new start by releasing the inner child to play and rediscover who he truly is and what his real work is meant to be.

PAST

5. THE PAST

This card is not so much about specific events in the past as what needs to be remembered from our past that is pertinent now. What have we learned or experienced that we want to take further or let go of? The Tower in this position would represent a tendency to burn one's bridges and have eye-opening and possibly shocking experiences that propel us forward. You could ask for confirmation of this and talk about different ways to make transitions that are more constructive.

FUTURE

6. THE IMMEDIATE FUTURE

From this card on, you are in the world of probabilities and it is important to remind the client of this aspect of the reading. The future is not set in stone and if it looks daunting, the cards are here to help show a way through the labyrinth. In other words, the future is what will probably happen if things continue as they are now. We always have a choice. If we can't change a situation or a person, we can always change our response.

In continuing on this imaginary reading, let's look at the effect of the Seven of Swords in this position. Sevens suggest growth and new ideas trying to surface. But fear, reinforced with logical explanations, gives a feeling of futility. The positive take on this would be that something new is trying to manifest and it's time to take the hand of The Fool into the future, but fear of the unknown (Moon influence) and false logic are defeating his joie de vivre. The client is immobilized. How can this change? Let's proceed to the inner self in the future and see what's going on inside.

7) INNER SELF

What is transpiring or transforming inwardly that could help in the outer world? Say the Two of Wands shows up. This card is Mars in Aries and that combines the influences of two Major Arcana already in the reading, The Emperor, Aries, and The Tower, Mars. This card represents the need to burn down an old way of being in the world, to find one's true Dominion. Sometimes this comes as a shock, but when it appears in the inner self it offers us the opportunity to change internally our direction and persona and come out fresh to the world. Taking off an old mask, we are once again linked to our soul's journey and not in reaction to others' opinions or ideas about who we really are. This card could show the client that he can find his true place in the world and does not need to keep drawing these challenging confrontations to himself over and over again. If he would open his spiritual vision, the third eye in The Tower, and explore the inner battle, then he could become his own peace negotiator.

This process would release all the pent-up energy that we saw in the past, The Tower, and in the subconscious, the Five of Cups.

8. THE ENVIRONMENT

I find this position extremely useful in examining the people and situations surrounding the client. It could be informing the reading about relocation, often symbolized by Aces, or a need for a luxurious holiday, which is one way of interpreting the Four of Cups in this position. Or the Three of Cups might indicate the need to create more stimulating social interaction within the home (Mercury, inspired communication, in Cancer, the home). Or if it is a Court card, it almost always means an individual who is strongly influencing the client's home, work, or social life.

Often all the cards in a reading have a common feel to them and this card will stand out as completely different. If this card is a Major, explore with the client the kind of milieu that would be most rewarding.

Let's imagine The Hierophant appears here. This card could bring up authority issues the way The Emperor does, as it represents the traditions passed down to us through both religious and educational institutions. It is often tainted by a memory of being told what one should or shouldn't do in life. If The Child/Fool has had this kind of experience, then any kind of learning situation could cause a negative reaction. Let's say the client had gone through school and received a degree in business and, with the help of his father, gotten his first job in the stock market, just like his dad. Now an environment of learning is calling him, but a sense of futility blocks him because he doesn't want to be told what to do yet again. But what if he goes back to school to learn something he loves and can walk out of any class he doesn't like? Then he could change his whole relationship to learning. Sometimes, to completely drop out of the work world, as The Fool might advise, and go back to school might seem too drastic, but what if you suggest just taking one class in something he always wanted to learn, to begin the transition gradually. This might work better and avoid the tendency to burn bridges and repeat old patterns.

9. HOPES AND FEARS

What we want we often fear, so within this paradoxical position there is a wide range of possible interpretations. This is a very good time to ask the client what they think about the card in this context and go from there.

Let's examine the effect of the Five of Swords in this position. First of all, you should take note that this is the third five in the reading and the nature of five is revolutionary change and movement. The three fives are the Five of Cups in the subconscious, The Hierophant V in the environment, and now the Five of Swords. This card shows an inherent fear of defeat and a dislike of competition. Challenge cards like this one are often pushing us so far that we finally just decide that anything is better than being stuck in the past and we take a risk.

What risk to choose is often guided by the astrological sign that is indicated in the card. The Five of Swords is an Aquarius card and if we look to the Aquarian Major (The Star) we can receive some valuable information. The Star shows us a beautiful vision of bringing loving light into the world and reminds us that we are each as unique as the stars when we follow our own course. If we are bringing our unique dream into the world, then the element of competition is eliminated and the joy of manifesting our destiny comes closer than we thought possible. Aquarius is the age we are entering and it often represents healing, technology, science, and communication. Mentioning these words may trigger a response in the client about something he always wanted to learn.

10. THE OUTCOME

This is probably what will happen as a result of the present circumstances. If the Two of Swords were the outcome, it would imply that the most important result at this time would be to find inner peace so that the Two of Wands, his true domain, can become clear to him. So possibly doing some healing (The Star), through counseling about his relationship to power, and taking a small step of one class in something he loves, might start the process of change in a way that is gradual and has great potential to lead in a realistic way to the resolution of old patterns and arriving at a state of peace.

The small changes would also break the pattern of bridge burning and start him on the road to mature adult decisions instead of mere reactions to power that represent child-like rebellions.

When you find yourself thinking a card always means the same thing, it is time to reintroduce yourself to this divine archetype. For example, let's take the Prince of Cups. This is the Scorpio Court Card; therefore, there is an aspect of secrecy and privacy. The image is misty and the Prince is focused only on the snake rising out of the grail as if he only cares about his own will. There is coldness and mystery, just like a scorpion backing into his cave. We all can develop a certain prejudice against a card. I have a Scorpio mother and my first love was a Scorpio, so I had unconsciously stereotyped the poor fellow and this card was an opportunity to rescue my prince from the Tarot ghetto and let go of the past for myself.

Looking at the card with fresh eyes I saw the eagle and thought about its significance. One of Scorpio's totems, the eagle is a powerful extroverted image as opposed to the internal and private ones I had been focusing on. When I consulted Ted Andrews' excellent book, Animal Speak, I found that the eagle is admired for its ability to soar and hunt. This bird's vision is so acute it could read a newspaper from the opposite end of a football field (if it could read). Therefore, perception, clarity, and getting what you're after are all part of the eagle. He also represents spirit in its connection to the heavens and the Sun, and its ability to hold the big picture in mind. Holding an overview of one's life is enhanced by eagle medicine.

I had my Scorpio backed in a corner, sinister and selfish, and now I blasted open my perspective by soaring with the eagle. In combining the Scorpio, snake and eagle, we can see the Scorpionic process revealed. The Scorpio guards the life force of the kundalini serpent until a clear desire or goal surfaces out of the heart or grail (the cup in the image); then the eagle soars to the heights in search of the fulfillment of this inner urge. It is what happens in the winter when the life force retreats and all seems to die into the cauldron of transformation. (The season of a card gives us another perspective on its significance.) The dark time of fall is played out when the skeletons dance for Halloween and the Day of the Dead, Dia de los Muertos.

The pumpkins are lit to keep light alive and remind us of the recent harvest that will come again. The jack-o'-lantern gives way to Thanksgiving candle lights, and Solstice/Christmas lights keep hope alive and pass the torch to Bridget. She takes hold at Candlemas and makes poets bold, to inspire us through the last days of darkness, till our eagle soars in springtime and the Sun is high on its upward journey.

Another way to refresh your relationship is to look at the image in another deck and read about it in the respective book. The Minor Arcana in the Crowley deck are all given positive or negative names; most other decks are merely numbered. These words have definitely been useful but they can be limiting and even distressing. The Seven of Disks is called Failure. But if you look it up in the Motherpeace deck, you find a lovely image of a pregnant woman on a vine, ripening along with the other pumpkins.

Thus, the idea of failure is transformed into something that is still gestating and should not be rushed. The idea or project will be born in its own time and the pressure of Saturn to push the stubbornness of Taurus too hard will often make us forget our original seed or vision and just try to get things done, now! (Saturn in Taurus is the astrological influence of this card.)

WHAT'S MISSING?
WHAT ISN'T IN A READING IS VERY TELLING.

No Majors

When there is no Major Arcana, it is as if the director of a play has forgotten the deeper meaning and message and is lost in the actor's ideas of how it should go. It suggests that the inner voice of clarity is not being heard by the personality; every day is a series of reactions to circumstances and people. The guiding principles are temporarily forgotten.

It may be wise to take a moment and pick again from the rest of the deck to get in touch with the archetypal guide that is needed right now. This could feel like a test and create worry that a Major still won't show up. Any card can point to a Major so I tell the client that if it is not a Major, not to worry, I will reveal what Major it is suggesting.

Any of the numbered cards can reference a Major. For example, an Ace will point to The Magician I, a Four points to The Emperor IV, a Ten points to The Wheel of Fortune X, and so on. All the numbered cards also have astrological designations, such as Saturn in Sagittarius in the Ten of Wands.

The Saturn Major is The Universe XXI, and the Sagittarius Major is Art XIV. Thus these Majors are reference cards for the Ten of Wands.

If a Court card is chosen, it is easiest to choose the Major that is the strongest influence in the card. For example, The Prince of

Disks covers the last ten days of Aries and the first twenty days of Taurus, so go with the Taurus Major, The Hierophant V.

Missing Suit

This section will give you some insight into the significance of each suit when it is absent from a reading.

No Wands

When there are no Wands it usually shows a lack of energy, no fire to get things moving. This means it is not a time of action but rather a time to consider more thoroughly the options. When a client has laid out a plan and everything in the reading confirms the plan but there is no fire, it would seem to be more of a pipe dream; smoke without a fire to keep it going. Many people imagine grandiose ideas but lack the spirited action of the wands of the Magician, the tools to make it happen. What will carry it along? Where is the will to ignite support from others?

A lack of fire in the reading can also signify a physical lack of energy and a need to take better care of the vital life force through diet, exercise, or spiritual practice. Illness, exhaustion, or depression are other possibilities to consider. If this is the case, there will probably be other cards that express this as well, such the Eight of Cups, Indolence, or the Ten of Swords, Ruin.

Other cards in the layout will suggest options, such as The Hermit, calling us into introspection and healing. It is probably an excellent time for a retreat, or possibly some soul searching through journaling about deeper needs and emotions. The Six of Swords would suggest a need for a holistic approach to health, possibly bringing in some alternative modalities such as acupressure, Reiki, or massage.

No Swords

When there are no Swords in the reading, it can often be a relief. Swords, representing the mind, are where our greatest conflicts arise. I find these readings usually show a life that is flowing and on course. There is no need for any big decisions and there is very little self-doubt. The person is likely to be very clear about knowing where she is going and why. No time to figure things out, just continue with confidence in the plan at hand. What a relief to find the mind being used as a tool to practically manifest one's will instead of flinging doubts and fears in our path. No Swords, no battle.

No Cups

The lack of Cups in a reading will be best understood by the questions being asked and the current path of the individual.

If the reading is focused on relationships, then there may be a lack of emotional engagement.

If the reading happens at the end of a relationship and there is a focus on work, this could be a healthy approach to keeping one's head above water. It could also signal a fear of facing the pain, anger, or grief that the breakup has activated and detaching to avoid emotions.

In general, when there is no water, feelings are probably being suppressed.

No Disks

Disks are the suit of the Earth, so if the question concerns work it could signal that nothing meaningful is actually being manifested in the current career choice. Look to the other cards for possible suggestions about direction.

Disks signify a need to be in the body, so healthy eating, exercising, and being outside are definitely indicated. Grounding activities are key at this time.

When the concern is about buying a house, relocating, or the current living situation, it would suggest that the individual is not "at home" yet and more options need to be considered that will allow real grounding to take hold.

It is risky to buy a house or any property when no Disks appear. If a specific place is being considered, it's possible that the client should do further inspection of the property and the structure itself.

LIFE AND YEAR CARDS

PRIESTESS YEAR

The Priestess Year is calculated by subtracting the total of your birth date from the year 2000.

Example:

$$
\begin{array}{cc}
\begin{array}{r} 9 \\ 18 \\ +1950 \\ \hline 1977 \end{array} &
\begin{array}{r} 2000 \\ -1977 \\ \hline 23 \end{array}
\end{array}
$$

Subtract 1977 from 2000 and you get 23. This means your Priestess year was when you were 23 years old.

The Priestess Year is meant to represent a profound initiation into the deeper meaning of your life journey. I have found so many interesting ways that this formula reveals our transitions.

Story I

My own Priestess Year was focused on my second child, April Faith. She was conceived on July Fourth after a rousing game of baseball in Golden Gate Park. All the men were playing while the women watched and took care of the kids. After a little something to drink, I was feeling my oats, and gathered a group of women together and took to the field, demanding to be part of the game. Everyone was laughing and joking but we were determined. I don't recall how well we did but all that mattered was that we got out there and did it!

Afterwards I was feeling so high that it was easy to, well, you can tell where this is going, so I'll spare you the details.

After being misguided in my first birthing experience I refused to go to the doctor and predicted that I would give birth to my second child on April Fool's Day, which is her father's birthday. I was absolutely positive that this would happen. On the morning of March 31, I felt my first contractions and stayed home, relaxing and enjoying my labor until 11pm, when I knew the baby would arrive very soon. I got to St. Luke's as a soft rain started to fall and was feeling no pain. My two other births were very difficult but this one was just hard work, as in "labor," but not painful. It seemed that I knew exactly what was happening and just rode the waves joyously until she arrived shortly after midnight. I turned to my then-husband and said, "Happy Birthday!" and there she was. We called her April Faith, and I can tell you it was an absolutely ecstatic experience. The doctor did not interfere in any way. The next day when I looked in the mirror, I saw tiny blood vessels had burst on my shoulders and my cheeks and I laughed, thinking I had gotten a bit carried away with the bliss of being a conscious Priestess of the door between the worlds. Labor can be hard work without pain when we are allowed to "Priestess" our own process! I believe that every birth is a miracle and a mystery so I am not implying any judgment about pain in birth. I certainly had my share and I learned exactly what I needed during my other births and did the work that was necessary. But April's birth definitely revealed my power to me in a very unique way. I also think that April had something to do with it from the other side, preparing her pathway and me so all would flow easily. April is an artist and I think this was her first installation!

To further demonstrate the Priestess aspect of our relationship, in the early '90s the goddess movement was thriving in Sonoma County and April and I discovered our first all-women ritual together. We were so happy to find a spiritual path that celebrated all that is feminine. At this point April was becoming an accomplished belly dancer and reclaiming this ancient dance into the realm of the sacred, and I had begun teaching the Tarot for the first time, so April and I became each other's teachers. For five years I took belly dance from her and she took Tarot classes from me. She was an avid learner and followed me around outside the class with her notebook in hand ready to get me to talk about the cards. Of all my students, she (an Aries, of course) was the most determined to learn. We loved sharing our stories of synchronicity and picking cards together on a regular basis. April is now an accomplished professional reader in her own right and I am proud to say she is in no way an imitation of me. We have done readings for the same people and they enjoy each one as a unique experience. In my classes, I emphasize that each of us must create our own relationship to the cards and weave them experientially into the internal web of our own psyche. That is why certain cards work for certain readers in very different ways even though the essential nature of the symbol remains intact.

April and I started making altars in our home and going to all the events, rituals, and classes that were available.

My youngest daughter, Allegra, was a pre-teen and wasn't sure how cool this whole goddess thing was, so we stepped back and let her express her feelings without judgment. She gradually joined us of her own accord. At the same time, April was teaching Allegra and her homeschool classmates to belly dance.

It was a miracle of our image-obsessed culture to see thin girls and full-figured ones, tall and short ones, all dancing together, looking in the mirrors and enjoying their bodies.

Isis is our family goddess as she represents all we love: belly dance, Tarot, the wisdom of the divine mother, and of course, magic.

As you can see, my Priestess was born in my Priestess Year and she has been instrumental in my personal development. I am profoundly grateful for her presence in my life and fascinated by using the Priestess Year formula as a lens to understand our relationship. In fact, it was April who suggested I write this book and then kept urging me on until I began.

Story II

The next example of the Priestess Year is the story of "Alan," who was raised by alcoholic parents and spent a lot of time in Vietnam during the war. He was addicted to drugs and alcohol until he turned 36 and woke up to reality. He became clean and sober and two months after his awakening, his abusive, alcoholic father died. At 54 years old, he was still clean and had become a productive writer. He was also developing an online service that helps people invest in ecologically-conscious businesses and make money at the same time.

His numbers are as follows:

$$
\begin{array}{ll}
\begin{array}{r} 9 \\ 5 \\ +1950 \\ \hline 1964 \end{array}
&
\begin{array}{r} 2000 \\ -1964 \\ \hline \mathbf{36} \end{array} \text{ years old in his Priestess Year.}
\end{array}
$$

Story III

My favorite story about the Priestess Year is the one about "Gupta," a young man in his early 30s. I don't have the numbers anymore but I remember that his Priestess Year was when he was two years old. I said, "You probably don't remember what happened when you were two." He responded immediately that he was initiated as a Hari Krishna priest when he was two and his particular training was for guiding souls through death to the other side! I was truly amazed at how applicable this formula is and how much it tells us about crucial transitions in our lives.

Story IV

"Lupe's" Priestess Year was also when she was two years old. I was well into the reading before I brought in this lens to help her understand her current challenges.

I had actually developed a certain theory in my mind and was pretty sure her Priestess Year would illuminate her life story.

Lupe was Latina. She was approaching her relationships with men by offering to help them in numerous ways in order to ingratiate herself into their lives.

She was almost 42 and I suggested that often, big changes can happen when we are in our Uranus opposition that seemed impossible before. (Uranus takes 84 years to orbit the Sun so at 42 we are halfway there.)

I figured she probably had a sibling born when she was two, as she had told me that she was one of six and she was the third of three girls and then three boys came along.

The first boy, "Juan," was born when she was in her Priestess Year. Culturally, worldwide, there is a tendency to celebrate the birth of a male child over a female. This is very strong in the Latino culture.

Since she was the third girl and closest to the first son, it was probably a very exaggerated moment for her, but she was too young to be really conscious of what was happening. I suggested that she probably internalized the messages that she was receiving from her family and social situations. Her importance became measured by her care for her brothers from then on, and her own light was eclipsed. She developed the strategy of finding approval by helping and nurturing the men in her life, but they rarely showed interest in her life path or her needs.

Consequently, she temporarily gratified her deeper needs for love by shopping and eating, symbolized by the Seven of Cups in her reading, when what she really wanted was validation of her worth and her work in the world.

When we can shed the light of awareness on the source of our actions and become conscious of their roots in our early years, we can dissolve some of the unconscious powers that these patterns exercise over our actions.

KABALA

The Kabala, like the Tarot, is a "map of life" that shows pathways and stations that we encounter on our journey. In fact, three world-renowned experts, Aleister Crowley, Eliphas Levi, and Dion Fortune, insist that they are inextricably bound to each other in their mutual origins. According to Dion Fortune, "They dovetail into each other at every imaginable angle." Although there is no actual "proof" that the Kabala and the Tarot were once one system, it is definitely uncanny how the two systems naturally flow into one another.

For example, there are 22 letters in the Hebrew alphabet that name the pathways on the Tree of Life. Likewise there are 22 Major Arcana or archetypes in the Tarot. For example, the Hebrew letter that represents the Priestess is called Gimel, whose literal translation is a camel. On the Tree this path traverses the abyss correlating to the initiatory path of the Priestess through the dark, lunar night. Both cross this "desert," the unknown, to gain a deeper understanding of the mystery, while learning to trust the inherent intuitive wisdom of the divine feminine.

Ten sephiroth or spheres create the structure of the Tree while each suit has ten cards. The nature and value of these numbers are given symbolic meaning in both systems. For example, the crown of the Tree, called Kether, is the root force of the infinite, while all the Aces are the seeds of the elemental suits they represent.

The Court Cards correspond to sephiroth two, three, six and ten, representing Father, Mother, Son, and Daughter in that order. In the Crowley/Harris Tarot they are called Knight, Queen, Prince, and Princess.

Thus, it is evident that all 78 cards find their energetic correspondence within the Tree of Life.

In my work as a reader I often show my clients the Tree of Life diagram and explain how the cards in their reading are further understood through this system. Bring it out when you do a reading; just enjoy meditating on the tree and you will start to create your own relationship with this ancient system.

Simple patterns will begin to emerge:

When you receive an Ace, Six, Nine, and Ten in a reading, you will notice that those cards occupy the central column of the Tree in complete balance between the left and right hand columns.

Note: The energy moves down the Tree from 1-10 as a lightning bolt bringing imagination into reality and slithers up the Tree as a serpent returning to the unmanifest.

TREE OF LIFE / KABALA

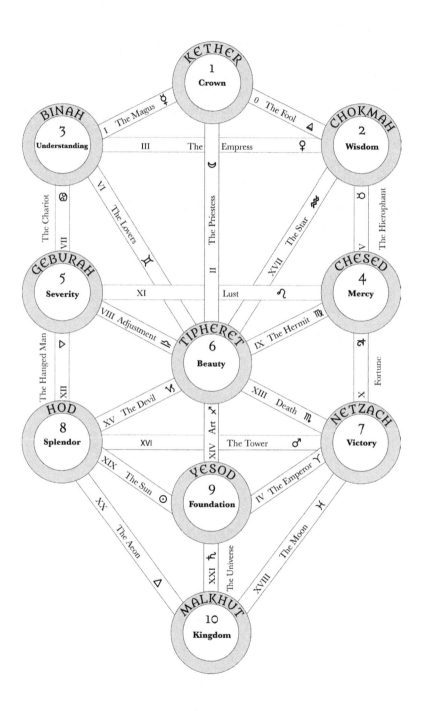

When you get three or more tens in a reading, you have taken the materialization of the last imagination as far as possible and it is time to return to the one again.

Or if you receive a predominance of fives, then you will see that position on the tree is called Severity and symbolizes revolutionary change and the challenges that come when we move past the probable, moving into the possible and eventually into the real.

Although explaining the Kabala in depth would be a whole other book, if this interests you I suggest you obtain a basic book on the Kabala, such as The Witches Qabala. If you want to go in depth, try Robert Wang's excellent book, The Qabalistic Tarot. Dion Fortune's book, The Mystical Qabalah, is very esoteric and considered a classic in the field but a challenge for beginners, so I would save that for later on.

I have also included a diagram showing the correspondences for your use.

Note: On the Crowley cards you will see the Hebrew letters showing you where they live on the Tree. Some decks actually picture the Tree on each card and highlight the path that is applicable.

THE RIGHT DECK
AT THE RIGHT TIME

The Tarot is in reality a universal filing system and that is why it is possible to create a Tarot deck using the symbolic language of any given mythic or modern structure.

There are decks based on many of the cultures of the world from Celtic and Italian to Native American and French.

My friend, Allen Gunn, who is up on all the latest on the Internet, even found The Silicon Valley Tarot, a tongue-in-cheek deck that was created for the corporate world with cards like the Four of Cubicles, the Eight of (Computer) Disks, and Major Arcana such as the Flame War that correlates to The Tower. The Court Cards include The Marketeer of Networks and the CIO of Hosts. Just to give you an idea:

Marketeer of Networks

The Marketeer clings tightly to one of the few jobs in which her gender is grudgingly represented in the Silicon Valley. Her smile is forced. She is relentlessly upbeat. She is well fortified from slings and arrows by industrial-weight shoulder pads within her smart Armani frock. Optimism, enthusiasm. Reversed: denial, deer-in-the-headlights. Appearances begin to crumble.

Which Deck?

The deck you choose to use for a particular situation often reveals an even more specific symbolic synchronicity than always using the same one. The following stories illustrate this phenomenon.

The last two stories show that Rachael Pollack, creator of The Shining Woman Tarot, has tapped into and evolved this ancient wisdom to serve us now.

The Voyager Deck

My daughter, April, had just left on a trip to Turkey and I was looking for some understanding and confirmation of her purpose. I also wanted to know what I needed to focus on to hold the best energy to support her on her journey. At this time the U.S. military was attacking Iraq, which borders on Turkey, and although my daughter was heading for a small tourist town, I was deeply concerned.

Since she was on a voyage, so to speak, and she had been using the Voyager Tarot deck a lot before she left, I decided to use it for the divination.

The card I picked was the Nine of Wands and the image was of a solitary woman entering the Blue Mosque in Istanbul (where April was landing!). I suggested she go and see it. I felt so reassured by this card because I had never seen it before and I would venture to say it is probably the only image of a blue mosque in any Tarot deck. The first e-mail I received from April revealed that she had seen the Blue Mosque on her way from the airport and she would later visit and actually go inside.

Not only was the image a strong confirmation that she was on the right path but the description in the Voyager Tarot book by Jim Wanless fit her purpose as well.

All the nine cards are an aspect of The Hermit and she was traveling alone, following her inner light, turning away from what was not right for her and respecting and protecting her inner spirit. It represented the courage and ability to stand alone.

This helped me to accept her choice and led my Priestess self to reassure my mother self.

The synchronicity of the day continued to unfold in rather magical ways. April departed on March 27, a week after the Spring Equinox. It so happened that a friend of mine had scheduled a Spring Ritual for March 28, so I was blessed with a circle of eight women, including myself, to send energy in support of my daughter and to help me ground myself with my community.

When I entered the sacred space, my eyes fell on the beautiful altar the women had created. Spreading out from the center were nine archery arrows, the traditional symbol of the Nine of Wands!

I shared my story with the other women and asked them for support for my daughter and myself. Tears unexpectedly welled up in my eyes and I was comforted by the words of my friend, Eoanna, who said that April was the ninth woman in our circle and that her presence was felt. We all sent protective and encouraging energy to my adventurous Aries as she set out to the Middle East.

The Tarot and rituals have helped me many times in my life to come to a calm and centered place in myself.

As the moon rose that evening and was hanging out directly above us, we invoked Artemis and aimed our arrows from the altar to a giant heart attached to some bales of straw. It was a powerful feeling to draw back the bow and let loose my intentions for the safety of my daughter and my own will to create as the new season unfolded.

The Nine of Wands card is ruled by the Moon, Artemis in Sagittarius, which is symbolized by the arrow. As I drew back the bow and looked to see the Moon above me, I said a silent prayer and felt the powerful stance of the divine archer in the limbs of my own body. I even managed to hit the bale, as Artemis guided me from her celestial throne.

The Battle for Seattle

In 1999, I joined the action in Seattle to shutdown the World Trade Organization's (WTO) meeting. Over 50,000 activists swarmed the streets, including labor unions like the AFL-CIO and environmental groups, known as the alliance of teamsters and turtles.

It was truly delightful to see burly teamsters talking and laughing with folks dressed as turtles, as the rain fell softly but failed to dampen our spirits.

These were heady times and the whole city was alive with the power of democracy in the streets. We succeeded in our mission to win what is now known as the Battle for Seattle.

As I walked the streets, I saw that every café and bar was filled with folks gathered around TVs, watching and cheering in amazement as this historic moment unfolded.

I didn't have my cards in my backpack, so I went into a bookstore and grabbed The Shining Woman Tarot book by Rachel Pollack.

I closed my eyes and opened the book to the card named Awakening which is traditionally called Judgment or The Aeon in the Thoth deck.

The description starts with a short verse:
"They rush from their houses.
 They stop all the traffic.
 They shout from the windows.
 They build homes for their neighbors."

And continues "What restores the city is the life energy of a spirituality based on the Earth....The urban setting and the presence of a family, implies responsibility to others. When we Awaken we understand our connections: to the Earth, to people around us, to our society and to the web of life..."

The specific image of stopping traffic and building community offered such a profound confirmation of the work we were all doing to prevent corporate interests from trumping the rights of people and the Earth itself. I am sure there is no other Tarot book in the world that mentions stopping traffic in describing this card, and that is exactly what we had just done.

There was a strong Earth-based spiritual element to this protest, especially through the presence of The Reclaiming community. This reading on the run gave me great encouragement to continue our work toward a system of Earth Justice for all.

Cracking The Da Vinci Code

While reading The Da Vinci Code, I thought it would be interesting to see what the cards had to say about this magical mystery tale.

Would there be clues that pertained to the story?

I picked the Speaker of Rivers, from The Shining Woman Tarot. In the card is an image of the inverted glass pyramid at the Louvre that was created by the Chinese-American architect, I.M. Pei. No doubt this is the only deck in the world that depicts the pyramid of I.M. Pei. This pyramid figures strongly in the whole storyline of the book.

The meaning of the last message found by the two main characters, Langdon and Neveu, is that the grail is buried beneath the small pyramid directly below the inverted glass pyramid of the Louvre. It is then concluded that Neveu is the descendent of Jesus Christ and Mary Magdalene.

The equivalent card to the Speaker of Rivers in the Thoth deck is the Knight of Cups where we see the winged Knight on a white horse lifting the grail to the heavens.

But in The Da Vinci Code, as in the Tarot, the meaning of the grail is actually the bloodline, the menstrual blood, the womb inside Mary Magdalene, and the womb inside every woman as well as the womb of life, the ocean itself.

This is revealed on a deeper level when we discover that the Ace of Cups, the grail in the hands of the Knight in the Thoth deck, is also depicted in The Chariot card as turned on its side and becoming a whirling disk, with menstrual blood in the center.

This is the astrological archetypal card of Cancer, the sign of the ocean, the mother, and the womb; implying that our true will is found in the very blood of life, not a physical object known as the grail. Just as the Philosopher's Stone is not really about turning gross metal into gold but about understanding the synthesis of all opposites when we recognize them as complementary and part of a whole.

This is yet another example that the Tarot loves specific questions and rises to the occasion to gift the most exact answer and validation possible!

APPENDIX

THE PASSIONATE MIND REVISITED
By Joel Kramer and Diana Alstad
Reviewed by Magick Altman

There is a way through to a brilliant future....

In these times of drastic change when unnatural disasters caused by our species are rocking the planet daily, and the social and political fabric is being torn asunder, what's a human to do? I highly recommend that you read The Passionate Mind Revisited.

The old paradigms filled with judgments, absolutes, and so-called truths that cannot be verified, must go into the compost heap.

This brilliant deconstruction of failed religions, social structures, and rigid fantasies of ideal human relationships will give you a refreshing approach to a both/and perspective that will help you become a trailblazer, aware and freed from the adolescent stage of human evolution.

Time to let go of all the forms of belief that claim to be "The Way" giving us absolutes and answers for all our questions. These parental substitutes play on our fears and insecurities so that we will surrender our own unique journey to the god, guru, or dictator that promises to take us to paradise.

Time to grow up into caring, curious, and creative humans who are willing to accept the full range of human complexity. Our hearts have an immense capacity for caring and love, and our mind's potential is constantly expanding, along with our physical prowess. The authors, Diana Alstad and Joel Kramer, show us ways to fluidly navigate the different dimensions of the human condition and come through it with our awareness, critical thinking, and compassionate hearts intact and thriving.

Yoga Journal calls it "a survival guide for the new world order."

For me, it succinctly exposes the lies of belief systems that basically dislike, disparage, and deny the beauty, freedom, and creative chaos that is life.

Earthlings who happen to love this blue-green gem will find a refreshing reassurance that being a fully engaged sensual, sexual, emotional, free thinking, cultural creative is really what it's all about.

The book unmasks the lie that religious institutions are, at heart, loving expressions of some alien almighty and reveals them as hierarchies bent on preserving their own power positions by manipulating the good/bad right/wrong limited perception of life on Earth.

Forget about the paths and get in the river and start swimming. It's a hell of a ride!

This book will show you the way out of the wormholes of a civilization gone bad.

MARS REVISITS GAIA: THE TELLING OF
A MODERN MYTHOLOGY

Mars stumbles exhausted toward Earth, appearing through the atmospheric veil, like a brutal, broken knight of the Middle Ages. His visor thrown back, he peers out at the war-torn continents, and falls to his knees in shock and horror. Everywhere he sees the devastation of this once lush and beautiful blue-green dream called Gaia. Tears tumble down his ruddy cheeks as he wails, "What have I done! O Great Goddess, forgive me, WHAT HAVE I DONE!"

Afghanistan and Iraq, Africa and South America, everywhere he looks he sees the aftermath of war. Where mighty forests once stood, barren mountains crumble, scorched by the Sun. 60,000 years since he came this close. He tries to remember the words of encouragement he had given to the fear-filled humans as they struggled to survive amidst the awesome forces of nature. Be strong! He bellowed to the larger ones. He chose the men to be his disciples and trained them to fight for their families to survive. Brute force would bring them through, he reasoned. He taught them to make weapons to fight the beasts and kill for food. He saw the women praying to Venus for protection and scoffed at their pathetic hopes.

"Come forth, O brave ones, worship me, and I will teach you all the Martial Arts, the science of weaponry, the tricks and deceptions, the traps and tools of my legacy as the Fiery One!" Then he had returned to the outer regions of space, continuing to answer the calls for more power from the men of Earth. From the weapons of mere bone and stone, he taught them to use iron and steel, to build the armies of the earth. But he failed to check and see the results of his teachings. Failed to hear the cries of the women and children and the creatures of the Earth, who were no longer a threat but now endangered, themselves.

Bloated with pride and blinded by the praises of the armies of men, he continued to grant them boons. Guns and cannons, jets and bombs, Mars became fascinated with the endless uses of his fiery force. Even the horror of the atomic bomb did not awaken Mars out of the trance of power.

But now the heavens had sent him back towards Gaia to look upon his wicked works and face the reality of his ruinous ways. "I only wanted to help them survive, they were so special in all the Universe, I could not let them perish, could I? But Venus, the Moon, and Mercury, whose had stayed close and seen the ruination, looked on in silence as the truth set in. Venus, in her sweet compassion, touches Mars on his shoulder, and points to the Piscean pools shimmering in the light of the starlit heavens, and whispers, "It is not too late, another age approaches, Aquarius beckons you to submerge yourself in Neptune's waters and re-dream yourself, my brother."

He looks into her deep green eyes and surrenders all defenses. Mercury and the shining Sun help him take off his heavy armor. Weapons fall all around this god, creating thunder in the skies. Lightning flashes, the oceans rise, and all the humans look to the skies and pray for the end to war. His body, naked, broken, weary slips into the sea, and all the heavens breathe a sigh of great relief. "Go deep, go deep," the Moon enchants, "face your demons one on one and don't come back until you're done! The hounds of hell will smell your blood if you do not cleanse completely."

It seemed like an aeon that he was under the purple wisdom waters, but bubbles began to break the surface, releasing the insufferable scent of sulphur, until at last the mighty war god broke through and reached out toward his brother Sun.

And redeemed Mars spoke, "Courage is reborn in me, no longer wed to fear. Courage is reborn in me, my passion pours from the cup of love, there are ways to work together. My resources are rich and many. Violence, so crude and temporary, will never rule again!"

The men of earth, confused and curious, look to their lord on high! O mighty one! They call to Mars, what do we do to stop our enemies? How will we keep your kingdom for you? Who will man the Keep?

"My sons, my sons, lay down your guns, You are not threatened by anyone. My Brother Sun will teach you new ways to use the power of Fire, while I retire for a long-needed rest and learn how to dance and paint and sing and experience the joy of fire as an inner light, a warming hearth, and a way to cook." They looked at him as if he had lost his mind and he gratefully agreed.

"But my heart is still pumping and Venus is coming to take me to her queendom. All is well. The spell of false power is now dissolving and we enter a time of resolving our differences with reason and mutual respect. Mercury will teach you logic but the Moon won't let you forget your instincts. They will take you on the path of your dreams, so give up your hopeless, conquering schemes. My old ways are no longer needed."

Although the men were dumbfounded, and pounded their fists in dismay, Mars walked away singing, "It's a beautiful day" and calling out "You'll find your own way!"

"Gaia had all the answers all along. Her order still underlies all the devastation. End your nation states, re-congregate around the systems of life. Imitate, reintegrate yourselves with nature's ways, and she will be glad to have you stay.

"I will be back soon to give you courage to be warriors on the path of enlightenment, to be warriors for peace, for love and light..."

OM HRDAYA NAMAH –GROUNDING RITUAL CHANT

It is combined with gestures that emphasize the words. Simply translated it goes like this:

1. First I bow down to my heart, (middle finger of right hand touches the heart),
2. That awakens my mind, (same finger touches forehead).
3. That connects me to the Super consciousness, (fingers of right hand pulls a few strands of hair from the top of the head up towards the heavens)
4. That protects me, (Cross both arms over chest, hands resting on the shoulders)
5. So I may see with my third eye (middle finger of right hand, index finger and ring finger create a triangle and the tips of the three fingers are placed on the forehead)
6. And manifest my will (palms of both hands, facing the chest, circle each other and then the three fingers used before slap the palm of the left hand, making the final connection).

This simple meditation gets the energy moving in a circular motion from the heart to the mind and down to the final gesture at the level of the bottom chakra. If it is hard to imagine this without seeing it, make it your own as best you can; it is the intention that counts.

THE CHARGE OF THE GODDESS

I who am the beauty of the green earth and the white moon among the stars and the mysteries of the waters, I call upon your soul to arise and come unto me.

For I am the soul of nature that gives life to the universe.

From me all things proceed and unto me they must return.

Let my worship be in the heart that rejoices, for behold—all acts of love and pleasure are my rituals.

Let there be beauty and strength, power and compassion, honor and humility, mirth and reverence within you.

And you who seek to know me, know that your seeking and yearning will avail you not unless you know the mystery: for if that which you seek, you find not within yourself, you will never find it without.

For behold, I have been with you from the beginning and I am that which is attained at the end of desire.

INDEX

A

Achilles, 178
Activist, 12, 13, 50, 52, 54, 125, 161
174, 311, 379
Adam, 100
Addiction(s), 89, 92, 120, 174, 192
202, 208, 301, 302
Adolescence, 130
alchemy, 77, 108, 111
Aleister Crowley, 9, 16, 24, 32, 92, 99,
121, 141, 156, 166, 230, 236, 311, 358,
367, 374
Alexandra Genetti, 234, 304
Alice Walker, 130
Allen Ginsberg, 64
Amethyst, 351
Amma, 188
Aphrodite, 86, 234
Apocalypse, 141, 144
Apocalypso, 144
Apollo, 13, 41
Aquarius, 38, 128, 144, 146, 157, 266,
280, 297, 365, 388,
Archetype, 13, 22, 34, 36, 42, 49, 60,
70, 82, 92, 113, 124, 125, 146, 162,
218-220, 229, 239, 253, 259, 262, 265,
279, 293, 298, 307, 321, 335, 358, 361,
366, 374
Artemis, 36, 38, 378
Astragalus, 165
Audre Lorde, 35

B

Bali/Balinese, 76, 122, 125, 126
Bellydance, 371
Beltane, 60
Bible, 98, 141
Bird(s), 166, 170, 184, 222, 272, 366
Bisexual/Bisexuality, 113
Bob Dylan, 48, 62, 64
Bridget, 366
Buddhist, 326
Buffalo Springfield, 64
Bull, 60, 61, 208, 290

C

Caduceus, 32, 33, 280
California, 340
Camel, 36, 41, 71, 314
Candle(s), 38, 84, 200, 351, 366
Career, 89, 100, 106, 112, 170, 195, 200, 205, 206, 236, 250, 266, 290, 317, 356, 369
Carl Jung, 124
Caroline Casey, 33, 50
Cary Grant, 92
Cat, 14, 176, 185, 300
Celtic Cross, 359, 360
Chant, 30, 294, 352, 353, 389
Christian, 97, 98, 118, 141
Ciranjiva, 301
Compassion, 38, 46, 70, 71, 86, 110, 125, 130-136, 141, 144, 157, 173, 176, 188, 280, 301, 306, 355, 386, 387, 390
Computer, 131, 377
Cormac Cullinan, 77
Cree, 74
Cupid, 64

D

Death, 33-40, 76, 82, 102, 104-107, 121, 131, 149, 162, 294, 302, 345, 346, 356, 357, 372
Demeter, 36, 38
Devil, 116, 118, 119, 120, 121, 169, 115
Diogenes, 80
Dion Fortune, 374, 376
Drugs, 44, 64, 67, 74, 115, 118, 302, 372

E

Eagle, 108, 195, 196, 366, 367
Educere, 45, 15
Einstein, 56
Eliphas Levi, 374
Environment, 14, 24, 48, 94, 95, 113, 158, 204, 234, 262, 275, 282, 287, 306, 311, 316, 364, 365, 379
Equinox/ Equinoxes, 60, 162, 356, 378
Eve, 100

F

G

H

I

J

Jefferson Airplane, 64
Jerrigrace Lyons, 82
Jesus, 59, 98, 110, 219, 355, 380
Jim Wanless, 378
Jimi Hendrix, 121
Joel Kramer and Diana Alstad, 54, 385
John Lennon, 34, 64
Joni Mitchell, 124, 132
Joseph Campbell, 92, 144
Juno, 140
Jupiter, 86, 106, 236, 254, 284, 286, 290, 294, 296, 308, 325, 328
Justice, 12, 27, 73- 78, 82, 156, 164, 173, 174, 185, 254, 265, 272, 307, 356, 379

K

Kabala, 218-222, 229, 239, 253, 265, 279, 293, 307, 321, 345, 374, 376, 375
Kali, 11, 58, 104, 105, 162
Karen Vogel, 47, 256
Katherine Hepburn, 92
Koran, 141
Kundalini, 32, 59, 98, 121, 146, 236, 302, 266
Kwan Yin, 39

L

Labyrinth, 363
Lady Frieda Harris, 9, 16, 158, 188, 290
Lavender, 84
Lemniscate, 30, 307
Leonard Cohen, 66
Lesbian, 64
Lion, 46, 91, 108, 174, 182, 205, 298, 300
Lotus, 195, 224, 234, 290
LSD, 64

M

Mala Kabbala, 94
Marge Piercy, 125
Mark Twain, 275
Mars, Martian, 121, 124, 125, 126, 195, 218, 243, 249, 250, 263, 272, 298,

Printed in Great Britain
by Amazon

44672049R00225